Middle Innings

A DOCUMENTARY HISTORY

OF BASEBALL, 1900–1948

COMPILED AND EDITED BY

DEAN A. SULLIVAN

UNIVERSITY OF NEBRASKA PRESS

LINCOLN & LONDON

Acknowledgments appear on page 225, which
constitutes an extension of the copyright page.

(∞)

First Bison Books printing: 2001
Most recent printing indicated by the
last digit below:

10   9   8   7   6   5   4   3   2   1

Library of Congress
Cataloging-in-Publication Data
Middle innings: a documentary history of
baseball, 1900–1948 / compiled & edited by
Dean A. Sullivan.
    p. cm.
Compilation of baseball writings from work that
appeared between 1901 and 1948.
Includes bibliographical references (p.)
and index.
ISBN 0-8032-4258-1 (cl: alk. paper)
ISBN 0-8032-9283-x (pa: alk. paper)
1. Baseball—United States—History—20th
century—Sources. I. Sullivan, Dean A.,
1963– .
GV863.AIM52 1998
796.352'0973—dc21
97-36995
CIP

Contents

CHAPTER 5. LIGHTS, ACTION, HISTORY

CHAPTER 6. BASEBALL IN WARTIME AND PEACETIME

Illustrations

Preface

The best sports writing captures the excitement and immediacy of the game. *Middle Innings* presents rarely seen and little-known documents that permit readers to share with their predecessors the experience of reading these pieces for the first time. With luck, a reader will get a sense of the world of baseball in the first half of the twentieth century, and the society in which this world flourished.

In these pages we encounter the shock of turn-of-the-century Southern Californians at a successful Japanese baseball team, the profusion of baseball songs, the impact of radio on baseball, and the chill caused by the Black Sox scandal. The impact of Jackie Robinson becomes clear through articles on race, ethnicity, and religion in baseball. These are accompanied by accounts of teams and players in the Negro Leagues, on amateur and semipro clubs, and on college and youth teams, and how these teams were as representative of baseball as the major league clubs.

Due to the richness of the subject matter and the abundance of documents, it was not possible to cover every notable event and player in this era. *Middle Innings* strives to provide as representative a look at baseball as one volume can. The objective was to cover as many topics as possible, drawing connections and explaining contexts, and to persuade readers that they share more than they realized with their predecessors.

I would like to thank Society of American Baseball Research (SABR) members Bob Bailey and Paul Debono for providing me with documents. Larry Lester, research director of the Negro Leagues Baseball Museum, contributed a document and offered valuable advice. George Russ, curator of the Joyce Sports Research Collection at the University of Notre Dame, helped with documents on the All-American Girls' Professional Baseball League. SABR members Fred Ivor-Campbell, Larry Gerlach, and Jerry Malloy provided encouragement. At the University of Maryland, Nancy Struna (president of the North American Society for Sport History) has taught me more about sports history than I could have imagined, and for this I cannot thank her enough.

The support of my family has been invaluable. In the three years spent preparing this book, on many occasions my spirit needed lifting. My brothers Steve and Jay Sullivan, my sisters Lisa Rodriguez and Laurie Barden, and above all my father, Donald Sullivan, never hesitated to help me when asked, and even when I didn't ask. I hope *Middle Innings* will serve as partial justification of their faith, and as the basis for an even closer relationship in the future.

Introduction

Americans greeting the twentieth century saw a revolution in communication that had a significant impact on leisure activities, including baseball. The invention and popularization of the telegraph, telephone, phonograph, motion picture camera, and radio helped create a new world of leisure opportunities for the consumer who, thanks in part to active labor unions and government regulation of work and wages, had more free time and ready cash to spend on amusements. Baseball took full advantage of the situation and, despite increased competition for recreational time and expenditure, grew dramatically during the period.

The first major issue in baseball in the new century was the attainment in 1901 of major league status by the American League (AL). Despite opposition from the National League (NL), the claim of parity by the AL was accepted by the baseball press and public because of the talent the new league demonstrated. Among the AL's accomplishments were the placement of franchises in major cities occupied by NL teams, which did their utmost to block the entry of rival teams into their territory, and the signing of top NL players to AL contracts. Faced with escalating player salaries in the bidding war, the NL agreed to recognize the AL as an equal early in 1903. Together the leagues created the National Commission, consisting of each league president and a third, neutral party, which ineffectively ruled both the major and minor leagues until 1920.

The new National Agreement, which formalized the structure of organized baseball, did not include a provision for a postseason championship series. In 1903 the winning clubs in the NL and AL, Pittsburgh and Boston, planned a series themselves. The teams were following the precedent of the 1880s, when similar "World Series" took place between the NL and the American Association between 1884 and 1890. Even though both clubs considered backing out because of injuries, the 1903 World Series was a great success that seemed to seal the peaceful coexistence between the two leagues.

After the 1904 NL pennant series, NL champion New York refused to play Boston, the defending Series champions, claiming the AL did not deserve such an honor. The resulting public outrage convinced Giants owner John Brush of his error, and he led the effort to formally establish the World Series. From 1905 on, the Series was played at the conclusion of every season, through world wars and economic depressions, until a labor dispute—one of many in baseball history—ended the string in 1994.

The decade before World War I was baseball's most successful era since the mid-1880s. Not only were the major leagues thriving, but the number of minor league teams increased annually. Often these leagues organized "Junior World Series" of their own. In addition, amateur, semipro, and youth baseball continued to garner considerable attention in rural and urban areas alike. Games between top clubs could attract more fans than many major league contests, in part because fans still believed that their local game and their athletes represented them, and embodied democratic values exemplified by players like Christy Mathewson and his fictional counterpart, Frank Merriwell.

The early twentieth century also marked the consolidation of baseball through-out popular culture. Well-known athletes had appeared on the vaudeville stage for years, and this trend accelerated in the 1900s as theaters generated more profits than ever. The new medium of recorded music celebrated the national pastime with dozens of songs of all kinds, including the most famous sports song of all, 1908's "Take Me Out to the Ball Game," originally written for a vaudeville routine. Baseball was represented in movies, poems, magazine fiction and articles, and children's stories. Sports editors and writers responded to the demand for more baseball news by expanding coverage and by creating new outlets for feature articles.

A representative new periodical was *Baseball Magazine*, which first appeared in 1908. From the very beginning it attracted talented writers who addressed subjects, like college baseball, umpires, and a "hall of fame" for the best players, which were too long or detailed for daily newspapers. This atmosphere also fostered the development of some of the finest baseball writers in this century. Four—Grant-land Rice, Fred Lieb, Damon Runyon, and Heywood Broun—all moved to New York City newspapers in 1911, signaling the beginning of a new era in sportswrit-ing. Other notable baseball writers of the era were Ring Lardner—who, like Run-yon, later became a successful writer of fiction—Hugh Fullerton, and former Tombstone, Arizona, sheriff Bat Masterson.

A writer whose work frequently appeared in *Baseball Magazine* was David Fultz, a lawyer, college football referee, and former major league player. In 1912 he wrote a series of articles advocating his new organization, the Fraternity of Profes-sional Baseball Players. The Fraternity was the third players union, following the Brotherhood (1885–90) and the Players' Protective Association (1900–1902). Fultz attracted star players like Ty Cobb and Walter Johnson, but antagonized owners. After several years of discussion the major league owners recognized the Fraternity in 1914 and granted a few of Fultz's requests, but his union faded away soon thereafter.

One of the consequences of the unrest the Fraternity represented was the Federal League (FL), a third major league, formed in late 1913, which, like the American League before it, did its best to lure other major league players to jump their contracts. Over one-third of all AL and NL players left for the new league, and many of those who remained received substantial salary increases. Despite two exciting pennant races, the FL could not attract enough fans to cover expenses and folded after the 1915 season. However, owners of the Baltimore FL franchise filed a lawsuit that ensured a lasting, if unintended, legacy of the failed league.

Claiming that they had not been consulted during negotiations among the three leagues that resulted in the death of the FL, the Baltimore owners filed an antitrust suit against the major leagues. They asserted that the NL and AL practiced interstate commerce, and that the two leagues conspired to defeat rivals like the FL by using their position as a monopoly to effectively prevent outsiders from hiring players. In 1919 a federal court in Washington ruled that the Sherman Anti-Trust Act was applicable since baseball was engaged in interstate commerce, and awarded the Baltimore plaintiffs nearly $250,000. Organized baseball won an appeal, which Baltimore in turn appealed to the U.S. Supreme Court. The high court's decision, announced in the spring of 1922, affirmed the judgment of the appeals court that major league baseball was not a business as defined under the Sherman Act. In spite of the apparent illogic of that decision, baseball's antitrust exemption has survived numerous legal challenges and has had a profound effect on labor relations in the sport.

A judge in the Federal League cases made his own mark on baseball history. A FL case was heard in the court of Judge Kenesaw Mountain Landis, who postponed a decision until the FL agreed to withdraw the suit as part of the agreement that settled the baseball war. In dismissing the case, Landis made an impassioned speech praising the game. The owners did not forget.

This legal combat took place against the background of the more sanguine First World War. When the United States entered the war in 1917, Secretary of War Newton Baker's "work or fight" order required ballplayers (and other able-bodied males) to either volunteer, enter the draft, or work in an industry essential to the war effort. While many players entered active military service, others obtained jobs with defense-related companies that sponsored baseball leagues. Some of these industries competed for major leaguers by arranging for them to spend the majority of their time on the ballfield, not in the plant.

The war effort resulted in the curtailment of the 1918 season, forcing baseball to stage the World Series in September. As compensation of sorts to baseball fans, the National Commission extended the Series to nine games starting in 1919. The first teams to meet under these conditions were the Chicago White Sox, the prohibitive favorites, and the Cincinnati Reds. When the Reds emerged victorious, fans across the nation were shocked. That shock turned into horror when rumors that the Series had been fixed were confirmed after several players admitted their involvement in the scheme.

Fans did not recognize, or perhaps care, that since the conclusion of the Federal League war salaries had plunged to their previous levels and that White Sox owner Charles Comiskey—a former player once active in the Brotherhood—was among the most penurious executives in the sport. Fans wanted assurances that the national pastime would take measures to prevent such an offense from happening again. The owners, who had been dissatisfied with the National Commission in any case, took a dramatic step toward meeting the demands of their consumers.

In 1920 the owners hired Judge Landis as baseball's first commissioner, at the then-astounding annual salary of $50,000. Landis accepted the position on the condition that he would be granted absolute authority over the game, and the owners, desperate to restore baseball's good reputation, agreed. His first important decision as commissioner was to ban permanently the eight recently acquitted "Black Sox" players. Landis took his mandate to combat gambling, and the slightest appearance thereof, very seriously. Only months before his death in 1944, Landis concluded his career by banning Philadelphia Phillies owner William Cox for gambling-related offenses.

Landis's hiring was not the only significant baseball event of 1920. In early January the New York Yankees announced that they had purchased the contract of Babe Ruth from the Boston Red Sox. That historic transaction launched the Yankees to forty years of dominance unprecedented in American professional sports.

Just six weeks after Ruth's signing, a group of men led by former pitching great Rube Foster met in a Kansas City YMCA to form the Negro National League (NNL). The NNL was organized only because of organized baseball's unwritten but unchallenged practice banning the signing of black players. After an uncertain beginning, the Negro Leagues—whose teams comprised one of the largest, best-known black-owned businesses in America (although several clubs, most notably the Kansas City Monarchs, were owned by whites)—flourished in the 1930s and 1940s. They staged their own World Series and All-Star games, and developed dozens of players who, given the opportunity, would have excelled in the majors. Ironically, the long-awaited integration of baseball in the late 1940s and 1950s killed the Negro Leagues, as its fans flocked to major league parks to watch their heroes and ignored the leagues that had entertained them for decades.

During this period African American fans were nearly as unwelcome in major league ballparks as black players, but one way in which they and everyone else could experience games was through radio. The first commercial radio station was founded in 1920, and just one year later that station, Pittsburgh's KDKA, first broadcast a baseball game. Shortly afterward regional then national networks were established, which allowed millions of listeners to "attend" the World Series and other important sporting events. Although some teams resisted having their games broadcast, fearing that it would decrease attendance (an indication of the medium's strength), executives like Cincinnati's Larry MacPhail convinced them that radio actually increased the fan base. By hiring an obscure radio announcer named Red Barber to narrate Reds (and later Dodger) games, MacPhail demonstrated the importance of personalities to baseball broadcasts. Fans quickly developed ties to their announcers as they had with their players. Less than two decades after its introduction to the medium, baseball without radio seemed inconceivable.

Major league games were not the only baseball contests broadcast on radio. A growing number of minor league teams also developed ties with local stations, but with the onset of the Depression these clubs needed an additional attraction to pull in fans. The solution they settled on, night baseball, had been attempted intermittently for fifty years but did not become practical until the Kansas City Monarchs invested in a portable lighting system and proved that baseball in the evening was a lucrative endeavor. Starting in 1930, scores of minor league teams found the money to finance lights, and by the middle of the decade night baseball was commonplace. Nevertheless, the major leagues, which had been slow to recognize the promise of radio, dismissed night games until the maverick Larry Mac-Phail installed lights in his Cincinnati park and saw attendance skyrocket. Still, his peers were slow to follow. The number of night games was limited until World War II, when the federal government asked organized baseball to increase the number of night games to provide entertainment for working men and women.

Depression-era fans also experienced the heyday of amateur and semipro baseball. Spectators seemed to appreciate athletes who appeared to play more for the love of the game than for money. Two tournaments in particular, the *Denver Post* Tournament and the National Baseball Congress, attracted semipro teams, often featuring Negro League stars and white professionals, from across the country. The American Legion's national championship tournament, initiated in 1926, gave thousands of young boys (and one girl) the opportunity to compete in structured, highly competitive contests. However, it was not until 1939 that the first organization devoted exclusively to youth baseball, the Little League, was created. Both Little League and the American Legion hoped that by teaching boys baseball they were instilling in them uniquely American values which would aid them in maintaining democracy.

Such values seemed more important than ever with the onset of World War II. Baseball owners, nervous about the fate of their game, sent President Franklin D. Roosevelt a letter through Commissioner Landis inquiring about the wartime status of baseball, and were immensely relieved to receive a presidential "green light" to continue playing. Nevertheless, the quality of play understandably declined as more major and minor leaguers enlisted or were drafted, and materials used in manufacturing baseballs became scarce. In 1944 officials in the metals industry in Washington State even planned the manufacture of aluminum and magnesium baseball bats, but apparently very few were made. Troops abroad kept abreast of the latest action through newsreels, tours by baseball players and officials, and publications like *Stars and Stripes* and *The Sporting News*. In addition, some of the best players spent the war on military base teams.

On the home front even the acute shortage of skilled players did not persuade owners to sign Negro League players, although public pressure brought by the black press and sympathetic white sportswriters like the *Washington Post*'s Shirley Povich was increasing. One owner, the Cubs' Philip Wrigley, responded to the desire for more baseball (and to the popularity of softball) by organizing the All American Girls' Professional Baseball League in 1943. The AAGPBL, based in the Midwest, was seen initially as a novelty; the players wore short skirts and were instructed in deportment and makeup application as well as in baseball fundamentals. During its twelve-year existence the rules of the AAGPBL moved closer and closer to those of baseball, and its fans saw firsthand the athletic ability of women. Despite the league's success, it was largely forgotten until the early 1990s, when documentary and feature films, followed by a number of books, revived memory of the AAGPBL.

After the war's conclusion the service of black soldiers made baseball's racial segregation more appalling than ever. Still, the announcement by Brooklyn Dodger president Branch Rickey that the club had signed Jackie Robinson to a minor league contract in late 1945 jolted the baseball world. Some players vowed that they would never take the field with or against Robinson's club, but in spite of all obstacles, Robinson led his Montreal team to the International League championship in 1946. Promoted to the Dodgers the following season, Robinson became a hero in the black community and eventually won the respect of rival players and fans. His success on and off the field began the slow, long-overdue movement toward integration in baseball. Nevertheless, the extraordinary pressures he endured during his battles are thought to have contributed to his death at the young age of 53, in 1972.

Shortly after Robinson's dramatic ascent to the major leagues, another baseball hero died at 53. Few can deny that Babe Ruth was baseball's greatest symbol and greatest player. Though his quest to become a manager was denied, Ruth served as an ambassador for the game, even after he was diagnosed with throat cancer. When he died, in 1948, Americans relived the pain they experienced when his teammate Lou Gehrig contracted a rare disease and died in 1941. Legendary sportswriter Grantland Rice concluded his obituary of Ruth with the sentence "One all alone," which was also true, in a different sense, of Robinson. The sport popularized by Ruth and humanized by Robinson has survived the loss of both and has seen the development of new heroes who have approached Rice's encapsulation of greatness, although not to the extent of the men who embodied their respective eras in baseball history.

Middle Innings

A New Century Dawns

The beginning of the twentieth century marked a resurgence of professional baseball after the turbulence of the 1890s. The ascent of the American League to major league status reestablished baseball as a two-league game, as it was in the glory years of the 1880s. Another reminder of the 1880s, a post-season championship series, was reborn as the World Series. With the new-found stability of the majors, other levels of baseball also flourished. The number of minor leagues expanded annually, and semipro and college ball were more popular than ever. Baseball also expanded internationally. Japan, for example, sent its top clubs to the United States to gain experience—and occasionally taught their hosts something about the sport. The new century also saw professional leagues formed by African Americans, who had been effectively exiled from the national pastime. The future of the game seemed limitless.

1

Buffalo Dropped from American League (1901)

SOURCE: *Buffalo Courier*, January 30, 1901

After transforming the Western League into the American League and enjoying a successful 1900 season, AL President Ban Johnson planned to further upgrade the AL to equal status with the National League. A key component in his strategy was to move franchises currently in midsize cities to larger cities; four AL cities—Kansas City, Milwaukee, Indianapolis, and Buffalo—were stripped of league membership at a meeting in Chicago on January 28, 1901. While this move may seem logical to modern baseball fans, it enraged supporters of the affected clubs. The writer of the article below angrily and sarcastically describes the circumstances under which Buffalo was demoted.

ALD. FRANKLIN HAS RETURNED

"UNCLE JIM" SADDER BUT WISER, LOVES BAN JOHNSON NO LONGER— OFF FOR NEW YORK TODAY ON PRIVATE (?) BUSINESS

James Franklin, owner of the Buffalo baseball interests, returned to this city from Chicago yesterday afternoon. When seen by a Courier reporter last night the local magnate was not in a very loquacious mood, but after a dozen or so queries had been propounded to him Franklin supplied the writer with not a little information.

Buffalo's chief baseball mogul left for the town of many winds at the upper end of Lake Michigan last Sunday night. Down deep in his yearning heart "Uncle" Jim did not anticipate getting a franchise in the new league, but he knew that there was something coming to him, and he was on the ground when the meeting of the other magnates was held last Monday.

Months ago Franklin was promised by that great blubberous expounder of gaseous talk, Ban Johnson, that Buffalo would undoubtedly be a member of the new American League. Buffalo's impresario thought that the balloonish Johnson was a man of his word, but subsequent events inundated, so to speak, the dry land on which Franklin thought he stood. Reports emanating from reliable sources weeks ago hinted of the fact that Buffalo was doomed, and although decidedly reticent when interrogated on the baseball situation last Sunday evening, a few hours previous to his departure for Chicago, Franklin admitted yesterday that when he left he did not have hopes of being made an American League owner.

The meeting of the interested chieftains was held at the Grand Pacific Hotel, and while there Franklin was the recipient of further ill-treatment at the hands of the corpulent, wind-pudding-eating Ban (Wagon) Johnson. The latter relegated Franklin to the atmosphere of the hotel corridor while the meeting of the magnates was in progress in one of the parlors. After the lid of Buffalo's coffin had been nailed on and the big "mucky-mucks" had finished their business, Franklin was invited to enter. James did so and in a tone full of pathos and in that suave way for which Ban Johnson has become famous as a salve advancer, Franklin was informed of the fact that he and his Pan-American crew weren't wanted; and after being handed the $500 which he deposited last year, Buffalo's Napoleon was told to "take his clothes and go."

When asked if he took Johnson's measure by a pyrotechnic display of caustic rhetoric after learning of the ultimatum set down, Mr. Franklin told the writer that if he had given Johnson a scathing word-picture of his own feelings he had forgotten what was said, and on that theme Franklin was not very glib.

It is rumored that a meeting of the Eastern League was held in New York City last night. Tonight Mr. Franklin will, according to his words of yesterday, leave for the metropolis. His trip to New York is very significant, although "Uncle Jim" was uncommunicative on the subject. The only plausible deduction which one can made [sic] from the local leader's movements is that he will go to Gotham to interview our old friend, Patrick Powers, president of the Eastern League, and essay to become a member of Pat's circuit. Powers hasn't evinced any desire to have Buffalo in his fold; on the contrary he has been quite frigid in his manner towards the Buffalo club's future. Just what Mr. Franklin's jaunt to New York will bring forth will cause the wiseacres considerable conjecture. It is hoped, if the Eastern League gives Buffalo the cold stare, that the State League will take compassion on Franklin, and admit him. Should the State League tell us to look elsewhere there will be still another choice organization to have aspirations for; the Squashville Association, composed of Mud Center, Potato Hollow, Squirrel Creek and other baseball-mad centers, will possibly open its arms to poor Buffalo.

The story published in the Chicago papers of yesterday that Mr. Franklin has sold the players on his list to Koch, the Milwaukeean, is untrue. Mr. Franklin denied the rumor yesterday.

A. L.

2

Charles Comiskey Plays Prank on Ban Johnson

(1902)

SOURCE: *The Sporting News*, October 18, 1902

Johnson and Comiskey were allies in their fight to transform the Western League into a major league—the American League. After the AL's second season Comiskey accompanied Johnson on his annual hunting trip, where Johnson hoped to impress all with his marksmanship. However, Comiskey replaced Johnson's shells with blanks. According to Johnson's biographer, Eugene Murdock, Johnson never recovered from the humiliation and until his retirement in 1927 remained bitter toward Comiskey.

This article was written by Hugh Fullerton, who would become one of the best-known baseball writers. He was one of the few reporters to correctly predict that the Chicago White Stockings would upset their mighty cross-town rivals in the 1906 World Series, and was the first reporter to publicly question the integrity of the Chicago White Sox in the 1919 World Series (see documents 43 and 46).

PROMPTED BY JEALOUSY

Comiskey brought back one story from the wilds of upper Wisconsin which is not a "fish" story, but founded on absolute fact. It had to do with an attempt to convince Ban Johnson that his reputation as a clever marksman was based on good luck in the past rather than ability. Some one in the party of four which made the fishing and hunting trip to the unexplored regions beyond Fifield conceived and executed a plan to substitute a supply of blank shells for the carefully loaded affairs with which the American League leader invariably provides himself for such a trip. The execution was aided by the haste of Ban's departure consequent upon his arrival from the East only a few hours before the party was scheduled to leave Chicago.

Repeated failures to bring down a bird at short range aroused Ban's suspicions naturally and, reloading his gun with one of the "latest and most up-to-date smokeless powder" shells, he took careful aim at a tree not far away, fired, and then examined the tree thoroughly. Not a scar broke the weather marks of hundreds of years. Another shell was inserted, and at a distance of 10 feet Ban shot again. One big black spot where the wadding struck was all there was to show there had been a murderous assault on the monarch of the forest.

"Give me that knife of yours," snapped Ban to the guide, and with tightly closed lips he cut into one of the unused shells, only to find a triple dose of wadding, the usual allowance of explosive, but not a sign of anything harder. Ban "hiked back" to camp and patiently awaited the return of the others, when the explosions that occurred were louder but more harmless than the "phoney" shells which had so nearly ruined his reputation as a wing shot.

H. S. FULLERTON

3

National Commission Formed (1903)

SOURCE: *New York Times*, August 30, 1903

After a two-year battle for territory and players, the National League and the American League made peace in January 1903. The new National Agreement, signed in early September, created a three-man National Commission—consisting of the two league presidents and a third person—to rule baseball. The Commission never functioned effectively, and after the Black Sox scandal of 1919 the owners dissolved it in favor of a single commissioner. Also of importance to the delegates was the relationship between the majors and the National Association of Professional Baseball Leagues, the governing body of the minor leagues. Although on August 31 NAPBL President Pat T. Powers announced he would not sign the National Agreement because it ceded too much power to the major leagues, he soon changed his mind and subordinated his organization to the National and American Leagues in exchange for the protection from player raids they offered to minor league teams.

NATIONAL BASEBALL AGREEMENT

Minor League Organizations Will Discuss Provisions of Proposed Uniformity of Rules To-Day—Professional Interests in the Game Throughout the Country to be Protected

An important meeting of minor league baseball representatives will take place today at the Victoria Hotel, Broadway and Twenty-seventh Street, at which the new National agreement, adopted by the National League and the American

League delegates at Buffalo, last week, will be discussed in detail. This meeting has been called by President P. T. Powers of the National Association of Minor Baseball Leagues, an organization which embraces all the professional baseball associations in this country, with the exception of the two big leagues.

Ever since the baseball war between the major organizations was amicably settled by the signing of the Cincinnati peace pact last January, most of those who have interests in baseball clubs throughout the United States and part of Canada have been urging the adoption of a new National agreement for the protection of every person, club owners as well as players, connected with the game. . . .

The Presidents of the major leagues, with two representatives from each organization, were in conference recently in Buffalo, and the outcome of the conference was the adoption of a lengthy document embracing, seemingly, every point of importance for the absolute government of professional baseball. One of its articles created a National commission for the purpose of enforcing the terms and provisions of the agreement. The members of this body were named as August Herrmann of Cincinnati, Chairman; President Johnson of the American League, and President Pulliam of the National League.

The most important objects of the new agreement are as follows:

(1) Perpetuation of baseball as the National pastime of America by surrounding it with such safeguards as will warrant absolute public confidence in its integrity and methods, and by maintaining a high standard of skill and sportsmanship in its players.

(2) Protection of the property rights of those engaged in baseball as a business without sacrificing the spirit of competition in the conduct of the clubs.

(3) Promotion of the welfare of ball players as a class by developing and perfecting them in their profession, and enabling them to secure adequate compensation for expertness.

(4) Adoption of a uniform code of rules for playing baseball.

The agreement is to be indissoluble except by the unanimous vote of the parties to it. Each party to the agreement retains the right to conduct its affairs and govern its players according to its constitution and by-laws, but there shall be no conflict between such constitution and by-laws and the objects and terms of the agreement. Should the measure be adopted by the National Association of Minor Leagues, these minor organizations will have absolute control of their own affairs. . . .

The practice of "farming" is prohibited. All right or claim of a major league club to a player shall cease when such player becomes a member of a minor league club, and no arrangement between the clubs for the loan or return of a player shall be binding between the parties to it or recognized by other clubs.

The right of a minor league club to its players shall be absolute, except that from Aug. 15 to Oct. 15 of each year major leagues shall have the privilege of selecting players from National association clubs for the following season upon payment of $750 for each player so selected from clubs in Class A leagues; $500 for each player so selected from clubs in Class B leagues; $300 for each player so selected from clubs in Class C leagues; and $200 for each player so selected from clubs of a lower class.

A major league club may at any time purchase the release of a player from a minor league club, to take effect forthwith or at a specified date, provided such purchase is recorded with the Secretary of the commission for promulgation within five days of the date of the transaction.

Many of the articles in the agreement are designed to protect the interests of the players, one of which gives a player suspended for a period of longer than ten days the right to appeal to the commission. The leagues are strictly enjoined to enforce the provision in the constitution against open betting on baseball grounds, and club officials are obliged to cause the arrest and prosecution of those who may engage in such a practice. . . .

Articles of the agreement which do not find favor with the minor league representatives are the drafting clause and the method of paying for players drafted. Under the terms of the agreement the major leagues have two months in which to draft players, while the old rule gave them only one month.

4

Will Pittsburgh Bow Out of the World Series? (1903)

SOURCE: *Sporting Life*, September 19, 1903

On the eve of the first modern World Series, rumors circulated that the contest would not be played due to injuries suffered by both teams, especially Pittsburgh. Not only was "the incomparable" Honus Wagner hurting, but sixteen-game winner Ed Doheny had just abandoned the team. This left Fred Clarke's squad with only two dependable pitchers, Sam Leever and Deacon Phillippe. That such a rumor could arise indicates that the Series was still considered an exhibition, albeit an important one. The Series was played, and Pittsburgh lost despite a good performance by Wagner and a heroic effort from Phillippe, who threw five complete games.

The first paragraph is a news story, and the remaining material is an editorial. Both were written by Francis C. Richter, Sporting Life's prolific editor.

A WORLD'S SERIES

MAY NOT BE PLAYED THIS FALL AFTER ALL
The National League Champion Team in Such a Crippled Condition That It May be Compelled to Decline to Enter an Unequal Contest

Pittsburg, Pa., Sept. 15.—Editor "Sporting Life:"—There are indications that the post-season series between the champion Pittsburg team, of the National League, and the champion Boston team, of the American League, will not come off. There are several things which may prevent it. But the most serious is the present physical condition of Pittsburg players. During last week the team played like a lot of school boys, and the only excuse that could be made for them is that they were most all fit subjects for hospitals. The injury of Wagner was the crowning blow. While the big fellow was in the game on Saturday, still he is in bad physical condition, the tendons in his right leg being in very bad shape. Without him in the series Pittsburg would have no more chance of winning than the St. Louis team has of taking the pennant from Pittsburg. Dreyfuss and Clarke both know this, although they will not admit it. The question of pitchers is a serious one. Since Doheny deserted the team he has been in the dumps. Monday week he was taken out of the game because of indifferent playing, and on Tuesday he disappeared. It was claimed that he was sick, but other persons allege that he was looking on the wine. He did not appear on the grounds again until last Friday and has not pitched since. Without Doheny Pittsburg would have but two pitchers upon whom they could depend, Leever and Phillipi [sic]. Dreyfuss and Clarke, when questioned as to whether the post-season series could be pulled off, stated that they could not tell until the latter part of the week.

THE WORLD'S SERIES

It will be a matter of keen regret if the Pittsburg Club shall be compelled, by reason of injuries to indispensable players, to decline the proposed world's championship series with the American League champion team. In such event the successful season of 1903 would be robbed of a glorious climax, the base ball world deprived of some royal sport, and the major league partisans cut out of much food for winter discussion.

Nevertheless, either the Pittsburg or Boston Clubs will be amply justified in declining the gage of battle if either team be not in perfect condition for the hardest series of the year. For either team to be minus its full strength would make of the battle an unequal, and therefore unsatisfactory, contest; and afford no fair test either of the strength of the teams or of their respective leagues for whose honor and glory the teams would battle quite as much as for their own prestige and satisfaction.

However, the Pittsburg and Boston teams are in all respects so evenly matched, and the inter-league rivalry is so keen, that it would be a pity if the series should fall through. Here's hoping that Pittsburg's tower of strength, the incomparable Wagner, may recover from his injury before the close of the season, inasmuch as in such event there is little doubt that the two great champion teams will meet to settle the stirring question of team and inter-league superiority.

New York Giants Refuse to Participate in World Series (1904)

SOURCE: *Sporting Life,* July 9 and October 15, 1904

At the midpoint of the 1904 season New York baseball fans faced the prospect of having their two major league teams, the Giants (NL) and the Highlanders (AL), meet in the World Series. The Giants enjoyed a commanding lead in the National League, while their crosstown rivals trailed defending Series champion Boston by a small margin. However, John Brush, the owner, and John McGraw, the manager of the Giants, both hated the AL and its president Ban Johnson. Brush's antagonism with Johnson dated from their days in the Western League, while McGraw's dislike stemmed from his perceived mistreatment while a player-manager with the AL Baltimore Orioles club.

On July 5 Brush declared that his Giants would not meet the Highlanders in a championship should the AL club triumph. Brush was angry that the AL had placed a club in his city, and did not want to give them the opportunity to claim superiority in New York. He released a more general refusal on September 25. When Boston clinched the pennant on the season's final day, Brush and McGraw repeated their refusal to play a postseason series, and in spite of the ensuing uproar among baseball fans, they stuck to their decision. However, Brush soon recognized his error and led the effort to draft an agreement for an annual World Series, starting in 1905.

Below is the initial story on Brush's stance on the Series. The statement that an agreement had been made to ensure the playing of a World Series is misleading; pennant winners were not obligated to participate in a postseason series. The second article is a statement by McGraw at the conclusion of the season in which he takes responsibility for the decision and outlines his reasons for making it. The most complete account of the affair is in Benton Stark, The Year They Called Off the World Series: A True Story. *Information on McGraw's relationship with Johnson and Brush's establishment of the Series are in Sullivan,* Early Innings: A Documentary History of Baseball, 1825–1908 *(Lincoln: University of Nebraska Press, 1995).*

BITTER BOSS BRUSH STILL RETAINS EXTREME HATRED FOR RIVALS

Authoritative Announcement There Will Be No World's Championship Series if The Two New York Clubs Win Major League Championships

New York City, July 5.—The statement is made here on the highest authority that the New York Nationals will refuse to play the New York Americans for the world's championship if each wins the pennant in its respective league. President Brush, of the New York Nationals, has repeatedly asserted that under no circumstances would he allow his team to play the rival organization in this city. From one of Mr. Brush's closest friends it was learned to-day that Brush will go so far as to violate the agreement made by the both leagues at the beginning of the season to play a series of seven games for the world's championship. Mr. Brush will disregard the demands of the public for a series of championship games if both New York teams win pennants, and will be satisfied to let the Giants rest on their laurels.

SHOULDERS THE BLAME

MANAGER MCGRAW SAYS THAT HE AND NOT MR. BRUSH OR THE PLAYERS IS RESPONSIBLE FOR NON-PLAYING OF SERIES

New York, Oct. 10.—In a statement issued by John J. McGraw, manager of the National League Base Ball Club, he says that he, and not John T. Brush, president of the club, is the one responsible for not playing a post-season series of games with the New York American League teams. He further says that he is supported in his stand by every man on the championship team. He says his team is not afraid to play any team in the world, which is true, for there was not a man on his team that was not anxious for this series of games. Here is Manager McGraw's open letter to the public:

New York City, Oct. 8.—To the Base Ball Patrons of New York:

I want to go clearly and emphatically on record in the matter of the refusal of the New York Club to play a post-season series. I was never accused of being a coward. It is not my nature to hide behind any man; I never yet did it and I am not going to begin now. The people of New York have been kind enough to give me some credit for bringing the pennant to New York, and if there is any just blame for criticism for the club's action in protecting that highly prized honor the blame should rest on my shoulders, not Mr. Brush's, for I and I alone am responsible for the club's action. However, when the facts are known there will be no blame. Mr. Brush's only part in it is supporting me, as he has always done.

I have my reasons for my stand and they are good reasons. I am willing to stand before the public and the patrons of the New York Club with them and be judged by them.

When I came to New York three years ago, the team was in last place. Since that time, on and off the field, I have worked to bring the pennant to New York. The result is known. Now that the New York team has won this honor I for one will not stand to see it tossed away like a rag. The pennant means something to me. It is the first I have ever won. It means something to our players, and they are with me in my stand. We are not a lot of grafters looking for box-office receipts at the expense of our club. The club is not run on these lines. If we had wanted to sacrifice the sport for box-office receipts we would not have won the pennant as we did. We could have eased up and made it close, but we didn't. We never stopped until we clinched the pennant, even if it did rob the game of the interest of a pennant race. The club never complained. When the fight was hot we played to thousands. After the race was won we played to hundreds. But that was square sport and the stockholders never complained. If we didn't sacrifice our race in our own league to the box-office we certainly are not going to put in jeopardy the highest honor in base ball simply for the box-office inducements.

I know the American League, and its methods. I ought to, for I paid for my knowledge. They induced me to join them when they raided the National League and as a souvenir of my experience they still have my money.

I have not forgotten its boast when it entered New York last year. It promised to put the National League Club in this city out of business by June. That was the American League idea of sportsmanship then.

Never while I am manager of the New York Club and while this club holds the pennant will I consent to enter into a haphazard box-office game with Ban Johnson & Company. No one, not even my bitterest enemy, ever accused me of being a fool, and I am not going to give them a chance now to say that I am a candidate for Bloomingdale.

If the National League should see fit to place post-season games on the same plane as championship games and surround them with the same protection and safeguards for square sport as championship games, then and not till then will I ever take part in them.

Now about the team. A better team was never gotten together—we are afraid of no team. They are with me to a man in my stand. I put it up to them one by one, and they showed their colors.

We are here and here to stay; we will defend the pennant in 1905, and hope to for many years. We are willing to be judged by our patrons and the supporters of honest sport.

John J. M'Graw

6

Chesbro's Wild Pitch Ends Highlanders' Quest for Pennant (1904)

SOURCE: *New York Sun*, October 11, 1904

After pursuing the Boston Puritans, the defending AL champions, throughout the 1904 season, New York entered the final weekend of the season trailing their rivals by only one and one-half games. If they swept Boston in the season-ending doubleheader, the Highlanders would win the AL pennant, and thus increase the pressure on Brush and McGraw to play a postseason championship series. Their hopes were increased with the knowledge that their pitcher in the opener was Jack Chesbro, who had already won forty-one games during the season. Thanks to his pitching and hitting, the game was tied 2–2 entering the ninth inning. With two outs and a man on third, Chesbro threw perhaps the most famous wild pitch in baseball history, allowing the winning run to score and ending New York's pennant dreams. The Highlanders won the meaningless closer 1–0 by scoring with two outs in the bottom of the tenth—which, if accomplished one game earlier, could have changed baseball history and the reputation of one of baseball's finest pitchers.

Throughout this pivotal game, Puritans supporters sang their unofficial anthem, "Tessie," a song from the Broadway musical The Silver Slipper *first recorded by Billy Murray in the spring of 1903. They also sang the song during Boston's 1903 and 1912 World Series victories. Murray also recorded the most popular version of "Take Me Out to the Ball Game" (see document 22).*

BASEBALL GLORY FOR BOSTON—AMERICAN LEAGUE PENNANT NOT FOR NEW YORK

First Game of Double Header Won by the Champions, and an Immense Crowd on Hand to See—Errors Costly for Griffith's Men—Locals Take Second

The American League championship stays in Boston, and, incidentally, the world's championship, since the New York Nationals will not test their strength against Collins's conquerors. The Bostons retained their position as the premier baseball team of the country by beating their most formidable rivals, the New Yorks, in the first game at American League Park yesterday afternoon. The score was 3 to 2, and the game was as close as the score. In the second game the New Yorks shut the Bostons out in a ten inning battle, but the first settled the pennant's abiding place. The second game was therefore but an aftermath but there was no cessation of effort on that account, and a splendid tribute to popularity of American League ball and a splendid evidence of appreciation of the hard fight made by Griffith's men were to be found in the fact that the bigger part of the immense crowd remained throughout the second game.

American League Park held its banner crowd. An attendance of proportion seldom surpassed in the history of baseball outpourings filled the big stands to overflowing. It became necessary to stretch ropes across the front of the right field bleachers, and restrained by these and out in the grass several thousand found elbow room not to be had in the congested stands. Along the right field fence also were a few scattering thousands. Somebody in the grand stand dug up a ladder, and there was a rush for the roof as a vantage point, but the folks up there were chased down in a hurry. The crowd was well handled and there was very little fuss or confusion.

The rooting of the different factions was something strenuous. Naturally New Yorkers predominated, but the Hub was ably represented by a strong lunged delegation in the left wing of the grand stand. Between the rival camps things sizzled and seethed. The Bostonians had a band with them, and their paean of victory was the famous "Tessie." In a way the Hub horde was hoist with its own petard by this ditty. The New Yorkers improvised megaphones out of cardboard placards and sang "Tessie" as fervently as did the Bostonians when things broke their way.

As a mascot the Boston brigade had an aged darky along, and when the band played "Dixie" the old chap capered nimbly on the roof of the Boston team's bench. When the band played "Old Black Joe" he moved back and forth with measured tread. Attached to a broom which the Bostonians had was a banner with this strange device:

> Mr. Brush, we're on plush,
> Where are you?
> Give us a game, don't be vain;
> One or two.

The whole afternoon was one of stir, hurrah, bustle, excitement, thrills and exuberance such as are to be found at sporting contests of unusual importance. The size of the attendance was a distinct rebuke to those who pretended to believe that it was on the cards for the New Yorks to win. One of these individuals in the grand stand who kept telling how the New Yorks were bound to win because it was so arranged hurried away after the first game. The Boston players were as happy as schoolboys after their victory and danced around like a lot of collegians.

The Boston club owner, John J. Taylor, is to issue a formal challenge to the New York Nationals for a series of games, and just to show that it is not a box office scheme on the part of the American League he will suggest that the players divide all the gate receipts. Several of the New York National players were at the games yesterday and went down to shake hands with the New York American players at the latter's bench before the game.

BOSTON (A.L.) 3; NEW YORK (A.L.) 2   FIRST GAME

The New York's were outplayed in the first game, both in batting and fielding. they lost on the merits of the play. The Bostons fielded faultlessly. Dineen pitched a stronger game than Chesbro, though he was wavering badly once or twice. Chesbro, however, pitched strongly enough to have won had he received clean support. It was errors that lost the game for New York.

There was a mighty cheer for Chesbro and his fellows as the New Yorks took the field, and three Boston batters were cut off in a hurry. For New York, Pat Dougherty, on whom the effects of malaria were plainly visible, walked and Willie Keeler sacrificed. But neither Elberfeld nor Williams could make any headway against the pitching of the burly Dineen. The Bostons sent five men to bat in the second inning, Freeman and Ferris making hits, but no score was forthcoming. Freddie Parent threw out Ganzel and Conroy in the second after making wonderful stops of hard hit grounders.

As Chesbro came to the plate in the third inning a fur lined overcoat, a present from North Adams friends, was presented to him. That was not the only presentation of the afternoon. The New York players presented a diamond and gold fob to Abe Nahon, the club secretary. Chesbro's response to his gift was a slashing three bagger to right with only one out. But just here Bill Dineen showed his mettle. He struck out Dougherty with three drop balls and also made Keeler of the eagle eye fan the atmosphere. In the third and fourth innings not a Bostonian reached first base, and only one in the fifth, on a base on balls.

There were two New Yorkers out in the fifth when Kleinow sent a line single to right. Chesbro also hit safely, a scorching liner to Dineen, which the big fellow could not handle. The cheering shook the stand when Dougherty singled to right and scored Kleinow, and the embanked thousands went into a frenzy of delight. Dineen was shaky, and a base on balls to Keeler filled up the bases. Another base on balls to Elberfeld forced Chesbro over the plate. There were still three on bases when Williams hit to Dineen and was thrown out at first.

A bad throw by Elberfeld and a fumble by Chesbro made things look squally for the New Yorks in the sixth. But there were two out when the two men were on bases, and Freeman gave Williams an easy fly. Anderson led off with a hit to left in New York's half of the sixth, but was caught napping, Dineen using a motion that was so nearly a balk it was hard to see the difference.

The Bostons tied the score in the seventh. Lachance hit a slow grounder to Williams, which was good for a base. Ferris ripped a single to right, Lachance being held at second. Criger sacrificed, very cleverly, Ganzel fielding the ball to Williams at first base. Then came a play that made the home contingent groan. Dineen sent a grounder to Williams and the latter had an easy play on Lachance at the plate. But he threw too low to Kleinow, the ball bounded away from the latter, and not only Lachance, but Ferris as well, scored. Ferris's run could have been shut off had Chesbro been spryer in getting to the plate to help out Kleinow.

Kleinow hit hard to centre in the seventh, Stahl's good fielding limiting the hit to a single. Kleinow was forced by Chesbro, Dougherty flied to Dineen, and Keeler forced Chesbro. The eighth inning was hair raising. Stahl began with a single to left. Collins struck out, Freeman singled, Stahl going to second. Lachance sent a fly to centre just out of Anderson's reach, and Stahl, when he saw Anderson could not get the ball, tore for the plate. He jumped up in the air and leaped for the rubber like a circus performer doing a double somersault over a pack of trained elephants. But his vicious approach did not disturb Kleinow, who tagged him out, the ball having been beautifully relayed in by Elberfeld from Anderson.

In the ninth Criger beat out an infield hit, Dineen sacrificed, and Criger went to third when Elberfeld threw Selbach out. With two out, Chesbro made a wild pitch and Criger scored. It was a most unfortunate play. It was not a case of being unnerved on Chesbro's part. Happy Jack is always a cool customer in the box. It simply happened that at this most crucial of moments he made a wild pitch. Parent made a hit, on which Criger would have scored anyway, though he might not have made the hit had the discouraging play not just preceded it.

Ganzel struck out in the ninth. Conroy drew four balls. Kleinow flied to Ferris, and McGuire drew four balls. Then Dineen zipped three over for Dougherty, the big fellow struck out and the championship, which flirted so long with Griffith and his brave boys, took wings to Boston.

7

"Semi-Professional Base Ball" in the Northern Midwest (1905)

SOURCE: *Spalding's Minneapolis–St. Paul Amateur Base Ball Year Book*, 1905, pp. 21–22

In the early twentieth century A. G. Spalding expanded his already formidable sports library by publishing baseball guides for specific cities. These guides featured discussions of all the notable local teams, along with numerous photographs and statistics, and concluded with a lengthy essay by the venerable Henry Chadwick. The following article recounts the 1904 season among independent clubs in Minnesota, the Dakotas, and Wisconsin. Such clubs occasionally boasted future major leaguers, and the teams described below starred players like Russ Ford, who enjoyed three twenty-win seasons for the Yankees; George Hildebrand, whose brief major league playing career had already ended but who would umpire in the majors for over twenty years; and George Wilson, who was a prominent pitcher for top turn-of-the-century black clubs like the Page Fence Giants and the Chicago Union Giants.

SEMI-PROFESSIONAL BASE BALL

Interest in base ball was never greater in the smaller cities of Minnesota, Wisconsin and the Dakotas than during the season of 1904, and a large number of very strong clubs were supported by the enthusiastic fans, in spite of the fact that the Northern and Iowa State League had attempted to secure all of the best players at the beginning of the year. In North Dakota the Lisbon team played phenomenal ball, especially late in the season, when the breaking up of one or two Northern League clubs filled the northwest with a number of players who were eager to take on for the remainder of the year. Russ Ford, brother of Gene Ford of the Minneapolis American Association staff, and a great twirler, with several others, were snapped up by Lisbon, and this club was unbeaten during July and August, finally disbanding because it could secure no worthy opponents in its section.

Webster in South Dakota, Renville in Minnesota and Chippewa Falls and Eau Claire in Wisconsin, also had remarkable teams in the field, and games between any one of these clubs always resulted in small scores, because of the phenomenal pitching and fast fielding of the opposing clubs.

The impartial critic of independent base ball would without question place Webster in the first rank because of the pitching of Hildebrand. With this versatile twirler in the box no club in the West, and probably no American Association team, could have a chance to win, because he was invincible. He lost games, but not when any championship was at stake, and was always just a little better than the batter who was opposing him. The club behind him gave him fair support, and contained enough batters to bat out a victory against the best of pitchers.

To Chippewa Falls must be given the second honors, and this club also won because of strength in its pitching staff. George Wilson, the colored pitcher, who has been connected with the best independent teams in the West for years, was the Hildebrand of this organization, and won practically all of this [sic] games. He and Hildebrand did not oppose each other during the year, but the record of the latter pitcher is the better of the two. Wilson did not have the support of Hildebrand, and did not pitch as steadily, when all of the games are considered. The Chippewa Falls pitcher, however, should be given credit for being one of the best general players in the three States, as he batted over the three hundred mark, and fielded his position in faultless fashion.

Below these two clubs come a large number of teams of about equal strength. Eau Claire had a very fast fielding team, but was weak at the bat, winning its games through the ability of Speiser in the box. Speiser pitched such consistent ball as to attract the attention of professional managers and he will play in the Iowa State League this year. With Eau Claire should be classed the Javas of Minneapolis, Renville, Stillwater, and Fort Snelling, such clubs as Faribault, Osceola, Arlington Mankato and St. Cloud being below the first named.

8

"Frank Merriwell's 'Dope Ball' " (1905)

SOURCE: *Tip Top Weekly*, no. 471, April 22, 1905

Frank Merriwell is one of the best-known fictional characters of the twentieth century. Created by Gilbert Patten, who wrote his Merriwell tales under the pseudonym of Burt L. Standish, Merriwell was a brilliant, brave young man who also happened to be one of America's finest athletes, starring for Yale's baseball and football clubs. He had an uncanny knack for winning the big games while at the same time foiling the efforts of criminals to vanquish him. Many of Merriwell's exploits were published in Tip Top Weekly, *whose subtitle, "An Ideal Publication for the American Youth," summed up Patten's intentions perfectly.*

In the following excerpt "Merry's" team was preparing to play the Stanford club while touring the west coast. Merriwell's arch enemy, Porfias del Norte, hypnotized Merriwell's catcher to induce him to play poorly, and performed other nefarious deeds calculated to crush Merriwell once and for all. Not surprisingly, he did not succeed.

FRANK MERRIWELL'S "DOPE BALL" OR THE
WIZARD TWIRLER OF LELAND STANFORD

Stanford went to bat first.

Lester Standing had appeared and was permitted to sit on the bench with the visitors. He seemed to be quivering with excitement as he pushed up beside Dick Starbright.

"Your team is bound to win this game," he said. "I consider it a sure thing, don't you?"

"There's nothing sure but death and taxes," answered Dick.

"Oh, but they can't beat you! They can't hit Merriwell's double shoot."

"He isn't going to use the double shoot to-day."

"What's that?" gasped Standing, in dismay.

"I say he isn't going to use the double shoot."

"Why—why not?"

"Because he made an agreement with Larkin that he wouldn't use it."

"When?"

"Just before the game."

"I wish I had known it in time!" half groaned Standing.

"In time for what?"

"Never mind. Here they go."

Merry delivered the first ball.

It was a high in-shoot.

Sidney swung and missed.

"One strike!" cried the umpire.

"Well! well! He has good speed!" shouted a Palo Alto man.

The next ball was wide, and Sidney let it pass.

"One ball!"

"Get them over!" yelled a voice.

Again Merry drove in a speedy one that almost seemed to lift Hodge off his feet. It was a rise, and Sidney struck under it at least a foot.

"Ow, wow, wow!" whooped a spectator. "Put on your glasses, Sid! You'll have to get a stepladder to reach those. Let 'em go."

Two strikes had been made, and Sidney had not even fouled the ball.

The next one was straight as a bullet and over the inside corner.

Sidney turned pale as he listened for the umpire's decision.

"Ball—too high!" cried the umpire, and Sidney breathed again.

"That was all right," he told himself. "I must look out. I thought he'd call me out on it."

He was on his mettle now, for something told him that Merriwell was trying to lead off with a strike-out.

Frank toed the slab and went through the movements of delivering a speedy ball, which nerved Sidney to be ready to strike quickly. What happened was that he struck too quickly, for the ball seemed to stop and linger in the air in a most astonishing manner, as if some unseen power checked it after it left the pitcher's hand. Really the ball was not much more than two-thirds of the distance from Frank's hand to the plate when Sidney swung at it. When it was too late to check the swing, the batter realized that he had been fooled. He flung down his bat in disgust and walked to the bench.

9

Japanese College Team Wins in Los Angeles (1905)

SOURCE: *Los Angeles Daily Times*, May 18, 1905

Learning the game from American missionaries, the Japanese quickly took to baseball. Before long they were regularly defeating teams from the American embassy staff and U.S. military personnel. Americans responded not with admiration but with contempt, hurling terms such as "brownies." When the Waseda University team toured the western United States, they were expected to lose in embarrassing fashion, but instead they impressed many of their American critics, starting with their performance in the game described below. Following the success of this tour, Waseda and other Japanese clubs regularly traveled to the United States, and occasionally American college teams and professional all-star teams reciprocated.

BROWN BOYS NETTLE HIGH

Japanese Students Defeat Ours at Baseball
Waseda University Strong on Diamond Here
Sizzling Contest Delights the Yelling Fan

The baseball tossers from Tokio proved their ability to play the American game yesterday afternoon, by defeating the High School boys, 5 to 3, in a sizzling contest at Fiesta Park.

The Japanese were expected to play ball, but the 800 or more fans crowded on the central bleachers scarcely thought the little short-legged, black-haired, base runners would demonstrate such a thorough knowledge of the game.

The High School team is slightly better than the average run of amateur base-ball nines in Southern California, and they were picked to trim the Japs. They failed to turn the trick. In the first two innings of the game they were affected with such a severe case of "cold feet" that the Japs circled the diamond three times with the utmost ease, and Thompson, the crack pitcher from the red schoolhouse, walked men in one-two-three order, because his mates declare he was rattled at the sight of the well-knit forms of the students from the University of Waseda.

Hundreds of Japanese attended. From the pocket of almost every enthusiastic brown spectator the well-thumbed leaves of a book on baseball rules protruded.

Bright-colored pennants with strange emblems floated over the Japanese contingent, who were dressed in their best, and were stirred to the yelling point, as their countrymen forged steadily ahead.

THE OPENING GUN

About 3:10 o'clock, when both teams had finished their preliminary practice, the game opened. High School won the toss, and sent the Japs to the bat. Hashido, captain of the team, connected with Thompson's delivery and sent the ball out into the right field for a safe hit. The little man fairly whizzed down the chalk mark to first base. This seemed to take the heart right out of the High School twirler, who promptly passed two men on balls. With the bases filled, a hard crack sent the spheroid out over the second baseman's head and brought in two tallies. This ended the scoring for the inning and the Japanese rooters opened their lungs and vented their delight.

The High School boys scored a goose egg for their inning, and thoroughly discouraged, scattered over the field for the second turn of the Japs to bat.

Some one among the High School players caught a difficult fly, the rest of the fellows did not care who it was, a Jap was out and their blood was up. A stiff liner to shortstop, which was fumbled, sent a brown man to the initial plate, but his mate went out on a pop fly. With two men out, a brown batter sent the ball over against the fence and scored the third tally for his team.

High School scored once in the second inning and new life was instilled into the nine. The Japs were held until the sixth inning with a score of 3 to 1. In their part of the sixth, the High School players sent two men over the home plate and tied the score.

The eighth inning closed with a tie score, 3.

The crowd expected a ten-inning game, and everybody was willing to remain to watch the pretty contest. Interest was intense and the rooters began to toot up their slogans. This was too much for the usually silent Japanese spectators. A short, fat, greasy-faced Mongolian in the center of a compact bunch of his countrymen rose and began a strange yell.

"WHATTA MATTA?"

"Whatta matta with high school? He's no good," he shouted and his fellows, greatly to the amusement of the other spectators, took up the refrain. It was the firm conviction of the Japs that the "white boys" could not play ball with the men from Tokio.

The brownies went in to settle matters in the ninth, and with a pretty series of bunched hits scored twice and won. The High School lads could not connect with the delivery of little Kono.

The line-up:

High School		Waseda
Thompson	pitcher	Kono
Colbath	catcher	Yamawaka
M. Mitchell	first base	Izumitani
S. Mitchell (capt)	second base	Oshikawa
Childs	third base	Suyama
Tufts	short stop	Hashido (capt)
Bradley	left field	Hosokawa
Ely	centerfield	Obaya
Wilkinson	right field	Shisiuchi

Score by innings:

	1	2	3	4	5	6	7	8	9	
Waseda	2	1	0	0	0	0	0	0	2	—5
High School	0	1	0	0	2	0	0	0	0	—3

The schedule of the Japanese players while in this city is as follows:

Saturday, May 20, Waseda vs. Sherman Indians.

Tuesday, May 23, Waseda vs. Pomona, at Pomona.

Wednesday, May 24, Waseda vs. University of Southern California, at Methodist Field.

Thursday, May 25, Waseda vs. St. Vincent at St. Vincent. This game is subject to change as an effort is being made to play it on Sunday.

This afternoon the Japs will cross bats with Occidental at Fiesta Park. The Presbyterian line-up will be:

Knight, pitcher; Clover, catcher; Dakin, first base; Field, second base; Thatcher, third base; Roth, second base; Merrill, left field; Hagerman, center field; Bird, right field.

10

The Scandal of College Players and "Summer Ball"

(1905)

SOURCE: *McClure's*, July 1905, pp. 260–63

In the summer of 1905 McClure's, a magazine in the forefront of the "muckraking" school of journalism, ran a two-part series by Henry Beach Needham on the hypocrisy of the "amateur" athlete in college. The first article, published in June 1905, focused on college football. The second also discussed football, but began with an analysis of the phenomenon of "summer ball," in which top college baseball players were hired to play for resort teams for high wages, despite rules which declared such players to be ineligible for college play. While Needham had an unrealistic view of amateurism, he cited numerous examples in which college football and baseball players, often with the knowledge of their coaches and athletic administrators, evaded the rules. Summer ball continued to concern college administrators for the next half-century.

THE COLLEGE ATHLETE

HIS AMATEUR CODE: ITS EVASION AND ADMINISTRATION
By Henry Beach Needham

PART II—"SUMMER BALL," THE GATE-MONEY EVIL, AND "UNNECESSARY ROUGHNESS" IN FOOTBALL

No question relating to the amateur standing of athletes engaged in intercollegiate sport has produced more rabid discussion, with opinion greatly divided, than the propriety of "summer ball." By summer ball is meant baseball played by amateurs, so-called, mainly collegians, on the "summer nines"—teams semi-professional in character, not members of any recognized league, which are organized to furnish entertainment for the visitors at summer resorts. It was fifteen years or more ago that baseball reached its first popularity in the White Mountains—the birthplace and home of the summer nine. The game indulged in by collegians of the day, and for some time thereafter, was regarded as an innocent past-time, not incompatible with proper amateur standards.

"In those earlier days," says The White Mountain Echo of August 20, 1904,

college ball players did not think it at all beneath their dignity to spend the summer at a swell hotel, in exchange for which pleasure they gladly gave their services on the diamond and cared not who knew it. And if, at the season's end, a purse was made up for the players by popular subscription, so much the better; there was no one to say that they should not take it, or that, by so doing, they forfeited their eligibility to the college team.

But those good old days are gone; and now, if a collegian wants to play baseball for money in the mountains, it is not as a short stop or pitcher that he receives his weekly stipend, but as a tray boy, bell hop, or the guardian of a casino or hotel bowling alley.

If collegians could play summer ball "in those earlier days," and not forfeit their eligibility as amateurs, it was because professionalism was not clearly understood. Furthermore, it was not realized that summer ball was to be productive of other and more serious evils. When the Conference on Intercollegiate Athletics met at Providence in 1898, the edict went forth that "playing during the summer on professional nines, or on so-called summer nines, should be wholly discouraged." Not content with adopting the general rule debarring athletes "who shall at any time have received for taking part in any athletic sport or contest any pecuniary gain or emolument whatever, direct or indirect," the Conference added a special provision proscribing summer ball. For the last seven summers, therefore, playing on the "so-called summer nines" has been in direct violation of the athletic code of the leading colleges of the East, including Yale whose eligibility rules (now being superseded by the Harvard-Yale agreement) disqualify students who have received "board for playing summer ball." It is in the light of such iron-clad restrictions, that this objectionable feature of intercollegiate athletics is to be judged.

DELIBERATE EVASION OF THE CODE

Certainly summer ball is officially recognized now, and Charles W. Towne, the writer of the article in The Echo from which quotation is made, explains how, "if a collegian wants to play ball for money," he goes about it and covers up his tracks. Mr. Towne knows whereof he speaks, for he arranged last summer a series of games played by the New Hampshire summer nines of Maplewood, Waumbek, Bethlehem, and Fabyan. These teams were composed largely of college and preparatory school players, a number of whom are representing colleges on the diamond this season. Maplewood, for example, had for pitchers, Cook and Heim, Exeter graduates who are now at Princeton. The pitcher of the Waumbek team was Keady, captain of this year's Dartmouth nine and left-tackle of the Dartmouth eleven of 1904. With Fabyan was O'Brien of the Dartmouth 'varsity ball team. There were other college players, but some of them were masquerading under names other than their own.

The practice of playing under an assumed name is growing. The act in itself makes a man a professional under the rules governing the Princeton-Yale track contests. But it is part of the game of subterfuge and evasion. Here is a letter written to a preparatory school-boy. It was misdirected, and fell into the hands of a lad other than the one for whom it was obviously intended.

St. Albans, Vt., April 26, 1904.

DEAR SIR:—I write thinking I might induce you to come to St. Albans to play summer ball on the league team here. I know both your school and league record and they are certainly very good ones. A gentleman who saw you work in the New York State League strongly advised me to get you, if possible. I think you will like this league far better than the one you played in last year, and will find the quality of ball played even better. If you come here, you will have two Harvard, two U. of P., two Dartmouth, a Georgetown, and, possibly, a Brown (not this year's team) or Princeton man on the team with you. The circuit is composed of five towns, all within a radius of fifty miles and peopled with as hot baseball "fans" as there are under the sun. The players, being for the most part good, clean college men are taken into the social life of the town.

The salaries paid in this league compare very favorably with those paid in any minor or independent organization and I think it will be well worth your while to write me your terms per week for playing here. You may play under an assumed name as you did last year, and nobody will be the wiser.

Awaiting the anticipated courtesy of an early reply, I remain,

Sincerely yours,

(Signed) J. J. THOMPSON, Manager

PREVALENCE OF "SUMMER BALL"

Brown's proposal to authorize collegians to play on summer nines met with deserved censure. But in the wide discussion which followed, the sins of other college baseball players did not receive merited attention. Look over the field and note a very few of the prominent college athletes who have played summer ball. Clarkson, captain of Harvard pitched for North Attleboro, Massachusetts. He is now with the New York American League team, having signed a contract with this professional aggregation while a Harvard undergraduate, for which he was debarred. Carr, who succeeded Clarkson as captain of Harvard, played with New London, New Hampshire. Cosgrave, Princeton, center-fielder of the "All-America"

team (Caspar Whitney's paper nine representing the strength of the college diamond), was a member of the Pittsburgh Athletic Club and the Orange Athletic
Club semi-professional teams. Cooney, catcher of the Princeton nine and captain-
elect of the eleven, caught for Maplewood, New Hampshire (season of 1903) and
for Lancaster, New Hampshire. . . .

Up to two seasons ago, Paul Smith's in the Adirondacks was a haven for Yale
baseball men, including the "hard-hitting" Barnwell, who had a reputation as a
summer-ball player. Concerning this Yale retreat, Mike Murphy made an interesting disclosure:

"Yale hasn't won a baseball championship," said the Yale trainer, "since the
summer-ball rule took effect."

"And yet, Mr. Murphy, Yale men play summer ball."

"I know it," said Murphy. "Those fellows who played at Paul Smith's might have
better played with fellows who'd helped their game more. I believe in it. I think it's
all right. A man has a right to get his board, and to take twenty-five dollars a week
to help him through college."

Murphy's opinion is the opinion of the majority of college baseball men. They
argue for their right to do as they please in vacation time. And they do as they
please, eligibility rules notwithstanding. They appreciate the difficulty of obtaining
proof. Few players could be convicted in a court of law on the charge of receiving
money, or its equivalent, for playing ball. It is easier to convict a legislator of bribe
taking—yes, the attorney for the big corporation of bribe giving—than to convict a
college gentleman of evading the rules he is pledged to live up to, and of taking
money.

11

Philadelphia Giants Win Black Championship (1906)

SOURCE: *Philadelphia Inquirer*, September 4, 1906

*In the early 1900s African American baseball teams enjoyed a resurgence in popularity.
Though the color line was still strictly enforced, top black teams gained the attention of
the local white press. In the article below, the writer credited the* Inquirer *with generat-
ing the publicity necessary to draw approximately twelve thousand fans to a game for the
championship of the International League, a short-lived black league organized by
William Freihoffer, a Philadelphia bakery owner. Leading the Philadelphia Giants to
victory were future Negro League founder and Hall of Famer Andrew "Rube" Foster and
second baseman Charlie Grant, whom John McGraw tried to sign to a New York Giants
contract.*

PHILA. GIANTS WON CHAMPIONSHIP CUP

**Landed International League Honor and Handsome Trophy
Wide Notoriety Given Games by The Inquirer Brought Out
Tremendous Crowd of Rooters**

INTERNATIONAL LEAGUE

	W.	L.	P.C.
Philadelphia Giants	7	1	.875
Cuban X Giants	6	2	.750
Wilmington Giants	4	4	.500
Philadelphia Professionals	3	5	.375
Riverton-Palmyra	0	8	.000

The Philadelphia Giants, the colored champions of the world, again demonstrated their ability and prowess to hold that honor by winning the International League championship and Freihofer [sic] Cup yesterday by twice defeating the Cuban X-Giants at the Athletics' grounds in two exciting ball games. The local champs played good ball in both games, and particularly in the morning game, on which contest depended the championship of the league.

Over 12,000 people witnessed both games, the afternoon crowd filling up the big stands with wildly enthusiastic rooters. The great booming The Inquirer gave the two games during the past week let all lovers of independent base ball know what was before them on Labor Day, and the widespread reputation of The Inquirer's well read sporting page was clearly demonstrated by the enormous turnout to the games.

The A.M. contest was the one which both clubs wanted badly, as it was the one which decided the championship of the league. The afternoon game was merely an exhibition one, and while the result did not mean much to either club regarding the cup or league honor nevertheless both exerted themselves to their utmost to win.

Both teams were keyed up to the highest pitch in the morning game, and every play was run out to the limit. The Cubes played in decidedly hard luck when men were on bases, and while Foster shone to brilliant advantage when the plate was menaced the Cubes' hoodoo worked overtime in keeping them from the plate. Twice did the Cubes fill up the bases with two men out, but each time Foster kept the "pinch" hitter out of the hit column and the third hand went out with the bases full in each occasion. Buckner was hit just at the time bingos meant runs.

PHILA. GIANTS	r.	h.	o.	a.	e.	CUBAN X GIANTS	r.	h.	o.	a.	e.
Grant, 2b. . .	0	0	1	2	0	Wins'n, lf. . . .	0	1	3	0	0
P. Hill, lf. . . .	0	2	4	0	0	Barton, cf. . . .	1	3	1	0	0
McCl'n, rf. . .	0	2	1	0	0	Buck'r, p.	0	0	1	3	0

PHILA. GIANTS	r.	h.	o.	a.	e.	CUBAN X GIANTS	r.	h.	o.	a.	e.
Harris, ss...	0	0	3	0	0	James, 3b....	0	1	3	2	0
Moore, cf...	0	0	1	0	0	Gate'd, rf....	0	1	0	0	0
Foster, p....	2	2	0	4	0	Will'ms, c....	1	1	9	1	0
Jordan, 1b..	1	2	5	0	0	Lloyd, 2b....	0	0	1	0	1
Francis, 3b..	0	2	3	1	1	Hill, ss......	0	2	3	1	0
Booker, c...	0	0	9	1	1	Wils'n, 1b...	0	1	6	0	0
Totals......	3	10	27	8	2	Totals.......	2	10	27	7	1

Two-base hits—Jordan, Foster, Barton. Stolen bases—James, Hill, Wilson, McClellan. Left on bases—Philadelphia Giants, 11; Cuban X Giants, 10. Struck out—By Buckner, 9; by Foster, 7. Bases on balls—Off Buckner, 3; off Foster, 4. Hit by pitched ball—Harris, Gatewood. Wild pitches—Foster, 1. Umpires—McLaughlin and Stricker. Time of game—2 hours.

12

Sol White on "Colored Base Ball" (1907)

SOURCE: *Sol White's History of Colored Base Ball, with Other Documents on the Early Black Game, 1886–1907* (1907; rpt., Lincoln: University of Nebraska Press, 1995)

Sol White was one of the better African American baseball players of the late nineteenth century. He participated in the short-lived League of Colored Baseball Players in 1887, and continued to play professionally until 1909. The last eight years of his playing career were with the Philadelphia Giants, a team he cofounded with two white sportswriters. One of those men, H. Walter Schlichter, published and edited Sol White's Official Base Ball Guide *in 1907.*

In the excerpt below White commented on the financial realities of black baseball , but defended the greatness of the game itself.

COLORED BASE BALL AS A PROFESSION

There is nothing like protecting the rights of the owners of base ball teams and while the ball players generally work in the opposite directions, they move under a false star and are only temporarily benefitted. The owner of a base ball team is in the business to make money for years to come, while the player is in the game to make the biggest rake off in the quickest time, never knowing just when he will have hard luck and fail to keep up a hot pace.

The colored ball player should always look before he leaps. He should remember that, although possessing the ability in every particular of the white ball player, he is not in a position to demand the same salary as his white brother, as the difference in the receipts of their respective games are decidedly in favor of the latter; thousands attending games of the whites to hundreds of the blacks. Leaving out the colored stars of the International League of 1887, the aggregate salaries for colored ball players, amounted to a little over $5,500 for a season of 5½ months. 1906, the banner year for colored base ball, when the number of teams is considered, with no less than 150 ball players employed in the professional ranks, they drew over $70,000 in salaries for the season, an average of $466 per man. An increase of over 785 per cent, from 1886 to 1907, or an average of 39¼ per cent increase each year.

These figures, in comparison, are expressly low to the salaries received and the business done by players and owners of white teams. Statistics of 1906 show the two major leagues alone paying over $600,000 per season to more than 300 ball players. While the minor leagues pay over $2,000,000 to 3,500 players.

These figures give the major league players an average of $2,000 per man for a season's work; and the minor league players $571 per man. The disparity in the salary of a major league player and a colored player is enormous, especially when it is taken into consideration that, were it not for color, many would be playing in the big league for $2,000, or more per season instead of less than $500 per season. As it is, they receive less than the minor league player.

Base ball is a legitimate profession. As much so as any other vocation, and should be fostered by owners and players alike. It is indisputably a masculine game, demanding all manly qualities and powers to the extreme. It is immune from attacks from all critics. From a scientific standpoint it outclasses all other American games. It should be taken seriously by the colored player, as honest efforts with his great ability will open an avenue in the near future wherein he may walk hand-in-hand with the opposite race in the greatest of all American games— base ball.

13

Kid Johnson Signs with Senators (1907)

SOURCE: (Boise) *Idaho Daily Statesman*, June 30, 1907

After beginning his career in Southern California, Walter Johnson moved on to the Idaho State League in 1906. The young Johnson dominated the competition, finishing the short season with a 7–1 record. His success attracted no attention, so Johnson returned to his Weiser, Idaho, club for a second season. In 1907 he was again magnificent, pitching two consecutive no-hitters, one of which was a perfect game with eighteen strikeouts. This achievement was noticed by a scout for the Washington Senators, which signed Johnson in late June. The best account of Johnson's exploits in California and Idaho is in the book written by his grandson, Henry Thomas, Walter Johnson: Baseball's Big Train (Washington DC: Phenom Press, 1995; rpt., Lincoln: University of Nebraska Press, 1998). According to Thomas, Johnson actually threw seventy-seven consecutive scoreless innings, not the seventy-five indicated in the headline below.

KID JOHNSON SMASHES WORLD'S RECORD FOR PITCHING

Weiser Twirler Chucks 75 Innings Without
Score Made Against Him
HIS RECORD FOR THE SEASON TO DATE
Accepts Offer to Join Washington, D.C., American League Team
But Remains with Weiser to End of State League Season

WEISER, June 29.—The wonderful record of Walter Johnson, the Kids' twirler, started last year when he was with Weiser in the state league and which Johnson continued with such remarkable success this year, has attracted the attention of ball players and managers all over the country and the offer of Joe Cantillion, manager of the Washington, D.C., American league team, is only one of many the phenomenal youth has received of late.

With his record of shut out games this season, Johnson has smashed to smithereens the world's record for pitching. He has pitched 75 innings without a run having been made against him. The former record was 54 innings. Some may not consider this remarkable because of the fact that Johnson has not pitched against the big leaguers. This fact does not in any way make Johnson's record less remarkable. No matter who is batting him the record would stand the same. In the 75 innings 230 men faced Johnson.

The complete record of Johnson for the entire season is as follows: He has struck out 166 batters; is credited with 18 base hits out of 37 times at bat, assisted 26 times and has 8 putouts to his credit. He has not made an error and only five runs have been made by his opponents. Twenty-five base hits have been made off his pitching during the season to date.

Walter Johnson was born at Iola, Kan., and is 19 years of age. He is six feet and two-fifths of an inch in height in his stocking feet and weighs 180 pounds. His home is at Fullerton, Cal., where he attends school. His first ball playing away from home was with the Weiser team last season.

Johnson has frowned on a number of good offers received lately and unlike many young pitchers who, through their eagerness to get into the big leagues have spoiled bright prospects for a successful career, turned them all down, concluding that it would be better for him to get more of such experience as he is now getting before meeting the big hitters. But Joe Cantillion sent a man from Washington to persuade Johnson to go to the national capital and Johnson has decided to go and take a chance with the big fellows. He will probably not be pitched in a regular game this season, but will be carefully coached, it is likely, during the remainder of the season and put in the game next year.

Johnson will be with Weiser through the remainder of the Idaho State league's season, which closes July 14.

14

Agreement for Minor League Championship Series

(1907)

SOURCE: *Columbus Evening Dispatch*, September 20, 1907

The minor leagues—or, more formally, the National Association of Professional Baseball Leagues—had no provision for a postseason championship series until 1919. Prior to that, champions of top leagues occasionally challenged each other to play for the unofficial NAPBL *title. The document below details the terms under which American Association pennant winner Columbus and Eastern League champion Toronto agreed to conduct their series; Toronto defeated Columbus in the series, four games to one. Their agreement is similar to that drafted by Boston and Pittsburgh that made possible the 1903 World Series.*

AGREEMENT IS FRAMED FOR TORONTO SERIES

Columbus Will Play Eastern League Champions Beginning Next Wednesday—The Conditions for the Games Are Agreed on at Buffalo Meeting

Columbus will play Toronto for the minor league baseball championship. All the conditions have been agreed on and the series is assured. President Bryce returned from Buffalo today, where he yesterday held a conference with the board of control, when rules were adopted and the conditions agreed on. The series opens at Toronto, September 25. The umpires will be Kane, of the American Association, and Owens, of the Eastern league. The agreement in full and the list of players eligible, follows:

RULES AND REGULATIONS

Rules and regulations governing a series of games between the Columbus, Ohio, club representing the American Association, and the Toronto, Ontario, club, representing the Eastern league:

ADOPTED BY BOARD OF CONTROL

First—All games shall be played under the supervision and control and direction of the board of control.

Second—Schedule: Columbus at Toronto, September 25, 26, and 28 (September 27 open); Toronto at Columbus, September 29, 30, and October 1, and until series terminates.

Third—Players eligible to participate: The following players, under contract to the respective clubs on or before September 1, are eligible to participate, and no others: Columbus—Upp, Wicker, Geyer, Townsend, Hall, Robertaille, Blue, Fohl, Kihm, Wrigley, Huslwitt, Friel, Gessler, McCreery, Jude, Jackson, Riley, Clymer.

Toronto—McGinley, Rudolph, Moffatt, Hersterfer, Mitchell, Applegate, Hurley, Carrigan, Flynn, Schafly, Frick, Phyle, Wotell, Welch, Weidensaul, Kelly, Thoney.

Fourth—Series to terminate when one club has won four games.

Fifth—A championship pennant, suitably inscribed, to be presented to the winning club.

Sixth—Guarantee: Each club shall post with the chairman of this board the sum of two thousand dollars ($2000.00) as a guarantee that the series shall be played as above described.

Seventh—Umpires: One to be selected by the president of each league, assigned to duty and subject to orders from the board of control. Umpire Kane has been selected by the American Association, and Umpire Owens by the Eastern league.

Eighth—The board of control to be sole judges as to the fitness of playing ground.

Ninth—Expenses: All traveling and hotel expenses of players to be paid from the gross receipts by the board of control. Umpires' salary and traveling and hotel expenses, championship emblem, to be paid by the board of control.

Tenth—Division of receipts: Ten per cent (10 per cent.) of the gross receipts shall be paid to the board of control for expenses, including umpires' salary, etc. Any balance remaining to be converted into the players' pool. Ninety per cent (90 per cent.) of the gross receipts from all games shall form a pool for the players, to be divided—sixty per cent (60 per cent.) to the winner and forty per cent (40 per cent.) to the loser.

Eleventh—The amount to be paid to the players' pool shall be paid to the board of control, who shall distribute to the players after the series is finished.

Twelfth—All questions arising out of the playing of the games not provided for herein, or covered by the playing rules, to be decided by the board of control.

Thirteenth—The rates for admission shall be twenty-five, fifty and seventy-five (25, 50 and 75 cents).

Fourteenth—Official scorers: Robert Reed, of the Ohio State Journal, Columbus, Ohio, and Edward Allen, of the Toronto World, Toronto, Ontario, are hereby appointed official scorers.

Fifteenth—Time of game: All games shall be called at 3 p.m.

Sixteenth—The players participating to be subject to control and discipline during the series the same as during the regular playing season.

Seventeenth—The board of control shall establish headquarters in the cities of Columbus, Ohio, and Toronto, Ontario, during the playing of the series.

> J. H. FARRELL,
>
> J. D. O'BRIEN,
>
> C. D. WHITE, Board of Control.
>
> J. J. MCCAFFERTY, President, Toronto.
>
> T. J. BRYCE, President, Columbus.

15

Detroit 9, Philadelphia 9, Seventeen Innings (1907)

SOURCE: *Philadelphia Record*, October 1, 1907

As the 1907 AL season entered its final week, the Philadelphia Athletics and the Detroit Tigers were still battling each other for the pennant. A victory for either team, according to the Record *reporter, could virtually clinch the league title. But after a furious, controversial seventeen-inning battle, the game ended in a 9–9 tie, which helped the first-place Tigers maintain their slim lead and win their first pennant. Among the most memorable performances in this contest were those of future Hall of Famers Ty Cobb (who later ranked this game as the most exciting of his career), Eddie Plank, and Rube Waddell. Perhaps the most impressive showing was that by Tiger pitcher Wild Bill Donovan, who threw 231 pitches in his complete game effort. The pitch count, along with a detailed statistical analysis, accompanies a brief article that follows the main story. For Cobb's account of this game see* My Greatest Day in Baseball as Told to John P. Carmichael and Other Noted Sportswriters *(1945; rpt., Lincoln: University of Nebraska Press, 1996).*

DRAWN BATTLE FOR PENNANT

**Athletics and Detroit Play a 17-Inning Game,
With the Score a Tie at 9 to 9**
MACK ACCUSES UMPIRE
**Charges That O'Loughlin Robbed the Athletics of a Victory
Because of Old Grudge**
OVER 30,000 SPECTATORS
**Paid Admissions 24,127, With Housetops and Windows Also
Crowded—10,000 Shut Out**

Before the greatest gathering of baseball enthusiasts that ever witnessed a game in this city, the Athletics and Detroit yesterday battled 17 long desperate innings to a tie, the score standing 9 to 9 when darkness brought the great struggle to a close. It was the longest American League game ever played in this city.

It was a virtual victory for Detroit, and the team left for Washington last evening with a lead of seven points over the Athletics. Over 30,000 people, including about 5000 in windows and on house-tops, witnessed the battle, which will go down in history as one of the most exciting ever decided in this city. The paid admissions numbered 24,127, which is the largest of the season, and there is little doubt that there were more people inside the grounds than ever before, for a great many scaled the fences, while a big list of complimentary admissions helped to swell the vast total. About 12,000 followed the progress of the game in front of "The Record" office, where every play was shown on the electrical scoreboard.

MACK BLAMES THE UMPIRE

If yesterday's game decides the championship, which is possible, then Umpire O'Loughlin will be blamed by Manager Mack and the Athletic players for knocking them out of it. O'Loughlin, in the fourteenth inning, declared Davis out after Crawford had muffed the ball he hit close to the crowd in left field. It is the first time in history that the batsman has been declared out when the fielder lost the ball after going to the ropes after it. As Murphy followed with a clean single or in fact a two-bagger and a single (the two-bagger having been called foul), the Athletics would have earned their victory in this inning.

ALMOST CAUSED A RIOT

The incident almost caused a riot, and in the heat of the argument over the play Monte Cross and Rossman, the big Detroit first baseman, came to blows, though Rossman's punch failed to land. Players and policemen rushed onto the field, and Rossman was hustled away by the "cops." The crowd in the outfield swarmed in, but when made to realize that the Athletics might lose the game by forfeit the police had little difficulty in driving them back.

It was a long time before the umpires rendered a decision. Connolly said he thought Davis was safe, but claimed it was not his place to make the decision. O'Loughlin, after considerable deliberation, declared Davis out.

"Silk" was plainly rattled, as he did not know how to get the game going again, ordering Donovan to pitch before the Detroit players were in their positions. Jennings wanted Rossman back on first and rushed out to bring him onto the field. When he got back Connolly refused to allow Rossman to play and Pitcher Killian finished the inning in Rossman's place. It was the general impression that Rossman had been placed under arrest for assaulting Cross, but such was not the fact.

Play was resumed with Murphy at bat and he sent a long drive to left, which struck to or on the foul line. Murphy reached second on the hit, but was called back to bat over and the crowd yelled "Robber!" at O'Loughlin. Two balls and another foul strike were called on Murphy when he singled to left. . . .

A VERY BITTER BATTLE

There was so much at stake yesterday that the two teams fought as bitterly as they knew how, producing the most thrilling struggle that has ever been seen in this city. Never before have two teams come together here under the conditions of yesterday's game. A victory for the Athletics meant the saving of the pennant almost to a certainty, while a win or a draw would nearly make the flag safe for the Tigers.

Entering upon the struggle with the idea that two games would be played, Jennings figured it would be best to take the first, and for this reason he sent his great pitcher, Donovan, in against little Jimmy Dygert. The way the Athletics pounded Donovan early in the game made it look like a runaway race, for at the end of the fifth inning the score stood 7 to 1 in favor of the home team. But those tenacious Tigers wouldn't lay down. Two bad errors, a base on balls and a timely two-bagger in the seventh gave Jennings' men four runs and the encouragement they needed to go in and save the game in the last two innings. It was the most sensational uphill battle ever put up by a visiting team in this city.

DYGERT WEAKENED QUICKLY

Dygert, who started the game for the Athletics, was pulled out in the middle of the second inning, with one run in and the bases full, and to "Rube" Waddell was left the task of pulling the team out of the hole. Waddell went at his work like a hero, the crowd giving him a great reception. Jones was the first man to face "Rube," and when the first one was called a strike, the crowd yelled with delight. The next one was a ball, another strike was called, a foul tip and Jones missed his last one, returning to the Detroit side of the field with thunderous applause ringing across the diamond.

This spurred "Rube" on, and he shot the first one over the plate on Schaefer. The next two were balls, then a foul, and Schaefer missed on the next one, retiring the side. Two strikeouts at such a critical stage was a great pitching feat, and the crowd on the field danced for joy, while almost all who were seated jumped up, threw their hats into the air and almost yelled themselves hoarse. From that time on until the ninth inning Waddell had a big lead to work on.

HOME RUN TIED SCORE

When the Tigers came up for their ninth inning the score stood 8 to 6 against them. Crawford, the first man up hit the first ball for a single. Waddell got himself into a hole, and with three balls and one strike he was trying to put over another strike when Cobb took a good swing and caught the ball fairly, sending it into Twenty-ninth street and tying the score. That was the end of Waddell. He was replaced by Plank, and then the real pitching duel began. Donovan grew stronger every inning after the seventh, and when Plank came into the game he was going at his best.

Plank pitched nine full innings and held Detroit to one run and seven hits. Donovan in the same nine innings held the Athletics to one run and three hits. Detroit secured two hits off Dygert and six off Waddell. . . .

DETROIT	AB.	R.	H.	TB.	O.	A.	E.
Jones, lf.	7	1	0	0	6	0	0
Schaefer, 2b.	9	1	3	3	6	7	0
Crawford, cf., 1b.	8	2	3	4	7	0	0
Cobb, rf.	8	2	3	7	1	1	0
Rossman, 1b.	7	1	2	2	12	1	0
Killian, 1b.	0	0	0	0	1	0	0
Downs, cf.	1	0	0	0	2	0	0
Coughlin, 3b.	7	0	0	0	1	3	1
Schmidt, c.	1	0	0	0	2	1	1

DETROIT	AB.	R.	H.	TB.	O.	A.	E.
Payne, c.	6	0	1	1	8	1	0
O'Leary, ss.	8	1	2	3	2	2	1
Donovan, p.	7	1	1	1	3	7	0
**Mullin	1	0	0	0	0	0	0
Totals	70	9	15	21	51	23	3

ATHLETICS	AB.	R.	H.	TB.	O.	A.	E.
Hartsel, lf.	9	1	4	7	3	0	0
Nicholls, ss.	6	1	1	2	4	10	2
Seybold, rf.	6	2	1	2	1	0	0
Davis, 1b.	8	3	3	7	19	1	0
Murphy, 2b.	7	1	4	4	2	5	0
Collins, 3b.	8	1	1	2	3	3	1
Oldring, cf.	7	0	3	5	3	0	1
Schreck, c.	4	0	0	0	9	1	1
Powers, c.	4	0	0	0	4	0	1
Dygert, p.	0	0	0	0	0	1	1
Waddell, p.	4	0	0	0	1	0	0
Plank, p.	4	0	1	1	2	1	0
*E. Collins	1	0	1	1	0	0	0
Totals	68	9	19	31	51	23	7

*Batted for Oldring in 17th.
**Batted for Killian in 15th.

Detroit   0 1 0 0 0 0 4 1 2 0 1 0 0 0 0 0 0—9
Athletics 3 0 2 0 2 0 1 0 0 0 1 0 0 0 0 0 0—9

Earned runs—Detroit, 3; Athletics, 5. Two-base hits—Crawford, Cobb, O'Leary, Hartsel, 3; Nicholls, Seybold, Davis, Collins, Oldring, 2. Home runs—Cobb, Davis. Sacrifice hits—Crawford, Schmidt, Nicholls, 2. Stolen bases—Cobb, Schmidt, O'Leary, Payne; Struck out by Plank: Crawford, Payne, Jones; by Donovan: Nicholls, 2; Oldring, 2, Schreck, Powers, 2; Seybold, 2. First base on balls—By Dygert: Donovan; by Waddell; Jones; by Plank, Cobb; by Donovan; Seybold, 2; Murphy. First base on errors—Detroit, 4; Athletics, 1. Left on bases—Detroit, 17, Athletics, 13. Hit by pitched ball—By Plank; Jones. Wild pitch—Donovan. Time—3h. 40m. Umpires—O'Loughlin and Connolly.

DOPE ON THE GAME

How the Pitchers and Batters Worked in Great Contest

Donovan pitched 231 balls in the 17 innings, of which 32 were called strikes, 27 strikes struck at, 28 foul strikes and only 7 other fouls. He wasted 71 balls by failing to get them over. The fact that only six Athletic men hit the first ball pitched shows how hard "Bill" was forced to work. On 33 men the first one was a strike and on 27 a ball, pretty near an even break between the batter and the pitcher.

The Athletics didn't make Donovan work as hard yesterday as they did last

Friday, and in most instances the ball was hit after one or two had been sent up by "Wild William." Seybold waited them out better than any man. The first time up Socks forced Donovan to pitch seven balls, five in the fourth and six in the eleventh. In all Donovan sent up 31 to Seybold in eight times up. Socks cut down his average by hitting the first one in the sixth.

Hartsel was successful on hitting the first ball and in two instances lined out two-baggers, but as a rule the ones who hit the first ball were easy outs.

Dygert pitched only 28 balls, three of which were called strikes, three missed strikes, eleven balls and two fouls. Waddell pitched 108 balls, 17 being called strikes, 15 missed strikes, 34 balls and 20 fouls. When Rube first went into the box he had great control, only three of the first 19 deliveries being called balls. Jones was the hardest man for Rube to pitch to. Though he didn't get a hit, Jones forced Rube to send up 18 balls out of four times up.

Plank in nine innings pitched 100 balls, only 7 of which were strikes called by the umpire, but 15 were missed by the batsmen. The foul-strike rule helped Plank to 14 strikes and only two fouls didn't count for Eddie. The Gettysburg wonder wasts [sic] few balls, and yesterday had only 29 balls called, four of which were intentional, when he passed Cobb in the fifteenth inning. The Detroit men were quite impatient at bat, 15 hitting the first ball pitched. This accounts for the few balls used by Plank after the thirteenth inning. The Athletic pitchers used 235 balls, or four more than Donovan.

DETROIT.

Innings.	Balls Pitched.	Strikes Called.	Strikes Struck at.	Fouls St'es.	Fouls Tips.
First	13	2	2	0	0
Second	25	5	2	3	1
Third	9	4	3	1	0
Fourth	15	2	3	3	1
Fifth	21	2	2	3	0
Sixth	11	0	3	2	1
Seventh	20	3	0	2	2
Eighth	16	2	3	2	0
Ninth	17	0	2	3	1
Tenth	8	0	1	1	0
Eleventh	12	0	3	3	0
Twelfth	19	1	2	4	0
Thirteenth	14	1	2	3	0
Fourteenth	6	1	0	0	0
Fifteenth	9	0	0	0	0
Sixteenth	9	1	3	1	0
Seventeenth	11	3	2	0	1
Totals	235	27	33	31	7

ATHLETICS

Innings.	Balls Pitched.	Strikes Called.	Strikes Struck at.	Fouls St'es.	Fouls Tips.
First	33	3	4	5	3
Second	9	2	1	2	0
Third	12	3	1	1	0
Fourth	13	2	1	0	1
Fifth	18	5	1	4	0
Sixth	9	2	0	0	0
Seventh	14	1	0	3	0
Eighth	14	3	0	1	1
Ninth	8	1	0	0	0
Tenth	12	1	3	2	0
Eleventh	23	2	3	3	1
Twelfth	10	0	4	3	0
Thirteenth	12	1	4	2	0
Fourteenth	10	0	2	1	0
Fifteenth	10	0	2	1	0
Sixteenth	7	1	2	0	0
Seventeenth	17	5	1	1	1
Totals	231	32	29	29	7

Baseball and Early-Twentieth-Century Popular Culture

Tremendous growth in the number of baseball teams, and in the game's popularity, paralleled the growth of the coverage of baseball in the media. Fans demanded not only information about the day-to-day details of their local teams and leagues, but also more feature articles which the daily newspapers often could not provide. In addition, they saw baseball as a fit subject for poems, vaudeville, and the new medium of the recorded song, as well as humor by writers like Finley Peter Doone and Ring Lardner. One publication that sought to slake the thirst for baseball knowledge was *Baseball Magazine*, which debuted in 1908 and is considered by some to be among the finest sports periodicals of the century. A young sportswriter named Grantland Rice earned national attention for the verses that preceded every column he wrote. His poems and syndicated columns appeared in sports pages that, since their emergence in the mid-1880s, had evolved into separate sections offering more information than ever before. Even ballplayers (with the help of ghost writers) published their own views on the game, hired by newspapers involved in circulation wars with their many rivals. Baseball had entered the American mainstream.

16

Cubs Protest Precursor of "Merkle Blunder" (1908)

SOURCE: *Pittsburgh Post*, September 5, 1908

The most celebrated play in baseball history, the "Merkle blunder," had its roots in a similar play in a game nearly three weeks earlier. On September 4 the Chicago Cubs and the Pittsburgh Pirates, locked in a fierce struggle with the New York Giants in the NL *pennant race, played a ten-inning contest that ended 1–0 in favor of Pittsburgh. As the winning run scored, Cubs second baseman Johnny Evers touched second to record what would have been the third out on a force play. Evers complained to umpire Hank O'Day that a run could not be allowed under these circumstances, but O'Day denied the appeal, backed by* NL *President Harry Pulliam. Nevertheless, O'Day must have realized that Evers had been correct, for when Evers made a similar appeal on September 23, he ruled baserunner Fred Merkle out, thus denying the Giants a crucial win. The Giants and Cubs ended the regular season with identical records, with the Pirates—who lost to the Cubs on the final day of the season—only one-half game back. Cubs President Charles Murphy used the incident to promote a the use of a second umpire to complement the single umpire assigned to each regular season game.*

A different account of the incident described below, from the Chicago Tribune, *appears in G. H. Fleming's account of the 1908 season,* The Unforgettable Season *(New York: Fireside, 1981).*

CUBS PROTEST YESTERDAY'S BALL GAME . . . CLAIMING CLARKE'S RUN SHOULD NOT GO

PRESIDENT MURPHY Insists That Gill Failed to Touch Second Base in Tenth Inning and Was Legally Forced; Retiring the Side—Sends Telegram to Pulliam

President Charles W. Murphy, of the Chicago world's champion club, has protested yesterday's ball game at Exposition park, on the ground that Warren Gill, the runner who occupied first base when Owen Wilson made a single with the sacks filled in the tenth, failed to advance to second, but turned and left the field as soon as he saw Fred Clarke scampering across the plate. According to the owner of the Cubs, Slagle fielded the ball to Evers, who stepped upon second base, thereby retiring Gill on a force, putting the side out. In a telegram to Harry C. Pulliam, president of the National league, sent last night, Mr. Murphy says:

"Chicago protests to-day's game here. With the bases full and two out, Wilson hit safely to center. Gill, of Pittsburgh, failed to run to second base from first. He ran a few feet down the line, then turned out and went to the club-house. Evers, who covered second base, received the ball from Slagle and called the attention of the umpire to the force-out. The umpire simply said, 'Clarke has crossed the plate.' Chicago claims Gill should have touched second base before he ran to the club-house, and will prove by the affidavits of a number of persons that he failed to do so. This protest is filed by Chicago despite the fact that you have never yet allowed one, because Clarke's run should not count, as Gill was plainly forced at second base on the play."

As soon as Clarke crossed the home plate, Umpire Hank O'Day turned and walked to the players' bench to get a drink of water. The Pirates and most of the

Cubs trotted for the exit, but Evers hustled over to second base and yelled at Slagle, who had picked up the ball. Shorty threw it to Evers, who called "O'Day, O'Day," but Hank failed to hear him owing to the noise made by the crowd leaving the park. Tinker, however, ran to the hydrant and called the thirsty's [sic] umpire's attention to what had happened, but Hank merely remarked: "Clarke has crossed the plate."

"I do not expect the protest will be allowed," said Mr. Murphy last night, "but it is certainly a just one, and should prove a strong argument in favor of the double-umpire system. Had there been another umpire on duty yesterday to look after the plays in the field Gill would have been declared out and Clarke's run would never have been allowed. The score at the end of the tenth inning would have been nothing-nothing. The National game has progressed to a stage where two umpires should officiate on every occasion."

17

Francis Richter on Fred Merkle (1908)

SOURCE: *Sporting Life*, October 3, 1908

Francis Richter, editor of Sporting Life *("A Weekly Newspaper Devoted to Base Ball, Trap Shooting and General Sports"), was one of the most opinionated and influential baseball journalists of his time. His periodical was more colorful than the staid* Sporting News, *three years its junior, and Richter's love of the game was evident in every column he wrote. Richter was an advocate of the Brotherhood and the Players' League in 1890, and was a strong supporter of the minor leagues. In the following editorial, however, he blasted the players and umpires whose mistakes made possible the "Merkle blunder." The incident would not have occurred, according to Richter, if Hank O'Day had granted Johnny Evers's appeal in Pittsburgh three weeks earlier and if that decision had been discussed with all players, especially with young players like Fred Merkle.*

A REGRETTABLE INCIDENT

The unfortunate termination of the New York-Chicago game of September 23 with its subsequent complications and recriminations, and certain aftermath of dissatisfaction and bitterness, must be a matter of keen regret to all friends of the National League and for all lovers of the game. It was hard for New York to have an assured victory thrown away through the stupidity of a player who failed to obey one of the elementary rules of the game—a stupidity absolutely inexcusable in view of the fact that only a few weeks ago the very same play was made the subject of a protest, of press discussion, and of an official Presidential decision. At the same time it was not to be expected that the Chicago team should permit itself to be deprived of a chance to tie or win a game just as important to itself as to its opponent through sentimental disregard of its opponent's failure to play the game according to the rules; especially as the Chicago club had already lost a game to Pittsburg through that same blunder, aided and abetted by an umpire's carelessness.

Abuse of the Chicago club is therefore as unjustifiable as is criticism of President Pulliam for his acceptance of the umpires' report on the status of the game. When the official umpires' report showed the game to be a tie on their decision, the President had no alternative but to declare the game a tie. Only a question of fact and judgment was involved, and even the President cannot overrule an umpire in such a case. The New York club has appealed from the umpires' decision to the President and may even carry an appeal to the Board of Directors, but what either power can do about it is not clear, even assuming that the New York club establish the fact that the umpire erred in his judgment. It may, however, be accepted in advance of the decision of President Pulliam or of the Board of Directors that it will be in accordance with the law and the facts, and that no injustice will be done. Nevertheless, it is to be hoped now that the pennant will be won by the successful club, whichever that may be, by a margin so large that this disputed game will not be the decisive factor.

The Chicago club's claim for a forfeiture would be a different proposition were that club to urge it. That would involve construction of an ambiguous constitutional clause, in which this particular case is only covered by inference, and the National League has never yet lent itself to the winning of games or pennants on technicalities. The only real question up for proper solution now is whether the disputed game was a tie game or a victory for New York. Should the latter club lose the decision the only parties at fault will be young Fred Merkle directly, and the team manager indirectly. The Gill incident should have been so well discussed in every players' dressing room as to render its repetition so soon and in such an important game, by even such an inexperienced player, impossible.

18

Nashville Wins Pennant With 1–0 Victory on Season's Last Day (1908)

SOURCE: *Nashville American*, September 20, 1908

In addition to the extraordinary pennant races in both the AL and NL in 1908, the Southern Association season came to an equally thrilling climax. On the final day of the season New Orleans, having played and won two more games than Nashville, was one game ahead of that rival. The Volunteers had to defeat the Pelicans and their ace, former major league star Ted Breitenstein, in order to take the league title. In a stirring pitching duel, Nashville thrilled the home crowd by winning 1–0 and claiming the pennant by only two percentage points. Other former and future major leaguers participating in this game include Bris Lord and two-time stolen base leader Harry Bay.

NASHVILLE WINS LEAGUE PENNANT IN FIERCE FIGHT

Victory Comes in Final Game of the Series
PELICANS BEATEN IN GREAT STRUGGLE
Before the Largest Crowd Ever Seen On a Local Diamond
SITTON'S WONDERFUL PITCHING RESPONSIBLE
Men Behind Him Play the Most Brilliant Ball of Their Career— New Orleans Makes a Game Fight

In a game brilliantly played Nashville yesterday afternoon defeated New Orleans for the Southern Association championship in one of the most exciting contests ever waged on a ball field. The score was 1 to 0, both clubs fighting it out to the last. The best team won.

It was the seventh inning when the battle for the flag was decided. Up to this time neither club was able to make the circuit. There were chances, 'tis true, for each side to make a run before this were it not for the masterly pitching of Messrs. Sitton and Breitenstein.

Two men were down when Nashville started the victory. Ed Hurlburt placed a single into right field. The drive was clean cut, going between first and second. Sitton came up and bunted to Breitenstein, beating it out. The fleet Harry Bay was next in line, and he also tapped one to Breitenstein, which he was unable to field in time to cut the runner at first.

BASES WERE FILLED

The bases were occupied, two down and Wiseman up. What would "Doc" do? Could he connect? Such were the questions passed rapidly through the crowd. The little fellow had, in the opening inning, hit for two bags, and, having always been a reliable batter, it was the opinion that he would break it up. This he did and in great fashion, too. He met the ball squarely on the nose, driving it just to the left of Breitenstein. The ball was hard hit. Dundon made a great effort to accept it, but it took a bad bounce, and "scooted" over the second sacker's head. Ed Hurlburt came home. Sitton, too, tried to score on the hit, but Briscoe Lord made a fine return to the plate, outing the runner. The game was won.

RECORD-BREAKING CROWD

A crowd the equal of which has never gathered in Athletic Park, witnessed the battle. If there was one there were 12,000. The field was completely encircled long before play was called. The stands were jammed and packed, every bit of the available space on the ground was occupied; in fact, so great was the attendance that ground rules were necessary. Delegations were on hand from all the neighboring towns, from Atlanta, Memphis, Knoxville, Birmingham, Little Rock, Louisville, and from far-away New York.

Weather conditions were almost ideal. A brisk wind was blowing but this in no way interfered.

Vedder Sitton, recently recruited from the South Atlantic League, where he has established a fine record, was Nashville's dependence in the rifle pit. Charlie Frank elected to use Theodore Breitenstein, the Grand Old Man of the circuit, who has been the leading twirler in this league. With two such men on the hurling hill it was sure to be a battle between pitchers. Such did it prove to be. A better game has never been pitched in this neck of the woods by men. Sitton's work was especially brilliant. In the nine innings he gave up but four hits, every single one of them being to the infield. He struck out nine men. Off of Mr. Breitenstein, the Volunteers gathered in eight safe ones and of these only two were clean cut. It was all scratch hitting.

Young Sitton, who is destined to make a mark as a pitcher in the baseball world, had wonderful speed and fine control. He walked only two men. He depended almost entirely on the "spit" ball and the manner in which it broke over the corners of the plate for him was a revelation to the Pelicans. The college lad was cool. The enormous crowd, the largest he had ever performed before, had no tendency whatever to rattle him. He went about his work just as if he had been in the business for years and it was this splendid judgment that carried him through a stubborn contest to victory. Though great credit is due every single member of the team for their fight, the one important factor of the game was Vedder Sitton. But while we speak of Sitton don't overlook Mr. Breitenstein. This Grand Old Man pitched remarkable ball. He had all of his cunning, used a very deceptive curve ball and against any other club save Nashville would have won.

Nashville	AB.	R.	H.	PO.	A.	E.
Bay, l.f.	4	0	1	0	0	0
Wiseman, r.f.	3	0	2	1	0	0
East, 2b.	4	0	1	1	3	0
McElveen, 3b.	3	0	1	3	1	0
Seigel, c.f.	4	0	0	1	0	0
Daubert, 1b.	4	0	1	10	1	0
Butler, s.s.	3	0	0	1	3	0
Hurlburt, c.	3	1	1	9	0	0
Sitton, p.	3	0	1	1	1	0
Totals	31	1	8	27	9	0

New Orleans	AB.	R.	H.	PO.	A.	E.
Montgomery, r.f.	4	0	0	1	0	0
Rohe, 3b.	4	0	0	0	4	0
Lord, c.f.	4	0	0	0	1	0
Tarleton, 1b.	4	0	2	12	2	0
Dexter, s.s.	3	0	1	3	3	1
Rickert, l.f.	3	0	1	1	0	0
Dundon, 2b.	3	0	0	2	2	0

New Orleans	A.B.	R.	H.	PO.	A.	E.
Matthews, c.	3	0	0	4	0	0
Breitenstein, p.	1	0	0	1	3	0
Totals	29	0	4	24	15	1

Score by innings—

Nashville	0	0	0	0	0	0	1	0	*—1
New Orleans	0	0	0	0	0	0	0	0	0—0

Summary—Two-base hit, Wiseman. Sacrifice hit, McElveen. Base on balls, Sitton 2, Breitenstein 1. Struck out, Sitton 9, Breitenstein 3. Left on bases, Nashville 8, New Orleans 4. Double play, East to Daubert. Time, 1:42. Umpires, Carpenter and Fitzsimmons.

19

Baseball Writers Form Organization after World Series (1908)

SOURCE: *The Sporting News*, October 22, 1908

During the 1908 World Series, between the Chicago Cubs and the Detroit Tigers, reporters faced a familiar but frustrating problem. Team officials in Detroit did little to discourage fans from sitting in the press box, forcing writers to seek seats elsewhere, if they could find any at all. After the final game of the Series (the Cubs won four games to one), on October 14, the writers gathered and formed the Base Ball Writers' Association of America, which exists to this day. In December the writers met again during the annual NL and AL meetings in New York, and agreed on a constitution. A brief description of the constitution, and of the evolution of baseball writing, is provided by Jack Lang, "Baseball Reporting," in Total Baseball, *ed. John Thorn and Pete Palmer with Michael Gershman, 4th ed.*

The foundation for a Base Ball Writers' Association was laid at Detroit last week, when representatives of every major league city except Brooklyn became charter members, elected J. S. Jackson president, I. E. Sanborn secretary, T. H. Murnane treasurer, and instructed Hugh S. Fullerton, H. P. Edwards and W. G. Weast to draft a constitution for consideration at a meeting to be held in New York in December. . . . Before the start of the next season the name of every base ball writer of standing in a major league city will be on the association's roll. The scope of the organization can not be safely outlined until the adoption of a constitution, but the elevation of the profession and an improvement in the system and methods of scoring will be among its aims. The temporary officers should be retained. The membership is so representative in all respects that none who inspects its list can fail to realize the influence for good that their concentrated efforts will wield. A scorers' association has been agitated for years; it has arrived and will accomplish all and more than theorists claim for it. Those identified with the movement are earnest, energetic, experienced and enthusiastic and will soon get results.

20

Reports on Two Black Women's Teams (1908)

SOURCE: *Indianapolis Freeman*, December 26, 1908

Interest in African American baseball teams and women's baseball teams has increased dramatically in recent years, but almost no information on clubs formed by and for black women has surfaced. The following article, which discusses the planned formation of a "Colored American League for Girls," is intriguing; unfortunately, no further evidence of the league, or of the teams mentioned below, has been found.

BASEBALL AMONG THE FAIRER SEX COMING INTO PROMINENCE

Springfield, O., Team—C. L. Mayberry Expects a League to Be Organized

Efforts are being made to get the fairer sex interested in athletics. This line of pleasure has been practically neglected or overlooked by the women of our race. The men may have acquired fame, wealth and health in all lines of the athletic and sporting world. Why not the women? Our neighbors' wives and daughters (white) take interest in athletics, and why not those of our race? Athletics are not copyrighted; they are at the disposal of each and every one. To some degree last summer tennis was taken up by the fair ones of this city, and there promises to be more interest manifested in the coming season. A good thing. Push it along. Take up athletics, girls; take physical exercise; get interested in the games of the field, diamond, and in other pastimes of the like. Enjoy life as it is; don't make it what it isn't or what it should not be.

In Springfield, O., there has been organized a baseball team, not composed of the rugged ball players that have monopolized the spherical game, but composed of girls. Nothing better could be done along this line; nothing better could be done to make the game clean sport; nothing better could be done to abolish the physical inability and make healthy our women. Modesty? Well, that has caused the failure of more women than anything else known. Modesty should be possessed, 'tis true, by men as well as by women, but it can be carried to an extreme, as can timidness. Take up the game, girls, in your town. Learn the game of baseball in all of its phases; know it from start to finish.

Louisville should have a girls' baseball team, as she has about the best woman baseball expert in the country in the person of Mrs. Henry Newboy. Every one should take interest and give encouragement to the promotion of girls' baseball teams.

Springfield, O., has organized a baseball team of girls to take the diamond next season, under the leadership of Mrs. Sarah S. Brooker. A number of other Ohio and Indiana cities have fallen in line, several games have been arranged, and it is probable that an Ohio-Indiana League will be formed by May 1, which is the beginning of the baseball season for girls. An effort is also being made by promoters of baseball to form an eight-team league in some of the larger cities, to be known as the Colored American League for Girls. Information regarding same can be had by addressing President C. L. Mayberry, 1712 North Limestone street, Springfield, O., or Manager (Mrs.) Sarah S. Brooker, 313 East Front street, same city.

President C. L. Mayberry, of the Springfield, O., girls' baseball team, is very anxious for the promotion of the new project, and is devoting much time and labor to send it on the road to success. Mr. Mayberry is prompted to have colored girls organized into baseball teams from the fact that he believes colored girls can do, and do just as well, if not better, in some cases, what the white girls can do. He wants to create enough enthusiasm in athletic circles to get on foot a league for girl players for the season of 1909. He has the following to say in reference to colored girls playing baseball:

"I know that you are aware there is but little that the girls of our race can find to do, and I feel that if this project can be made a success, and I am sure it can, it will be opening fields for our girls which have hitherto been totally closed. Why not have our girls play baseball as well as the white girls? Why wait until the white girls have worn all of the "new" off, and then start, as we have done in so many other things? I feel that it is high time for us to begin to be original in some things at least, and to start some things ourselves, and not wait until the white man or woman, as the case may be, gets tired and throws it aside, and then we take it up. I believe that if this is encouraged by men of influence and men of means, it will mean worlds to our girls."

Louisville, Ky.—Mr. and Mrs. Henry Newboy are training their baseball club for next season. They expect to have a strong club. Mrs. Newboy is an expert at the game, and practices with the club. The club meets every Sunday morning at the residence of Mr. Newboy, who is manager. Mrs. Newboy is secretary. There are very few women, especially colored women, who even understand a game of baseball when they see it played, to say nothing of taking a part in a game. But Mrs. Newboy understands and can play baseball and enjoys the diamond dust. But it is just a question of a few months until women will ask no odds on the game.

21

League Planned in Rural Northern Virginia (1909)

SOURCE: *Fauquier Democrat*, January 9, 1909

Citizens of small towns were as passionate about baseball as their counterparts in the biggest cities. Seemingly every town, regardless of its size, had its own team. When passionate local rivalries inspired such clubs to form a league, however, economic realities of life in a sparsely populated area usually caused the league to fail within a year or two. The article below describes the efforts of promoters in Culpeper, Virginia, to sponsor a league with local towns. Perhaps they wanted to feature the talents of a seventeen-year-

old banker's son named Eppa Rixey, who would soon achieve stardom at the University of Virginia and in the major leagues. The league was never formed, but the towns' teams mentioned in the article continued to play each other regularly.

The first four paragraphs originally appeared in the Culpeper Exponent. *The remaining paragraphs express the views of the* Democrat, *which was based in Warrenton, the seat of government in adjacent Fauquier County.*

OF INTEREST TO THE FANS

There is some speculation now going on in Culpeper as to whether a base ball league will be formed in Northern Virginia this year or not. Friends of the movement here believe that such a league can be made embracing such towns as Culpeper, Orange, Warrenton, Manassas, with possibly Charlottesville on the south and Fredericksburg on the north.

That such a league could and would furnish much wholesome amusement and sport during the coming summer goes without saying, and some of the friends of the movement believe that it could be conducted with a reasonable amount of pecuniary success.

Of course it will require some time to settle upon the preliminary work of forming such a league, and to give all such towns as care to enter the league an opportunity to do so. If such a league is to be organized this year it will be for the friends of the movement to begin early, pick their players, elect their officers and start the ball rolling in order to be in readiness when the season opens.

There are plenty of good players in Culpeper to form a first-class club who could and would give all comers a warm welcome on the diamond, and is no doubt a fact that some of the towns named could also furnish good teams to amuse the Culpeper boys for awhile.—Exponent.

We heartily agree with the Exponent in this move, and it would give us great pleasure to see a league organized with the teams above mentioned and we are quite sure there is ample material for a good team in Warrenton. All lovers of base ball should take up this move all along the line and push it to a finish. A league can easily be formed if the team managers would get to work early, arrange a convenient schedule, get their men together and begin practice at the earliest possible moment and the league would be an assured success. Lets get together.

22

Descriptions of Baseball Recordings (1908, 1909)

SOURCE: *Edison Phonograph Monthly*, July 1908, July 1909

According to Jim Walsh, an expert in early recorded music, there was an explosion of baseball-related songs in the early twentieth century, especially in 1908 and 1909. In his article in Hobbies, *"Baseball Recordings" (vol. 76, no. 10 [Dec. 1971]), Walsh listed some*

56 baseball recordings released prior to 1920. Of that number, 25 were released in 1908 and 1909, and 40 in the period from 1906–11. This profusion of baseball recordings reflected an effort by the young industry to capitalize on the tremendous popularity of the national pastime to further its own advancement.

One of the giants of the early recording industry was Thomas Edison, the inventor of the first phonograph in 1877. Edison Records, like the other record companies of the day, depended on their dealers to sell their product. They used publications like the Edison Phonograph Monthly to describe for the benefit of the dealers the new releases so that they in turn would be prepared to recommend the recordings to their customers. Below are five descriptions of Edison baseball songs; note that Edison stressed the clarity of the recordings, an important consideration given the primitive state of recording technology at this time.

Other notes of interest: Edward Meeker's version of "Take Me Out to the Ball Game" was the third, and least popular, of those released in 1908. Comedian Cal Stewart first released a version of "Uncle Josh at a Baseball Game" in 1897, and released at least eight other versions for different record labels, under slightly different titles, in the succeeding twelve years. Digby Bell was not only a close friend of "Casey at the Bat" reciter DeWolf Hopper, but was also a renowned baseball fan in his own right. He recorded at least one other baseball song for Edison, "The Man Who Fanned Casey," released in 1910. The seldom-published lyrics of "Take Me Out to the Ball Game" will help to explain the description of Meeker's recording.

9926 Take Me Out to the Ball Game   Edward Meeker

The base-ball hit of the season—a home run at least. Katie Casey is a true-blue, dyed-in-the-wool base-ball "fan," and can give her big brothers pointers on "rooting" for the home team. She'd rather munch peanuts on the bleacheries than caramels at a matinee—which is saying a good deal for a girl. Meeker must have taken Katie to a game or two, judging from the interest he takes in singing about her. The tune is a jolly, infectious one and you get every word. Orchestra accompaniment; music, Albert Von Tilzer; words, Jack Norworth; publishers, York Music Co., New York. [Vol. 6, no. 7 (July 1908)]

4 Flanagan and "The Reillys" at a Baseball Game   Steve Porter

Over four minutes of solid fun. A spirited base ball game forms a highly interesting and exciting background. Flanagan and the Reillys landed seats in a hot-bed of enthusiastic "rooters," and Mrs. Reilly's ignorance of the game makes her the butt of much merriment. One of the most attractive features is the progress of the game, which is humorously pictured. Orchestra arrangement. Original sketch, not published. [Vol. 6, no. 9 (Sept. 1908)]

10169 Uncle Josh at a Baseball Game   Cal Stewart

The baseball season is now increasing in interest, the fans are beginning to get a line on the leaders, and everything in the way of baseball will arouse considerable interest. Uncle Josh's baseball experiences, as given on this Record, are therefore timely and the Record ought to be in great demand. The words on the Record are original with Mr. Stewart. [Vol. 7, no. 5 (May 1909)]

156 The Tough Kid on the Right Field Fence   Digby Bell
A doubly attractive Record. It is made by Digby Bell, one of the best-known men in comic opera and vaudeville, who hereby makes his initial bow to the Edison Phonograph public. Its other attraction is the realistic baseball talk indulged in by the youngster from a "deserved" seat on the right field fence. He tells the home team how to play the game and what he thinks of them when their playing isn't up to his standard. He is a type of baseball "fan" found alike on the grandstand and on the bleachers. The Record ought to be a real treat to everyone who understands the language of our national game. It ought to go a long way towards establishing Mr. Bell's popularity as a maker of Edison Records. [Vol. 7, no. 5 (May 1909)]

196 The Baseball Girl   Miss Ray Cox
Miss Ray Cox makes her bow as an Edison entertainer with an imitation of a baseball "fan" who accompanies her best fellow to the game. It is a monologue that has earned her a deservedly enviable reputation with the theatre-going public, for it is really a marvelous portrayal of the conflicting emotions, the startling inconsistencies, the changing moods and opinions that mark the game's "fan." It is a scream from start to finish—from the moment she takes exception to the umpire's voice (which she characterizes as "an awful thing") through succeeding expostulations with the "man in blue" over his decisions to the time the game is saved by what she persists in calling a "wallop." It is a succession of laughs. [Vol. 7, no. 7 (July 1909)]

TAKE ME OUT TO THE BALL GAME

Katie Casey was baseball mad
Had the fever and had it bad;
Just to root for the home town crew, ev'ry sou—, Katie blew—
On a Saturday, her young beau called to see if she'd like to go,
To see a show but Miss Kate said "no, I'll tell you what you can do:"

Chorus
Take me out to the ball game,
Take me out with the crowd.
Buy me some peanuts and Cracker Jack.
I don't care if I never get back,
Let me root, root, root for the home team,
If they don't win it's a shame
For it's one, two, three strikes you're out
At the old ball game.

Katie Casey saw all the games.
Knew the players by their first names;
Told the umpire he was wrong, all along—good and strong—
When the score was just two to two,
Katie Casey knew what to do,
Just to cheer up the boys she knew
She made the gang sing this song:
  Repeat Chorus

23

"Indoor Baseball" and "Kicking Baseball" (1910)

SOURCE: Emmett D. Angell, *Play* (Boston: Little, Brown and Co., 1910)

In the early-twentieth-century the study of childhood development became a serious concern. Many experts published books full of games, sports and other activities designed to prepare children to become healthy, moral adults. Angell, a professor of physical education at the University of Wisconsin, invented many of the games described in his book, including "Kicking Baseball."

INDOOR BASEBALL

This game is played like regular baseball, but is adapted to indoor use by having a soft ball about twice the size of a baseball and a small bat. The rules and material for the official game can be furnished by any athletic house. The game is splendid for indoor exercise and very interesting. Mr. Henry Etling, instructor in public school gymnastics at Pittsburgh, Pennsylvania, has varied the game in several ingenious ways. He places vaulting bucks in front of each base, and the base runner is compelled to vault before reaching base; or, with heels together, base runners are compelled to hop between bases. Another variation is to have mats between bases, and each runner must roll before reaching base. These exercises add much to the amusement of the game.

KICKING BASEBALL

This is played just the same as baseball, with a few exceptions. The ball is a basket-ball; the bat, the batsman's foot; and a player can be put out as in baseball, and also by being hit with the ball while running bases. The home plate is four feet wide and two feet deep, and the batsman stands on it. The bases are thirty or forty feet apart, according to the size of the field. The pitcher stands back of a line thirty feet from the batter. Three strikes put a batsman out if the catcher catches the last strike on the first bounce. A strike is a ball that crosses the plate lower than the batsman's knee. The first two fouls count as strikes, but after two strikes fouls do not count. If a foul or fly is caught, the batter is out. There may be five or more players on a team. The game seems to afford equal enjoyment to boys and girls. It gives girls a better understanding of the national game, and at the same time affords them an exercise that is not too violent and is full of fun.

24

Grantland Rice's "The Slide of Paul Revere" (1910)

SOURCE: Grantland Rice, *Base-Ball Ballads* (Nashville: The Tennessean Co., 1910)

Less than a decade after completing his baseball career at Vanderbilt University, Grantland Rice had already become a nationally known sportswriter, famed for his ability to dispense baseball "dope" and to write clever, often moving verse. A year after the publication of Base-Ball Ballads, *his first book, Rice moved to New York, where he would reign as the dean of American sportswriters until his death in 1954. For more details, see* Charles Fountain, Sportswriter: The Life and Times of Grantland Rice *(New York: Oxford University Press, 1993).*

THE SLIDE OF PAUL REVERE

LISTEN, fanatics, and you shall hear
Of the midnight slide of Paul Revere;
    How he scored from first on an outfield drive
    By a dashing spring and a headlong dive—
'Twas the greatest play pulled off that year.

Now the home of poets and potted beans,
Of Emersonian ways and means
In baseball epic has oft been sung
Since the days of Criger and old Cy Young;
But not even fleet, deer-footed Bay
Could have pulled off any such fancy play
As the slide of P. Revere, which won
The famous battle of Lexington.

The Yanks and the British were booked that trip
In a scrap for the New World championship;
But the British landed a bit too late,
So the game didn't open till half past eight,
And Paul Revere was dreaming away
When the umpire issued his call for play.

On, on they fought, 'neath the Boston moon,
As the British figured, "Not yet, but soon;"
For the odds were against the Yanks that night,
With Paul Revere blocked away from the fight
And the grandstand gathering groaned in woe,
While a sad wail bubbled from Rooters' Row.

But wait! Hist! Hearken! and likewise hark!
What means that galloping near the park?
What means that cry of a man dead sore?
"Am I too late? Say, what's the score?"
And echo answered both far and near,
As the rooters shouted: "There's Paul Revere!"

O how sweetly that moon did shine
When P. Revere took the coaching line!
He woke up the grandstand from its trance
And made the bleachers get up and dance;
He joshed the British with robust shout
Until they booted the ball about.
He whooped and he clamored all over the lot,
Till the score was tied in a Gordian knot.

Now, in this part of the "Dope Recooked"
Are the facts which history overlooked—
How Paul Revere came to bat that night
And suddenly ended the long-drawn fight;
How he singled to center, and then straightway
Dashed on to second like Harry Bay;
Kept traveling on, with the speed of a bird,
Till he whizzed like a meteor, rounding third.
"Hold back, you lobster!" but all in vain
The coachers shouted in tones of pain;
For Paul kept on with a swinging stride,
And he hit the ground when they hollered: "Slide!"

Spectacular players may come and go
In the hurry of Time's swift ebb and flow;
But never again will there be one
Like the first American "hit and run."
And as long as the old game lasts you'll hear
Of the midnight slide of P. Revere.

25

A Japanese Prince on Baseball (1910)

SOURCE: *New York Tribune*, May 15, 1910

In the following article a Japanese nobleman suggests that baseball could help make the United States and Japan closer allies, and that a true "World Series" might be initiated. Although these predictions proved false, the popularity of baseball in Japan has inspired many American professional clubs to visit. The New York Giants and the Chicago White Sox played several games in Japan during their 1913–14 world tour. They were followed in the 1920s and 1930s by several Negro League clubs and major league all-star teams. And a number of college teams followed the lead of the University of Wisconsin—whose pioneering trip across the Pacific is mentioned below—to play their Japanese counterparts.

BASEBALL MAY SOME DAY AVERT WAR BETWEEN AMERICA AND JAPAN

Prince Tokugawa Thinks the Game Will Cement National Friendship

Baseball has served to entertain, thrill and excite hundreds of thousands, yes, millions, of the American people, but how many of even the most rabid "fans," the most ardent enthusiasts, ever thought of America's great national game as a peacemaker between two imperial nations, an agent possibly of averting a "terrible war," or at least a means of bringing into closer commercial and social relationship two world powers? Yet this is just what the game may do.

Prince Iyesato Tokugawa, last of the Shoguns and president of the Japanese House of Peers since 1893, paid New York a visit last week, and while here talked of the great American game to a Tribune reporter. The prince is something of a "fan" himself. He is a believer in baseball, enjoys seeing a good close game, with plenty of hitting, and knows a lot about the pastime.

"Baseball in my country," said he, "is becoming more and more popular. Americans introduced the game in Japan. At first we did not know what it was all about, but we used to go out and watch the teams from United States men-of-war play, and after a time we got so that we could understand it, and the better we understood it the more we thought of it.

"By degrees some of our people learned enough about it to think they would like to play it, and then a few in Tokio started playing the game. The more they played the better they liked it, and more and more people became interested in it."

After a time, the prince said, some of the Japanese became pretty good at it, and then they decided it was about time to measure their skill with American teams. . . . "Your University of Wisconsin has sent teams over and played with our University of Tokio. And we have sent our teams over to your western coast and played with your universities there."

That the prince took considerable pride in the success of the Japanese ball tossers was easily apparent. He spoke of the showing of the Tokio collegians against the University of Wisconsin team with just pride. As a matter of fact, those Wisconsin ball tossers have been about as good as some of the best American college teams, and when they first began visiting the land of the Mikado they thought they had a "snap," to put it mildly, but the Tokio players gave them the surprise of their lives, and they now slap themselves on the back if they manage to get an even break in those sunny isles.

Prince Tokugawa said that he believed before long the national game of Japan would be baseball. He spoke warmly in favor of the game, and more especially of the idea of the United States sending ball teams over to play in Japan, and of his country returning the courtesy. If this was carried out to a wide extent, he thought it would result in the people of the two nations becoming better acquainted with each other and hence entertaining more cordial relations.

"Some day," said the prince, "you may see a Japanese team playing a championship series on your Polo Grounds right here in New York."

26

The Hall of Fame (1911)

SOURCE: *Baseball Magazine*, January 1911

The concept of a Hall of Fame first emerged a quarter-century before the first election was held in 1936. This article described the idea, and in succeeding issues the editors selected three players per month into their Hall. After the first six men—Cap Anson, Mike "King" Kelly, Ed Delehanty, John Ward, A. G. Spalding, and Buck Ewing—were chosen, the quality of the nominees diminished somewhat. Along with George Wright and Dan Brouthers, lesser players like Charles Bennett, Jerry Denny, and James Fogerty were chosen. By July players like Nap Lajoie, Honus Wagner, and Ty Cobb were being honored.

THE HALL OF FAME FOR THE IMMORTALS OF BASEBALL

Comprising the Greatest Players in the History of the Game

Established as a lasting tribute to our most illustrious players, based upon the judgments of the leading authorities of the nation's grandest sport, and maintained for the benefit of the many million ardent supporters of the greatest outdoor game in the history of the world.

At present there seems to be no satisfactory way to decide just who are the leading players in baseball. There is no authority given to anyone by common consent, for settling such a difficult question. It is true the newspapers at the close of the season usually give out their selection for the All-America nine, and also publish the opinions of their readers, but these are almost always widely conflicting and fail signally in solving the problem. . . .

There seems to be a genuine demand for some institution which has the confidence of the baseball public, to step into the breach and act as a court of last appeal, in deciding difficulties of this kind. Such an institution ought to be national in its scope, without any possible local prejudice; and it ought to be closely affiliated with the national game.

We believe that our magazine is peculiarly fitted to act in the general province of an umpire in such controversies. It is the magazine of baseball, all its interests are centered on the game, and it is striving in every way it can to make that game even better and more interesting than it is at present. . . .

It is a universal trait of humanity to wish to know who are the leaders, the tiptop men, in all kinds of human activity. We have ourselves, felt a keen interest in selecting the All-America nine for the past season; and we know by the large degree of enthusiasm displayed in the public press, as well as in our own correspondence, that the general public was interested too.

But the problem of selecting an All-America nine is a slight one compared with the task of picking out the greatest players in history. Here it would seem that the most ardent fan has the haziest kind of a notion, and the conflict among such opinions are as expressed, is very great.

The older generation of fans is pretty much of the opinion that the old-time ball players were in a class by themselves, while the younger generation can see nothing but the brilliant feats of some of our present-day stars. The real unprejudiced truth, we imagine, lies somewhere between these two extremes.

There are various ways of selecting the members for our hall of fame. For instance, as everyone knows, the choice of the stars of football has been left, by common consent, to the judgment of one man.

We have no reflections to cast on the selections obtained in that way, nor upon the method in general. But we do think that in baseball, which is, after all, far more of a national institution than football, there is no one man whose knowledge of the game, or whose judgment, is conspicuous enough to render him deserving of so much authority. . . .

Baseball Magazine is far from assuming such an authority even for its corps of assistants and contributors. What we do propose, however, is that all our readers who are interested in determining the leading players of the game, and we know they are all interested, should co-operate with us in this selection, by sending us any scrap of information in their possession, especially about the older players as well as their own honest judgment as to just what players are deserving to be enrolled in Baseball's Hall of Fame.

When we have gathered all the evidence we can in this way we will try to mould from the general consensus of opinion, with the help of our able assistants and contributors, a list which shall stand the test of time as the roll of honor for the leading baseball players of history.

We can think of no greater honor to confer upon a man than to credit him with being one of the foremost of his profession. Our baseball players are justly proud of their profession and we know they are ambitious to attain the very highest position it offers.

For a player to be enrolled in a hall of fame which, in the nature of the case, includes only the very best players in all history, seems to us, to be the highest honor which could be conferred upon him. The public is extravagant in its praise, but it is very fickle, too; and the many years' service of a declining veteran are frequently lost sight of in the brilliant showing of some previously unknown youngster in the game.

There can be only a few names in baseball which shine with lustre enough to be enrolled among the immortals, but it is our aim that those who are worthy shall be set on a sure pedestal, where they will be forever above the possible forgetfulness or neglect of the too careless public.

The only requirement we feel called upon to make, outside of genuine ability, is that any player, to render himself eligible for enrollment, must have served for at least five years on one or more of the big leagues. We do not think a player is justly entitled to the highest honors in his profession, on the strength of one or two seasons' work, whose fine showing depended, perhaps, on some particularly favorable circumstances.

And now that we have explained the methods of management in our Hall of Fame, and the purpose for which it was founded, we must turn over some of the intermediate work to our readers. We depend upon them in large measure for the information and advice so necessary to us in making our selection. In our next issue we will try to give three names of famous ball players who, we feel sure, would be entitled by almost universal consent, to a place in our list. We shall use these players as a nucleus of charter members, and about their names gather in time, perhaps a score of others. We are eager to do this work for our own satisfaction as well as yours. We can think of nothing more interesting in all baseball than a discussion of the greatest players which the game ever knew.

27

College Baseball's Decline (1911)

SOURCE: *Baseball Magazine*, August 1911

In the article below, J. R. Macgowan states that the lack of uniform records prevented an accurate assessment of the relative strength of different clubs, and that the popularity of the college game was fading as a result. However, other evidence suggests just the opposite. Historian Harold Seymour, in Baseball: The People's Game *(New York: Oxford University Press, 1990), noted that in 1911* Baseball Magazine *introduced a regular column on college baseball, and that the following year A. G. Spalding and Company published its first college baseball guide. In addition, managers like Connie Mack sought out players with a college background, which may have made college a more attractive option to major league hopefuls.*

THE FAILURE OF COLLEGE BASEBALL

Why the College Game Is Becoming Less and Less Popular
By J. R. Macgowan

College baseball is becoming less and less popular, less and less a major sport each year. In the colleges there is no comparison between the position the game holds now and that it held a dozen years or a couple decades ago. Then the result of a game between two of the major colleges was telegraphed all over the world, now the result of a game excites a great deal less interest than the result of a contest in football or in track. A sure reflection of public interest is the newspaper page, and there one finds now less emphasis put upon college baseball games than upon the games in some of the minor sports.

To begin with, it may as well be admitted that college baseball holds its interest principally because of college spirit, not because of any inherent merit in the playing of the game. I do not think the reader can turn to a single incident—certainly not many of them—where a person with special interest in neither team, and curiosity to see the rah-rah boys and their display satisfied, cared to see a baseball game between colleges. The very essence of college baseball lies in support by adherents of each college, a one-sided and weak basis upon which to put the national game in the colleges. College baseball is losing its ground because the potential excellence of the playing is not at all appealing to anyone, but more especially because the status of the teams is not settled—true universal rivalry, the very heart of interest in league ball,—is lacking absolutely.

There is positively no way to ascertain the standing of any college team. When this is written no one under the sun can tell whether Yale has a stronger team than Pennsylvania, although Yale has been defeated repeatedly and Penn has been fairly successful. Only Providence could ascertain in the relative standing of Dartmouth and Chicago. No percentages are maintained, no batting, no fielding, percentages, of any sort. Very few colleges play one another more than once in the same season, and that once, as everyone knows, may depend a great deal upon the stunt of some unimportant player or substitute who has a hand in the game.

This condition in a lot of institutions, each being flouted by its own adherents, with no means of comparison between them, is accentuated by the fact that every college has almost an equal chance in winning the championship. In track and football the major colleges have so great an advantage that the small schools cannot for an instant dispute their greater right to fight out the championship. In baseball this condition is altogether different. Every college in America can support a baseball team—one of the excellencies of the national games is the cheapness of its equipment. Some small college may have a pitcher who can win games all of his own ability, such as Martin, at Tufts, this year. The Tufts team could play the best team in the East a hard game. This was shown pretty conclusively when she defeated Dartmouth, but who in the world would have the effrontery to maintain that Tufts is entitled to the championship? Yet on the face of things she may have all the claim in the world to it. The only remedy for this demoralizing condition is the establishment of an impartial board to maintain percentages. This has never been done and every year the game becomes less and less popular.

For at the heart of things all amateur sports are based on rivalry—the more rivalry there is the more interesting and vital is a particular game. Consider how much more interesting a baseball game between Princeton and Yale would be if it were conclusively known that the college championship, clearly and irrevocably and beyond argument, depended upon that game. Now, no one but the adherents of the two institutions will maintain that the game will decide anything.

College baseball is coming to have less interest to the average person than some of the minor sports such as lacrosse. As one who has a vital interest in the development of the game in the colleges, the writer is eager to keep a great centre of interest, such as it used to be, from becoming but an incidental interest, as it tends to be. It is up to the colleges to do something.

28

Mathewson Editorial on Baker
World Series Home Run (1911)

SOURCE: *New York Herald*, October 17, 1911

By 1911 star players had begun lending their names to ghost-written columns during the World Series. The New York Herald *hired Giants pitching stars Christy Mathewson and Rube Marquard to "write" articles on alternating days. In the second game of the Series Marquard surrendered a home run to Athletics third baseman Frank Baker that provided the winning margin for Philadelphia. Mathewson, in his column, criticized Marquard for poor pitching strategy. However, in the next game—played on the same day the article appeared—Mathewson gave up a ninth inning home run to Baker that sent the contest into extra innings. The Athletics eventually won that game, and the Series. For his heroics Baker earned the nickname "Home Run," a well-earned moniker despite a lifetime total of only 94 home runs.*

CHRISTY MATHEWSON SAYS ONE STRAIGHT BALL GAVE PHILADELPHIA CHANCE FOR VICTORY

Giant's Star Twirler Describes Crucial Moment of the Game When Marquard, After Fooling Baker on Two Curved Balls, Accidentally Put a Fast One Over the Heart of the Plate That Was Smashed Out for a Home Run

By Christy Mathewson, The Giants' Star Pitcher

PHILADELPHIA, Pa., Monday—One ball pitched to Frank Baker in the sixth inning here to-day cost the Giants the game. That ball was right on the heart of the plate, came up the "groove," and Baker hit it over the fence for a home run, scoring Collins ahead of him. If the ball had been pitched on the outside or had been a curve the result probably would have been different.

The sixth inning was the critical inning of the game—victory hung on that one ball, and Marquard served Baker with the wrong prescription. I don't think for a moment "Rube" intended to lay the ball over the plate for him, but he did it, and this cost us the game.

The trouble started after two were out, and everything looked easy. But Collins doubled hard to left field and Baker, a very hard hitter, came up to the bat. Collins took only a short lead off second base, standing almost on the bag with the evident intention of trying to get Meyers' signals and then tipping Baker off, as a hit meant a run and almost certain victory. Meyers saw this scheme and walked out to the pitching box and said to Marquard:—

"Pitch him two curve balls, no matter what I sign for."

A big leaguer recognizes only two kinds of balls, a curve and a fast one, the latter ball coming up to the plate with all the speed the pitcher possesses. Meyers crouched down and gave the sign for a fast one for the benefit of Collins, and "Rube" broke a curve off the edge of the plate which the umpire called a ball. Meyers then signalled for another fast one to throw Collins off, and Marquard broke a curve over the plate for a strike.

These two had exhausted the Indian's reserve supply, and he had to go back to straight signs again, hoping by this time to have thrown Collins off with his "phony" signals. Collins and Baker were too clever. Marquard thought that he could sneak a fast one over the plate after pitching the two curves. But Baker was up there all set and waiting for it. Collins evidently had tipped him right. It was clever work on the part of both of them.

Marquard hadn't any intention of putting the ball over the heart of the plate in a pinch like that one, but he did not get it exactly where he wanted it, and Baker, knowing what was coming, was set and waiting for it.

BAKER FOOLED "MATTY" ON SATURDAY

I had been told before the series that Baker could not hit fast balls well. I gave him one in the first inning of the game on Saturday and he smashed it to right field for a base. I immediately switched the dose and began to feed him low curves on the outside corner. I told Marquard about this discovery, but he evidently thought Baker would not be looking for a fast one at that time and expected to sneak it over. The Athletics' third baseman outguessed Marquard very cleverly and made the hit that won the game for his club.

Aside from that one ball, Marquard pitched a beautiful game and deserved to win it. It was not a lack of ability or power or speed, but just the combination of a man on second base tipping the batter off, a perfectly legitimate proceeding, and quick work on the part of the hitter. But I have thought of a scheme to beat them at this game of getting our signs as soon as a man is on second base, and when I use it the next time I pitch some batter is likely to get beaned, if he walks into the plate expecting one thing and meets another. . . .

The teams are now even and to-morrow we get a new start. The mistakes of to-day will be forgotten, but that one straight ball was what cost us the game.

29

Defending the Cork-Centered Ball (1912)

SOURCE: *Spalding's Official Base Ball Guide 1912*

Although the dimensions of the baseball have remained essentially the same throughout most of baseball history, the center of the ball has often been the subject of controversy. The introduction of the "lively ball" in 1920 is commonly thought to have ushered in a new era of offense led by Babe Ruth. Yet prior to the institution of the major leagues teams openly advocated the use of either "dead" or "lively" balls, depending on their style of play. This pattern continued until the National League adopted the Spalding baseball as its official ball in 1879. Thirty-one years later Spalding introduced a cork-centered ball, and batting averages soared.

Was this new baseball detrimental to the game? Spalding Guide editor John B. Foster contributed a brief history of the baseball and, with the help of a poll of 143 National League players, defended the integrity of the new baseball. The tone of the article suggests that Foster was less than impartial in his investigation of his employer's product.

This cork center ball has a very interesting history. Some years ago base balls were made with rubber centers. Then, in response to a demand for more runs to make the games more interesting to spectators, the experiment was tried of making a ball with a small piece of cork in the center—in the heart of the rubber core.

This produced a little of the desired effect and since then the relative sizes of the rubber and the cork in the center of the sphere has been changed, until the present ball was evolved.

The making of a ball seems simple enough, yet the inspection which is paid to every ball that leaves the factory to be used in the major leagues, semi-professional, amateur and college games which are played all over the United States, is equivalent to that which is bestowed upon watches that are manufactured by a firm famous for its skill and the perfection of its work.

When the present cork center ball was placed upon the market in 1910, it was put into use without any heralding of trumpets or advance advertising of any kind. The manufacturers had experimented with that ball for over two years before they felt warranted in assuring the members of the major league clubs that they could produce a ball of improved construction that would prove superior to any ball that had ever been used in championship games by major league clubs.

As a matter of accuracy, it may be said that the players of the major league clubs were using the new ball before they were aware of it. The ball was used in the world's series of 1910, yet no particular attention was paid to it.

In the beginning of the season of 1911 there were several games of many runs and free batting. Suddenly, as such things will happen, there arose a great cry as to the effect which the cork center ball was having on the national game. Naturally, some of the players, who were not having the best of luck in their early spring games, and who were only too eager to grasp at something by which they could account for their temporary shortcomings, charged the cork center ball with being at the bottom of their difficulties. Rival manufacturers, for obvious reasons, were very active in decrying the cork center ball.

Others, who were honest enough in their desire to excuse the players, took up the cry, and the cork center ball, for the space of about four weeks, held the attention of the Base Ball public.

The season progressed and the players settled down to the steady game which is always more significant of the latter part of June, all of July, August and September, than it is of the few days of April and the month of May. The large scores became the rare exception. The batting averages, which had soared, took a tumble. While they fell, they did not drop to the lower level which had threatened to make the game uninteresting because of the over-prominence of the pitchers. They were nearer an equitable adjustment of the chances between pitcher and batter than they had been for many seasons.

Second thought convinced many that after all it was not so much the fault of the cork center ball that there had been larger scores and free batting in the early part of the season, as it was that the major and minor leagues had been trying a great number of young pitchers who had not possessed the best of control, and who were naturally nervous in their desire to please the managers and to retain their positions in the major circuits.

It will be conceded that there is no one who is better qualified to judge of the merit of a ball than the player who uses it daily in contests for the supremacy in the National League. It will also be conceded that the better the ball the better the game. Taking the expert testimony of the players as the best evidence which could be gathered, to ascertain definitely something about the new ball, the editor addressed letters to the members of the clubs of the National League, asking them for their candid opinion as to the new cork center ball.

These requests for a symposium on the ball were not sought until the playing season was almost at an end, in order that the players might have had the fullest opportunity to form their opinions. . . .

A summary of the information conveyed in the answers is as follows:

98 per cent. declare that the Spalding Cork Center Official National League Ball, used throughout the 1911 season, and the same in every particular as we have been supplying them since August 1, 1910, has increased the batting from 10 to 15 per cent.

95 per cent. declare that the Spalding Cork Center Official National League Ball is not too lively.

98 per cent. declare that it is well thought of by all National League players.

75 per cent. declare that it is pleasanter to handle and can be thrown more accurately and farther than the old discarded rubber-cored ball.

30

Charles Ebbets Plans New Brooklyn Ballpark (1912)

SOURCE: *Brooklyn Daily Eagle*, January 3, 1912

Brooklyn Dodgers president Charles H. Ebbets thrilled his club's fans by announcing plans to construct a new stadium. Ebbets was reacting not only to local needs and demands but also to the trend among major league clubs, which between 1909 and 1915 constructed eleven other new stadiums, including Fenway Park, Navin Field (later called Tiger Stadium), and Weeghman Park (later called Wrigley Field). Ebbets declared that his stadium would be state-of-the-art, including public telephones and a garage for "autoists," and that the field would debut on Flag Day in 1912. By the time Ebbets Field hosted its first regular season game on April 9, 1913, the park was found to be lacking many features—including a flag and a press box—but it soon became an icon to the people of Brooklyn.

For more information on Ebbets Field see Michael Benson, Ballparks of North America: A Comprehensive Historical Reference to Baseball Grounds, Yards, and Stadiums, 1845 to Present *(Jefferson NC: McFarland, 1989).*

EBBETS PLANS TO REAR BIG STADIUM ON NEW BALL FIELD

$750,000 Park on Bedford Avenue Site Will Be Home of All Kinds of Sport
Double Decker Grandstand of Steel and Concrete, With Pavilion and Bleacheries, to Seat 30,000 Spectators—Eighty Foot Circular Entrance and a Garage

Brooklyn is at last to have a baseball park and general athletic stadium in keeping with the size and importance of the borough. Not only that—it will be the largest, most convenient and best equipped stadium owned by several of the largest universities in the country.

The new structure will be the property of the Brooklyn Baseball Club, and within its confines will be played the Brooklyn games in the National League schedule. But as a matter of interest to the thousands who do not actively take an interest in professional baseball the general athletic features should not be overlooked. It is intended to lay out the best running track that scientific experts can construct, a football field, socker [sic] field, jumping and vaulting pits, and all the other accompaniments of a first-class field for sports of every variety. It will be alone of its kind in New York, and should result in the holding of many important events in this city that are either held elsewhere at present because of the lack of proper conditions or are held under unfavorable circumstances. . . .

WILL TRY TO OPEN THE NEW PARK ON FLAG DAY

It is Mr. Ebbet's hope to have the park ready for National League games on June 14 next, Flag Day, which will be observed by all the National League clubs this year. If that is too great a task, the opening will take place on August 27, the anniversary of the Battle of Long Island. The latter day is by far the more likely, and will also be exceedingly appropriate. American destinies turned upon the Battle of Long Island, which raged between the new grounds and the present Washington Park. It was George Washington's masterly retreat from that battle, across the marshes where Washington Park now is, over into Manhattan through the Bronx, and into Tarrytown that saved the Continental army from annihilation by the British troops. Sullivan and Montgomery streets are named after two of Washington's ablest generals, who aided him in conducting a maneuver which had such a tremendous bearing on future generations.

One mad wag suggested last night that if it had not been for the brilliant coup of Washington in that dark hour there would have been no Brooklyn baseball club. Everybody over here would have been playing cricket. . . .

HOW THE CROWDS WILL BE HANDLED

According to the plans, the facilities for entering the park will be the equal, if not the superior, of any in the country. They are the result of a very careful study of the new structures in both the major and some of the minor leagues. Every effort has been made to expedite the selling of tickets and forwarding within of patrons without undue rushing, no matter if the full capacity of 30,000 seats is taxed to the limit.

The solution of this problem has been no easy matter. Every new park since the Philadelphia Athletics began the latter-day movement with their splendid concrete stands, has been an improvement on its predecessors in the matter of handling the crowds. One of the first objections pointed out by critics of the Philadelphia plant was that the patrons for the different priced seats converged upon one small area inside the gates and created confusion as the lines crossed one another. Taking this tip, ambitious magnates devised various methods of getting around the difficulty, but it is believed that the new Brooklyn ground, which will probably be known as Ebbets Park, will, as the result of the combined experience of fifteen or sixteen other magnates, be the best that has yet been evolved.

While the entrances will be ample, the exits will be even more so, and it is figured that it will be possible to empty the grounds in six to eight minutes in case of a great emergency. There are eight street car lines and the Brighton Beach elevated passing the site one block away on the various sides. This distance to the cars will tend to prevent congestion at the gates of the park and result the better for both the club and the fans. . . .

GARAGE FOR AUTOISTS

That garage idea, by the way, is rather new. The cars will be parked far enough away not to interfere with the patrons entering and leaving the scene of the games, and yet will be so near that the autoists will have practically no distance to walk. That was one of the details of perfection which was obtained from a close observation of the conditions at other parks, few of which have adequate or convenient places where autoists may leave their machines without danger of interference.

One long-standing complaint will be done away with when the baseball home is opened. The latest device in methods of announcing all changes in the lineup will be adopted. There will be a central indicator station and a megaphone device that will inform the fans of every new face in the struggle, where he will play, his favorite author and what he thinks of the tariff. That will be a tremendous advance over the old way of doing things, when you always asked the man beside you what the umpire said, and the man always told you wrong, so that you did not know the difference until you read the papers next day.

Carrying out the telephone idea, there will be booths scattered throughout the double-decker grandstand. This will be a great comfort. The hasty fan who has forgotten to order the supper things can hustle up to a booth between innings, and telephone the order to the grocer, and his wife will never know the difference or that he was not slaving at the office. The phones will be operated from a private switchboard by a gentlemanly attendant, who will be guaranteed not to swear even if he stubs a sore toe in the dark.

Concrete stands have two distinct advantages. They do not burn up, and they do not fall down. The haunting fear of the owner of every plant like that of Washington Park is that his stands will fade into smoke, as they have in half a dozen major league cities. Another is that in case of a panic something will break and precipitate scores of perfectly good fans into a fatal mixup. At Ebbets Park a fire on the grounds will be a mere laughable diversion, like a fight in the bleachers. As for anything falling down, it will be earthquake proof.

Rumblings of Unrest

Dissatisfaction among major leaguers with owner dominance over the players led players to form a union. The Baseball Players' Fraternity, although short-lived, pressured the owners into some concessions. It also provided leverage to the promoters of a new major league, the Federal League (FL), which attracted many Fraternity members into its ranks. The FL was also short-lived, but player anger over the reserve system, particularly as it was used to keep salaries low, remained as strong as ever. This frustration manifested itself in the Black Sox scandal of 1919. The owners never acknowledged their complicity in creating the conditions that inspired the eight guilty players to commit the acts that earned them infamy.

31

Response to Congressional Resolution on "Baseball Trust" (1912)

SOURCES: *Congressional Record Index*; Francis Richter, *Richter's History and Records of Base Ball* (Philadelphia: Sporting Life, 1914)

On March 11, 1912, Illinois Congressman Thomas Gallagher submitted a resolution requesting that a committee be formed to investigate the "Baseball Trust" as an "illegal combination." The resolution, after being referred to the Committee on Rules, was shelved. In response to the resolution, however, former Brotherhood president John Ward drafted a letter supporting what he described as a "beneficent trust" in which the "players (were) never oppressed." In the twenty-two years following the demise of the Brotherhood—which Ward cofounded in 1885 as the first baseball players' union—and its league, the Players' League, Ward's trust in the ability of owners to administer the sport increased dramatically, and Ward became the business manager of the Brooklyn Federal League club in 1914.

H. RES. 450

IN THE HOUSE OF REPRESENTATIVES.

MARCH 11, 1912.

Mr. GALLAGHER submitted the following resolution; which was referred to the Committee on Rules and ordered to be printed.

RESOLUTION

Whereas this Congress is desirous of investigating and securing information to dissolve trusts or illegal combinations in restraint of trade and liberties of the American people; and

Whereas the most audacious and autocratic trust in the country is the one which presumes to control the game of baseball; its officials announcing daily through the press of the country the dictates of a governing commission; how competition is stifled, how territory and games are apportioned, how the prices are fixed which millions must pay to witness the sport, how men are enslaved and forced to accept salaries and terms or be forever barred from playing, and of other acts incident to trafficking in a national pastime for pecuniary gain: Therefore be it

Resolved, That the Chair appoint a special committee of seven Members authorized and directed to inquire of the Department of Justice as to what steps it has taken against the Baseball Trust as it has against other illegal combinations, to take testimony that may develop all the facts relating to the matter, to sit during the sessions of the House and the recess of Congress, to compel the attendance of witnesses, to send for persons and papers, to administer oaths to witnesses, and to employ such assistants as may be needed.

SEC. 2. That the costs and expenses of said committee shall be paid from the contingent fund of the House of Representatives. Said expenses shall be paid out on the audit and order of the chairman of said committee. The Speaker shall have authority to sign and the Clerk to attest subpoenas during the session or recess of Congress.

BASE BALL A BENEFICENT TRUST

Mr. Gallagher is correct when he says that Base Ball is now under the direction of an autocratic trust, but it is a good thing that it is. I think that Congress is no place to discuss Base Ball. The atmosphere is not right. The surroundings are not suited for it. Baseball is the National game, but not a subject for national legislation. It cannot be successful without organization. The public cares little about the administration so long as the game is honestly conducted and it gets a run for its interest. It wants to be sure that the contest is a real one, and it insists more every year on having the best players who can be found. Base Ball to be a success

NEEDS FIRM ADMINISTRATION

and regulation. It is at present a trust, no doubt, but whether it is a violation of the Sherman Anti-Trust law is not for me to say in offhand opinion. Fifty or so of the ablest lawyers in the country have been working on the Sherman Anti-Trust law for several years and they have not put over much on it yet. Much of the discussion these days revolves around "Ty" Cobb. I consider "Ty" Cobb one of the greatest ball players the world has ever seen. At the same time he has a swelled head, largely due to the American League. That league has boomed him for several years and now his boom has come back as a boomerang. Cobb now considers that he is a law unto himself. He is being paid now as much as any club can afford to pay him. There is a limit to the size of base ball salaries, for the sport will be made so costly if men demand such money as he does that the public cannot afford to pay the high admission fees which would have to be charged.

PLAYERS NEVER OPPRESSED

In my experience I have never been able to see where ball players were oppressed. Organized Base Ball is the strongest trust in the world. It maintains strict discipline. It regulates the sport. However, it does not corner the necessities of life. It does not affect the high cost of living. The home plate would be as bountiful without it. The leagues have created Base Ball. Some persons may think that the game is a necessity, but if we consider it from a strictly legal phase it is rather a luxury. The last men in the world who should attack the organization of Base Ball should be the players themselves. The trust feature of it made them. The trust sought them out, developed them, trained them, exploited them, brought them to public notice and then paid them liberal salaries.

GAME MADE THE PLAYERS

If Base Ball were not so highly organized the famous players of today might never have been heard of. Instead of the attention of the people being focussed upon the great games there would be little ones in the back lots all over town and the enthusiasm of the sport would be dissipated. The rivalry which is promoted by having clubs to represent the leading cities comes with the trust idea. We have the American League and the National. These organizations so arrange their dates that they do not conflict in their games. This keeps up a steady attendance in Base Ball and the people enjoy the games under both managements.

THE PRESENT ORGANIZATION

has given to this country its beautiful base ball parks, its splendidly developed players, a corps of capable and well trained umpires and every facility for the enjoyment of a wholesome and exciting sport. Such an organization cannot be maintained without large expenditures. I should say that the salary list of the average club alone for a season would be $75,000 at least. The organization of Base Ball requires discipline, and it must enforce it.

32

David Fultz on the Fraternity (1912)

source: *Baseball Magazine*, November 1912

Prior to his formation of the Baseball Players' Fraternity, the third players' union in major league history, David Fultz was best known to sports fans as a top college football referee who worked several Harvard-Yale games and wrote a number of articles for Baseball Magazine on referees (in the off-season Baseball Magazine covered other sports). However, Fultz was also a lawyer and a former major league player. The following article is the first in a series of articles by Fultz on the Fraternity printed by Baseball Magazine. Like his predecessor, Brotherhood leader John Ward—whose 1887 article "Is the Base-Ball Player a Chattel?" first described the position of the players— Fultz stressed the many abuses of the current system. Like baseball's labor leaders today, Fultz pointed to the recent explosion of ball park construction as proof that the owners were making healthy profits and could afford to pay the players fairly.

THE BASEBALL PLAYERS FRATERNITY AND WHAT IT STANDS FOR

A Brief Review of the Baseball Players' Fraternity, Its Origin, Final Incorporation, Its Purpose in Being and What It Aims to Accomplish

The gist of the following article by David Fultz, founder of the Baseball Fraternity, has already been given to the public press. We believe, in justice to the new organization, it should receive a fair and impartial hearing before it is either condemned or commended. Inasmuch as there seems to be a great deal of misinformation in various circles as to the aims of this organization, we are pleased to present the following article by Mr. Fultz with a brief word on the origin of the Fraternity, its early history, and a clear declaration of its principles and purposes.

The Baseball Players' Association is at last a reality. This institution, which has been the goal of the players' ambition for many years, of whose benefits he has dreamed in seasons of adversity is at last fairly started on its career. . . .

The history of the organization may be treated briefly. Some two years ago several players came to me personally as a man who had for years played the National game and also as a practising lawyer in the city of New York. They felt the need of co-operation among the players to entitle them to a fair discussion of those differences which inevitably arise between four hundred men and their employers. It was at this time that the great need for such an institution became deeply impressed upon my mind and I determined that if it continued to seem advisable to work for the establishment of such a brotherhood. Nothing of consequence, however, was accomplished towards this work until the early part of the season of 1912. At that time the feeling among the players for the need of such an organization seemed more widespread than ever, and this feeling gradually crystallized under the small amount of leadership which was given it till it culminated in that final act on the sixth day of September, 1912, when the organization was genuinely incorporated. In compliance with the membership corporation law of the State of New York a certificate was filed with the Secretary of State and the County Clerk incorporating this organization under the name of Baseball Players' Fraternity. As explained in the charter, the general purposes of the fraternity are as follows:

To have every reasonable obligation of the players' contract lived up to by both contracting parties. To secure adequate protection from abusive spectators. To discountenance and abolish as far as possible rowdyism on the field. To be of financial assistance to deserving ball players. To advise the player concerning any real or fancied grievance, and, in the event the former exists, to prepare his case for him. To instill into the player a pride in his profession and to use the strongest possible influence to induce him to keep himself in condition and to give his employer the best service of which he is capable. . . .

Purpose

It is argued that the player is well paid. That he is well paid is no reason he should not organize. The star is well paid, we are frank to admit; the average player not so well, and some players very poorly. Many people will be surprised to learn that there are men playing in the big leagues for $900 per season. A pitcher who led his league a few years ago and who is considered to have won the pennant for his team, was under a $1,200 contract.

No artisan is well paid who does not get a fair proportion of the money he helps to make. A glance around the big league circuits at the stupendous equipment recently completed or now under construction would convince the casual observer that after paying salaries, the magnate still has enough left to keep the wolf out of the garage. If this is not conclusive proof, let the skeptical one attempt to purchase a share of stock in any of the clubs; the price quoted him will remove all doubt.

But with this we have no contention, we are exceedingly glad to see the magnate prosper; he has made large investments in an uncertain business and deserves large profits; we do, however, object to having the player represented as overpaid. With the amount of salaries, we have little concern, as we most emphatically shall not foolishly attempt to standardize a wage scale; with the possible exception of re-questing that the young player who is brought from a minor league shall be paid at least as much as he has been receiving. . . .

The fraternity has a membership of 286; almost every player in the two big leagues is enrolled. The stars, while having nothing to gain personally, have un-selfishly "gone out in front" to aid their less fortunate brothers. The players have never before been so thoroughly organized nor so thoroughly in accord. For a man to go back now would be to exhibit a color distasteful to every athlete. There will be no deserters. We have every confidence that the players will "stick."

We expect no antagonism from the fair-minded progressive owner. President Johnson has gone on record as favoring the movement. He is a far-sighted man of business sagacity; he knew that an organization of some kind was inevitable, and, if we mistake not, he is much gratified that the movement has developed along the lines that it has. We expect the co-operation of not only President Johnson, but President Lynch and Chairman Herrmann.

33

Jim Thorpe Exposed as Professional (1913)

SOURCE: *New York Evening Post*, January 25, 1913

In 1912 Jim Thorpe starred on the college gridiron for the Carlisle Indian School and on the track in the Olympic Games in Stockholm. At the beginning of 1913 his accomplishments were tarnished by the revelation that he had played professional baseball several years earlier. Overlooking the well-known fact that many college athletes, especially baseball players, had played professionally during the summers (see document 10 above), sporting officials stripped Thorpe of his amateur status and his Olympic medals. This decision was not reversed by the International Olympic Committee until 1982.

FROM THE FIELD OF SPORTS

CHARGES THICKEN AGAINST THE CARLISLE INDIAN, THORPE
Should Be Easy of Proof—Amateur Athletic Union Investigating—
If He Played Professional Ball His Victories Are Void—
America's Model Discovered in Worcester
By Fair Play

It appears to be an easy matter to straighten out the tangle in regard to James Thorpe, the Carlisle Indian, who is charged with playing professional baseball in 1909 and 1910. The first statement that the great all-around athlete played with the Salem-Winston nine in the Carolina League is denied by those interested in the club, as the original charge practically falls to the ground, but a more serious one has been made by Charles McDonald, sporting editor of a Raleigh newspaper, and Sherwood Upchurch, an umpire, that Thorpe was a member of the Rocky Mount and the Fayetteville teams in those years. They say that they knew the Thorpe who played on those nines, that they have seen the pictures of the Indian, and are certain that there can be no mistake in identification. In those years Thorpe pitched against several players who are now in the big leagues and identification should be easy. The men are Fulenwider, of the Giants; Yerkes, of the Red Sox; and Hearn, of the St. Louis Cardinals. They could be confronted with James Thorpe and quickly decide whether he is the man. There can be no possibility of mistaken identity in the case, for Thorpe could not be mixed up with any other athlete or ball player.

The whole question of summer baseball is up again in the case, and some day there will be a ruling on the subject which will settle it for all time. At some of the colleges summer baseball is permitted and the amateur standing of the participants is not disturbed, while in others the summer ball player is disqualified. In these days when so many students work their way through college in various ways, the question as to what they may or may not do in the way of earning money and still remain an amateur is a serious one, and this summer baseball is the most disturbing of all. Those who are in favor of permitting summer baseball declare that it is far better for a student to play the game than to act as waiter at a summer hotel and put himself in the ranks of professional waiters by receiving tips. In that respect it would seem as if their arguments were well founded. It is undoubtedly necessary to have a strict definition of an amateur, but there are times when the rules might be stretched a little without injuring sport in the least.

Thorpe's case is somewhat peculiar in that the eligibility rules at Carlisle have always been lax, and if he played with the professionals he may have done so with no idea that he was wrong and making himself ineligible to compete as an amateur. James E. Sullivan, secretary of the Amateur Athletic Union, says that the conditions surrounding the case are different from any that could obtain anywhere else in the world; in that it has been the custom to make pets of the Indian athletes, and because of their origin, nothing back of their careers in the Government school has ever been delved into. So it probably became natural for the students, before they came into contact with the registration rules of the union, to go out and play summer baseball in their vacations, and boys brought up in that way ought not to be judged by the same standard as those whose upbringing has been along the best and most approved lines. At the same time Mr. Sullivan says that if Thorpe is found to have broken the rules of the union by playing with the Carolina team, he will be stripped of all his records, his name will be taken from the Athletic Almanac, and he will have to return all the prizes he was won since his infraction of the rules. This will mean that he will yield fourth place in the running high jump in the Olympic games to Grumpelt and Erickson of America, who tied in fifth place; first place in the pentathlon to F. R. Bie, of Norway, and first place in the decathlon to H. W. Weislander of Sweden.

According to Sullivan the remarkable feature of the case is that the baseball sharps of the country have not intimated this wrong doing before. It was known that the Pirates have had their eyes on Thorpe for some time, and that Thorpe had been advised by Sullivan not to sign a contract with them last year. Further than this, as the union has nothing to do with baseball in its regulations, it could not be expected to keep track of a sport it did not govern, with the many other things to look after. It is more than likely that the men in professional baseball would think nothing of Thorpe's playing with them and then competing in amateur track and field athletics, for there are sports in which professional baseball players take part as amateurs without question. For instance, take the case of John M. Ward, the great short stop of years ago on the Giants, who is a simon pure amateur in golf, and no question has been raised as to his amateur standing when he has won his championships. Warner, the Carlisle coach, is in New York, and the directors of the Amateur Athletic Union will have him before them late this afternoon, for prompt action is to be taken in the matter.

34

Federal League Formed (1913)

SOURCE: *Chicago Daily Tribune*, March 8, 1913

In the wake of labor difficulty and the formation of the Baseball Players' Fraternity in 1912, a small group of wealthy businessmen saw an opportunity and formed the Federal League. Other leagues, like the Players' League (1890) and the American League (1901), had capitalized upon owner-player discord to spring into existence. Like the Players' League, the Federal League would survive only for a short time—in this case, two seasons.

FEDERAL LEAGUE ORGANIZES TODAY

**Magnates of Six Cities Hold First Meeting in Hoosier Capital
CHICAGO CLUB IN CIRCUIT
St. Louis, Cleveland, Indianapolis, Detroit and Pittsburgh
Others in the Fold**
By Hugh S. Fullerton

A new league, independent, claiming to come to fill an unoccupied place in the baseball world, is a-bornin' today.

The Federal league, at present composed of six clubs, backed by real money and with serious intentions of becoming the third major league, will be born and christened at Indianapolis. The reason for the meeting at Indianapolis is that the new league is incorporated under the laws of Indiana, which require that the first meeting be held in the state.

The Federal league at present is composed of Chicago, St. Louis, Detroit, Indianapolis, Cleveland, and Pittsburgh, with Cincinnati, Milwaukee, and Kansas City represented and seeking franchises.

ALL CLUBS CONTROL GROUNDS

As to the guarantee of good faith each applicant for a franchise in the Federal league must today lay down proof that the club controls playing grounds and on top of that deposit a check to guarantee that his club will carry out the schedule through the season. Certified checks to the amount of $1,000 for each club already are on deposit.

The Federal league is the outgrowth of the United States league, which was started last season, but failed because of incompetent organization and failure of some of the clubs to carry out their obligations. The owners of franchises were not all discouraged and their receipts led them to believe that the field was open and lucrative provided the organization was solid. On top of that they received assurances from the powers of organized baseball that there is room for more clubs.

At the Indianapolis meeting today Pittsburgh will be represented by W. T. McCulloch and Maj. Marshall Henderson, who were interested in the league last year. In eighteen home games last season, seven of which conflicted with the Pirates, the Pittsburgh team drew 54,907 persons and made money.

POWERS TO BE PRESIDENT

Chicago will be represented by Charles Sherloch and J. T. Powers. Mr. Powers is scheduled to be elected president of the new organization. In St. Louis, Senator Mike Kenna is the backer of the club. In Cleveland and Indianapolis the franchises belong to the promoters of Wonderland park and Luna park.

The big money back of the new league, it appears, comes from the company which now owns nine motodrome and amusement parks in the central west. There appears to be more capital back of the new venture than ever has been behind a rival league, and less opposition. The promoters seem to understand that the major leagues cannot cover the entire field and that there is an opening. They are neither seeking war with the powers of organized baseball nor avoiding it.

The new league has no intention of trying to secure players from major league clubs. Instead of signing men to play under contracts such as are in vogue in "organized baseball," they are offering the players one, two, and three year contracts, the players to become free agents at the end of their contract, with liberty to sign with any club they may see fit.

COVINGTON TO GET CLUB

The Cincinnati franchise, it is asserted, is to go to Covington, with grounds that can be reached from downtown Cincinnati ten minutes easier than the National league park can be reached. The new league does not appear in the suit brought against Herrmann and the other members of the National commission, a Covington club being the catspaw.

35

Damon Runyon Reports Babe Ruth's First Home Run (1915)

SOURCE: *New York American*, May 7, 1915

Sports fans in New York in the early 1910s enjoyed the most illustrious group of sportswriters ever assembled in one city. They could chose between Grantland Rice (of the Evening Mail), Heywood Broun (Morning Telegraph), Ernie Lanigan and his successor, Fred Lieb (Press), former major league player Sam Crane (Journal), and Damon Runyon (American), among others. Rice, Broun, Lieb and Runyon were all elected to the writer's branch of the Baseball Hall of Fame, and Lanigan—a nephew of The Sporting News's Alfred and Charles Spink—was the sport's foremost statistician. Runyon typically focused on personalities, as when he wrote short stories on characters that inhabit Broadway, later assembled in Guys and Dolls (1931). The following article chronicles

Runyon's first encounter with the greatest character in baseball history, Babe Ruth. In this game Ruth pitched and lost a thirteen-inning 4–3 decision, and he hit his first major league home run, a third-inning solo blast against Yankee pitcher Jack Warhop. Runyon described the young Ruth as "quite a pitcher and a demon hitter—when he connects."

YANKEES TIE IN NINTH AND WIN IN THIRTEENTH, 4 TO 3

High's Single, Steal of Second and Cook's Hit Land Long Game from Boston Red Sox

By Damon Runyon

There is not enough of Hughy High to make one good-sized hero for our story this morning, and so we add to him Luther Cook and thus compile a sufficient subject. Hughy and Luther, bunched together, make something to talk about. They assisted this community in taking a notable decision over the municipality of Boston, Mass., yesterday afternoon.

The shades of the thirteenth inning were falling fast up at the Polo Grounds, and the Wild Yanks and the Boston Red Sox, champs-presumptive of the Amur-r-r-ick-kun League, as Ban Johnson calls it, were clustered in a tie. The count was three all, with Will Evans, the gesticulator, eagerly scanning the horizon for evidence of nightfall, when Hughy and Luther amalgamated and broke up the pastime, the final tally being 4 to 3 in favor of the grand old Empire State.

In our own garrulous way we shall now endeavor to tell you just how it happened, omitting only such details as we deem unfit for publication.

Hughy High, small, but efficient, opened that thirteenth with a single to centre. Walter Pipp struck out, Hughy High stole second. Luther Cook singled over Heine Wagner's head, just out of Heine Wagner's reach and mid the mad mumble of the multitude. Hughy High came tumbling in across the h. p. with the winning run. How was that for High?

Having described the most important incident of the game, we now feel constrained to warn the compositors to clear away all obstructions below, and to either side, so we can run right on down this column, and over into the next, in telling about the goings-on prior to the moment mentioned, beginning with that hour in the ninth when we boys tied 'er up.

Luther Cook figured in that, too. One was out in the ninth, when George Ruth struck Luther with a pitched baseball. George pitched the baseball left-handed, and by giving it the body-follow-through, he succeeded in raising a tumor on Luther's shoulder. Cap'n Roger Peckinpaugh subsided without a struggle, while Luther tarried at first, rubbing his wounded torso, and glaring at George Ruth. That made two out, and it looked as this story would have to open with sighs, when Luther Boone—but by all means a separate paragraph for Luther.

Luther Boone doubled to right, a solid, smacking, soulful double that knocked the bleacherites back on the butt of their spines from the crouch that precedes the rush for the exits, and which scored Luther Cook with the tying tally.

A moment later Luther Boone went on to third, when George Ruth made a bad throw trying to catch him off second, but Leslie Nunamaker could not bring him in, and the game passed on into extra innings and to the big punch in the story as outlined above.

Well, it was quite a pastime. Everybody said it was a great game to win. Everybody was so delighted that they almost forgot about Dominick Mullaney, who was cast for the character of the bad guy in this tale. Not that we intend to make Dominick out, because you know the size of Dominick. The day that we blacken the character of Dominick is the day after Dominick leaves town, and gets well beyond the confines of this newspaper's circulation.

COOK AGAIN ENTERS SCENE

In the seventh inning, with we 'uns needing a run to tie, Luther Cook singled. Peckinpaugh was duly expunged, and Boone hit the right field wall with a blow which put cook [sic] on third. The ball hopped back off the razor-backed sign in right into Hooper's hands, and Hooper threw to first, instead of second, as Boone anticipated.

Boone had taken "that old turn" after hitting first, in accordance with the advice of all the coachers, and was several feet off the bag when Hoblitzel got the ball. Dominick said he was out, and the rally bogged down right there.

The crowd discussed Dominick in audible tones on account of that decision, and some thought it might be a good thing to assassinate him at once, but no action was taken on account of Dominick's size, and the presence of Ban Johnson.

We have been wondering ever since the season opened why Wild Bill Donovan has been keeping little Jack Warhop warmed up down there in right field, and the reason developed yesterday. It was for the purpose of having Jack pitch this game, and Jack pitched very well indeed while he was pitching, proving the efficacy of warming-up.

In the eighth inning, Charles Mullen batted for Jack, but nothing came of it, as Mike McNally, the Sox's new third baser, and the noisiest man in the whole world, next to Baumgartner, the Phil pitcher, made a smashing play on Charley's drive. Fritz Maisel got an infield hit that inning, stole second, moved to third on Carrigan's bad throw, and scored on Hartzell's out.

Cyrus Pieh finished the game for the Yanks, and this story would be wholly incomplete without an eulogy of Cyrus. Tall, thin and very interesting, Cyrus would have a column all to himself did space permit. He compiled a masterly finish. Pieh had the crust, as you might say, to use a slow curve on some of the sluggers of the Sox, and he made them appear mighty futile and inefficient.

In the eleventh he gathered up Scott's slow roller and made a two-base bad chuck to Pipp. Then he fanned McNally. Henricksen, who once broke up a world's series pastime on Chris Mathewson—long and long ago, that seems—batted for Carrigan, who manages the Sox, and therefore has a right to refuse to hit against Cyrus Pieh any time he feels that way about it.

Henricksen singled and Scott took third, Henricksen moving to second on the throw in. Then Cyrus Pieh fanned Ruth and Hooper. How was that for Pieh?

RUTH BANGS OUT HOMER

Fanning this Ruth is not as easy as the name and occupation might indicate. In the third frame Ruth knocked the slant out of one of Jack Warhop's underhanded subterfuges, and put the baseball in the right field stand for a home run.

Ruth was discovered by Jack Dunn in a Baltimore school a year ago when he had not yet attained his lefthanded majority, and was adopted, and adapted, by Jack for the uses of the Orioles. He is now quite a pitcher and a demon hitter—when he connects.

In our boys' end of the eleventh, Pipp led off with a single, but Wild Bill had Cook up there trying to sacrifice, and after failing in two attempts to bunt, Cook struck out. Whereupon he flung his bat far from him and took on an expression of intense disgust. Evidently the only way Luther likes to bunt is from his shoe cleats.

It was in that inning that Luther Boone was purposely passed for the first time in his brief career. In other days pitchers would have passed the whole batting order to get at Luther, but yesterday Ruth let him go to fire at Nunamaker, and Leslie did not betray Ruth's confidence. He lifted a fly to Hooper.

36

Eighty Thousand Watch Amateur Match (1915)

SOURCE: *Cleveland Plain Dealer*, October 11, 1915

At a time when the largest major league stadiums held less than forty thousand spectators, an amateur game that could attract twice that many fans was stunning. Yet other top amateur and semiprofessional tournaments staged games that attracted tens of thousands of fans. This article focuses almost entirely on the crowd, relegating to the background the contest they assembled to watch.

80,000 HOWL WHEN WHITES SCALP LUXUS

**Baseball's Greatest Crowd Jams Brookside
as Autos Become U.S. Champs East of Rockies
'On to Frisco!' Roar Clevelanders, Wild With Victory
That Cheering of Throng Aids
OMAHA TEAM DEFEATED BY SCORE OF 11 TO 6
Leads Until Terrible Fourth Inning, Then Fades Before Onslaught**
By C. L. Kirkpatrick

Fringed at the top by a mass of humanity ten persons deep the entire circumference, the vast bowl at Brookside park yesterday afternoon was jammed with the greatest crowd of fans in the history of the national pastime.

In the semi-final battle for the amateur baseball championship of the world, fully 75,000 and probably closer to 80,000, persons saw the White Autos, city champions of Cleveland, batter their way to a 11 to 6 victory over the Luxus team of Omaha.

Over 10 per cent. of the population of the sixth city of the United States turned out on a chilly afternoon for what will go down in the history of amateur sports as the most notable event in all years up to 1915. Estimates of over 100,000 were made by many who saw the spectacle. This figure, however, is believed to be too high. Nevertheless, the crowd was the largest that ever attended a baseball game, either professional or amateur in the history of the sport.

MASS SWAYS LIKE SEA

On the western slope of the stadium, the people were jammed in a solid mass. The mass swayed and rolled like the waves of a swelling sea. On the eastern slope the massed humanity sat on the close cropped green, or, in the bare spots, stood the two hours of the contest. Banked along the fill of the Wheeling & Lake Erie railroad was a mass of humanity that extended the entire length of the stadium, fully 400 feet.

It wasn't the crowd so much that thrilled. It was the noise. That terrific bedlam which has helped the White Autos vanquish the best talent that such cities as Detroit, Columbus and Johnstown could send here, was doubled by yesterday's outpouring. Seldom during the game could two persons sitting side by side hold conversation. The deafening uproar drowned out any individual human voice. Men, gray with age, other young men, young men in their prime, thousands of school boys, women, many of them old, many grandmothers, young women whose cheeks were pink from the fresh cool wind, were all fired with the contagion of the occasion. They screamed, yelled, and roared in unison. . . .

The Whites took one run in the first inning, but for the next two innings Lefty Holland, the twirling sensation of Nebraska during the season just closing, appeared invincible. With all the speed of a Walter Johnson he shot them across the plate and mowed down the Whites.

In the second the Luxus scored twice, getting a one-run lead. They nicked Big Six Louie Crowley for three hits in this session, besides being presented with a pass and having one man get on base by virtue of being hit. They added two more in their half of the third, two hits, a pass and a wild throw being the contributing factors.

Then came that terrible fourth inning when the Whites opened up their heavy guns and mowed down all opposition. When the smoke of battle had cleared away eight White shirted runners had crossed the plate on four hits, three errors, a sacrifice and two hit batsmen. Before the carnage was over Holland, with perspiration streaming down his face, marched from the box, a beaten man. His place was taken by Dyck, but before the inning was over one run was scored while the relief pitcher was at work.

It was the end for the Luxus. They knew it, although they gamely fought on to the finish. They never ceased their attempt to overcome the damage inflicted in the fourth. Nor did the Whites let up in their attack. To make victory sure, they added two more tallies, the demoralized condition of the opposition being greatly responsible for this last brace of tallies. Three errors, a single and a sacrifice contributed to these runs.

When Salettel at second gobbled up Farley's grounder and threw it to Gage for the final putout in the ninth, the crowd broke loose. It swarmed out over the playing field. Louie Crowley was lifted from his feet and carried on the shoulders of the multitude. He might just as well have been riding on the deck of a storm tossed liner. He was absolutely helpless in the hands of his thousands of admirers for fully ten minutes.

"On to 'Frisco! On to 'Frisco!" shouted the thousands as they marched across the field. The band struck up "The Star Spangled Banner," and then drifted off to "Hail, Hail, the Gang's All Here," as it headed an impromptu procession across the stadium.

37

Federal League Signs Peace Treaty (1915)

SOURCE: *Cincinnati Enquirer*, December 23, 1915

In January 1915 the Federal League filed an antitrust suit against major league baseball, claiming that it was a monopoly in violation of interstate commerce as defined by the Sherman Antitrust Act. The case was assigned to flamboyant Chicago federal judge Kenesaw Mountain Landis, who postponed making a decision in the hope that the litigants could settle their differences out of court.

SIGNED, SEALED AND RECORDED

Baseball Peace Agreement Now a Fact Accomplished
Federal League Goes Out of Existence Forever
Cruel War is Over, and Normal Conditions Restored—
All Fed Players Are Eligible
By Jack Ryder

The Christmas present of the National League to the baseball fans of the country is peace. After a two-day conference, which ended at 9 o'clock last night, the joint peace committee of the two warring factions came to a final agreement on all details with one exception, and the peace agreement was signed and sealed by both parties to the conference. The Federal League no longer exists. Its suit against the National Commission in the United States Court in Chicago will be withdrawn at once, and the league which came within an ace of disrupting the national pastime vanishes into history.

The only point on which a final settlement was not reached is the terms on which the International League shall regain its lost territory in Baltimore and Buffalo. This matter was freely discussed and was finally left to a committee of seven members, who will meet in this city on January 3, at the time of the annual meeting of the National Commission. This committee was given full power to act, and both sides agreed to abide by its decision. Whereupon the peace agreement was drawn up, signed and sealed, and the cruel baseball war was officially declared to be a thing of the past.

The terms of the final agreement do not differ in any respect from these which have been forecasted in this column for the past week, ever since the first hint of peace came forth. Two Federal League magnates break into organized ball by the purchase of ball clubs, one in the National, the other in the American League. Charles Weeghman and his associates in the ownership of the Chicago Feds become the owners of the Chicago Nationals, having reached terms of purchase with Charles P. Taft and Charles Webb Murphy, the present owners of the Cubs. The Cubs and the Chifeds will be combined into one team and will play their games on the grounds of the Federal League in Chicago, on the north side of the city, abandoning the old West Side Park.

BALL GETS THE BROWNS

Joe Tinker will manage the team. Roger Bresnahan, present manager of the Cubs, who has a contract with two years more to run, will be fully taken care of. His contract for two years will be paid in full. He may be retained as catcher on the club, or he may be transferred to some other club, but he will lose nothing in either case. The chances are good that his salary will be paid in full and that he will be set free to take up the management of the new Toledo Club in the American Association.

The other club to change hands is the St. Louis club, of the American League, known as the Browns. This club has been purchased from Robert Hedges, John E. Bruce, C. J. McDiarmid and the other owners by Phil Ball and Otto Stifel, owners of the St. Louis Feds. The two clubs will be combined and will play their games on the present American League park in St. Louis. Fielder Jones will manage the team. Branch Rickey, the non-Sunday bench manager of the Browns, is not under contract for next year, and so is out of a job.

Members of the Peace Committee stated that there was no talk about the sales of any other clubs of organized ball to any Federal magnates. They denied explicitly that there had been any deal on, to their knowledge, for the purchase of the New York Giants, the Cleveland Americans or the Philadelphia Athletics. There was some talk about the St. Louis Cardinals going to some Federal capitalist, but this deal was declared off, when a price could not be agreed upon. So far no apparent provision has been made for Harry Sinclair, the main angel of the Feds since the death of Robert Ward, to continue in the game. It is firmly believed, however, that Mr. Sinclair will succeed in coming to terms with the owners of the New York Giants during the winter and that the club that occupies the Polo Grounds will be transferred to him before the season of 1916 opens. . . .

Yesterday's final session of the Peace Committee was taken up almost entirely with the settlement of the International League question. The Baltimore and Buffalo Clubs, of the Federal League, managed to kick up quite a disturbance by insisting on terms to which President Ed Barrow of the International League would not agree. The Baltimore Club wanted to retain its franchise and be transferred to the International League just as it stands. Manager Jack Dunn, of the Richmond Club, was present, and strongly opposed such a settlement, which, he said, would be very unfair to himself. Dunn and his partner, Charles Knapp, of Baltimore, who also was present, declared that they had been shoved out of Baltimore by the Feds and forced to transfer their club to Richmond after losing a great deal of money. They claimed that they should be given back the Baltimore franchise, and they were backed up in this attitude by President Barrow. They asserted that the Feds had no right to come in and drive them out of town and then reap the profit of their action after their own league had failed to make good.

At first the Baltimore Feds offered to sell the franchise to Dunn for $100,000. Dunn labeled this offer as a joke, claiming that it would simply be making him pay heavily for something that was already his own in all justice. Finally the Feds agreed to keep the franchise and to allow Dunn to come in as manager of the team, instead of owner, and he also objected very strongly to this solution.

MINORS ARE ANGRY

In Buffalo a somewhat similar situation prevailed. The International League club there was not driven out, but it wants to have nothing to do with the Feds, who lost nearly $170,000 in two years and are bankrupt. Robertson, the owner of the Buffalo Feds and a very heavy loser, wants to have the Buffalo franchise in the International, hoping to recoup some of his losses. The International owners object to this procedure, and put up a strong argument against it.

For a time it looked as if the peace agreement might be blocked by the insistence of the Feds on breaking into the International League, against the wishes of President Barrow and his club owners. Mr. Barrow came out of the meeting room early in the afternoon and stated openly that he would not stand for the terms offered by the commission and the Feds. Later he was recalled and a compromise was arranged by the appointment of a committee to go into the rights of the controversy fully and come to a fair decision. This was agreed to by both sides in order not to hold up the signing of the peace agreement.

The committee appointed consists of seven members, namely the three members of the National Commission, Herrmann, Tener and Johnson; President Barrow, of the International League; President Gilmore, of the Federal League, and a representative of the Buffalo and Baltimore Feds, to be chosen by Gilmore. This committee will meet and report here on January 3, at the time of the annual meeting of the commission. It has been given full power to act, and both sides have agreed to abide by its decision.

38

Final Showdown for Matty and Brownie (1916)

SOURCE: *Chicago Daily Tribune, September 5, 1916*

Christy Mathewson and Mordecai "Three Finger" Brown concluded one of the most celebrated pitching rivalries in baseball history on a rainy afternoon in Chicago. Both men were clearly at the end of their illustrious careers, and some seventeen thousand fans sat through a meaningless (for the standings) doubleheader just to witness history. This was their twenty-fifth meeting, and with Mathewson's 10–8 victory each man had beaten the other twelve times (one game had ended in a tie). As longtime Daily Tribune *reporter I. E. "Cy" Sanborn noted, "The dollar sign has not driven all the sentiment out of the nation's pastime."*

MATTY BEATS MINER BROWN; FIRST TO CUBS

Wins Second for Reds by 10 to 8 After Tinx Take Opening Game, 3–0

By I. E. Sanborn

Chicago fans turned out 17,000 strong in spite of a rainstorm to celebrate the Brown-Mathewson swan song at Weeghman park yesterday and the Cubs and Reds celebrated by breaking even in the holiday double header, of which the battle of veteran heroes was the feature.

Mathewson emerged triumphant from his farewell engagement with his ancient and honorable rival, beating Brownie by a margin of 10 to 8. The Cubs won the curtain raiser by a score of 3 to 0.

There was nothing but sentiment to attract a crowd that overflowed the plant to see these past masters of the slab art pitch their last game against each other. Gone are the days when they were the reliance of two great ball teams battling each other for pennants year after year. Their lots are cast with second division outfits now.

GREAT MASTERS ARE THROUGH

Gone are the days when Matty and Brownie could give the greatest batsmen in the game a winning argument nine times out of ten and when shutout scores were frequent when they performed. All that is left to them of their wonderful prowess are their lion's hearts and their master minds.

Gone was the fearsome and deadly hook with which the veteran of the Cub slab used to mow down his antagonists in the pinches; gone was the effectiveness of Matty's far famed fadeaway. Still a great group of baseball rooters stood in the rain for an hour before time to start the games and, soon after it was decided to play, filled the plant. The dollar sign has not driven all the sentiment out of the nation's pastime.

The Cubs and Reds proceeded to knock a lot of things out of the deliveries of the great hurlers who faced them and still the fans remained to the long delayed finish of a batting fest, partly because they realized it would be their last chance to see Mordecai and Christy pitted against each other on a green diamond.

Not that neither of them will pitch again, because each of them demonstrated that he has many good innings left in his arm, but that they never will hook up against each other in the same game is practically certain.

It was a see-saw battle of bats and wits. At first the tide favored Brown, as the Cubs gained a lead of two runs and held it for two rounds. Then the Reds got to Brownie for the lead in the third and held it to the end, although the Tinkers rallied at the finish and had the tying runs on the bases in the last half round when Mollwitz, batting for Pechous, flied the game over. This was the first substitution made on either side, although it was not expected either of the past master pitchers would finish the way they were being hit.

EIGHTEEN HITS AND SIXTEEN

Brown was tagged for eighteen safeties while Matty escaped with sixteen off him. They had almost perfect control, issuing one base on balls apiece, and again Mathewson had a slight advantage because Brown also hit one batsman.

Wingo was the most heartless cuss of the lot, as he peeled off four hits, but Saier came close to Ivy in lack of consideration by smashing a home run over the wall in the ninth inning with two men on ahead of him.

CHICAGO—SECOND GAME.

	AB	R	BH	TB	BB	SH	SB	PO	A	E
Flack, rf.	4	2	1	3	1	0	0	1	0	0
Doyle, 2b.	5	1	3	4	0	0	0	2	5	0
Kelly, lf.	5	2	1	3	0	0	0	4	0	0
Saier, 1b.	4	1	2	6	0	1	0	10	0	0
Williams, cf.	5	0	3	3	0	0	0	2	0	0
Wilson, c.	5	0	1	1	0	0	0	3	0	1
Pechous, 3b.	4	0	1	2	0	0	0	2	2	0
Wortman, ss.	4	0	0	0	0	0	0	3	4	2
Brown, p.	4	2	2	2	0	0	0	0	2	0
Totals	*41	8	14	24	1	1	0	27	13	3

*Mollwitz flew out for Pechous in ninth.

CINCINNATI.

	AB	R	BH	TB	BB	SH	SB	PO	A	E
Neale, lf.	6	2	2	3	0	0	1	3	0	0
Groh, 3b.	3	1	1	2	1	1	1	0	3	0
Roush, cf.	3	1	2	4	0	1	1	2	0	0

	AB	R	BH	TB	BB	SH	SB	PO	A	E
Chase, 2b.	5	1	1	1	0	0	0	4	5	2
Griffith, rf.	5	1	2	3	0	0	0	4	0	0
Wingo, c.	4	3	4	4	0	1	0	4	2	1
Louden, ss.	5	0	2	2	0	0	0	2	0	0
Huhn, 1b.	5	0	2	2	0	0	0	7	1	0
Mathewson, p.	5	1	2	3	0	0	0	1	2	0
Totals	41	10	18	24	1	3	3	27	13	3

Cincinnati .... 0 1 2 1 2 2 0 1 1—10

Chicago .... 2 0 1 0 2 0 0 0 3—8

Two base hits—Doyle, Groh, Saier, Mathewson, Neale, Pechous, Griffith. Three base hits—Kelly, Roush, Flack. Home run—Saier. Struck out—Brown, 1; Mathewson, 3. Double plays—Wortman-Doyle-Saier [2]. Hit by pitcher—By Brown, Roush. Time—1:50. Umpires—Rigler and Eason.

39

Antitrust Suit Dropped in Landis's Court (1916)

SOURCE: *Chicago Daily Tribune*, February 8, 1916

As an integral component of the recently signed peace treaty with major league baseball the Federal League agreed to drop its antitrust lawsuit against baseball. Some six weeks later lawyers from both sides met in Judge Landis's court to officially withdraw the suit. Landis, however, could not resist the opportunity to extol the sport. His paean to baseball's integrity would be remembered by grateful owners in the wake of the Black Sox scandal. An ominous note was sounded by representatives of the Baltimore FL club, who commented that the club reserved the right to pursue legal recourse for their claims, which had not yet been settled to their satisfaction.

LANDIS DROPS SUIT AND PAYS GAME TRIBUTE

Withheld His Decision in Baseball Case to Give Chance for Peace

"I want you gentlemen to leave this court with the understanding that there was not the slightest bit of evidence produced from which the most suspicious person could have obtained anything with which to impute the honesty and integrity of any player or the cleanliness of the game."
—Judge K. M. Landis

By James Crusinberry

Baseball, America's national game, received perhaps its greatest tribute yesterday when Judge Kenesaw Mountain Landis, one of the fans, delivered it from the throes of the courts with a clean title after it had been dragged through by belligerent magnates who had attempted to maim and destroy.

Attorneys for the Federal league and organized baseball came before his honor asking for the withdrawal of the suit which the Feds started against their enemies more than a year ago. And the suit was withdrawn after Judge Landis had listened to Attorney Jenney of Baltimore, who represented that club's interests.

In permitting the withdrawal of the suit Judge Landis apparently couldn't resist the temptation to say a few words in explanation of his delay in rendering a decision on the famous lawsuit. He never did give the decision, though the case was heard more than a year ago.

GAME NOT HURT, SAYS JUDGE

The reason the judge didn't give the decision, he said, was because he loves baseball and felt convinced that the game itself hadn't been hurt and that in time the quarreling magnates would make peace. Before the crowd of baseball men and fans left his courtroom he opened up with a little speech of his own which showed he was convinced the game itself is too good to be harmed by any one.

"My decision would not have allowed either of the litigants to leave the court the absolute victor," said Landis. "Therefore I decided that this court had a right to postpone the announcement of such an order, and that is the reason it was postponed."

NO KICK FROM BALTIMORE

The finish came yesterday when the attorneys on each side appeared in the courtroom along with a representative from the dissatisfied Baltimore club of the Fed side. When the latter said there was no objection from Baltimore regarding the withdrawal of the suit without prejudice the judge wiped it completely off his records, but he couldn't resist saying a few words because he wanted the fans, real lovers of the game like himself, to know that the game itself and the players who take part in it hadn't been given one single black mark through all the litigation and fighting between the magnates of the Feds and organized baseball.

The attorney who represented the Baltimore club admitted that although his clients did not object to the withdrawal of the suit, they had not been a party to the amalgamation which had brought about peace in baseball and that they might take some legal action for redress in the future.

40

Toney-Vaughan Double No-Hitter (1917)

SOURCE: *Chicago Daily Tribune*, May 3, 1917

The matchup between Fred Toney and James "Hippo" Vaughan, staged at Weeghman Park (later renamed Wrigley Field), was a masterpiece of "slab art." For the only time in major league history the regulation nine innings were completed without either pitcher surrendering a hit. The Reds' Vaughan allowed two hits and the only run of the game in the tenth inning, but his performance was by no means tarnished—even though modern officials have since stripped him of credit for a no-hitter.

CUBS HITLESS AS TONEY WINS IN 10TH, 1 TO 0

Two Bingles Off Vaughan with Error Score Tally for the Reds

RECORD!
Three thousand or more fans who saw the Cubs-Reds game yesterday witnessed a contest that will stand as one of the most remarkable in history. So far as can be learned, there never was a time in the major leagues when two pitchers went nine innings without a hit being made on either side, as did Jim Vaughan of the Cubs and Fred Toney of the Reds.

By James Crusinberry

Fred Toney and Jim Vaughan both attempted to enter the baseball hall of fame yesterday when the Cubs and Reds fought at Weeghman park, and the result was a pitching duel such as never before has been staged. When nine rounds had been played neither one of the stalwart hurlers had allowed a base hit, but in the tenth the break came, and it went against Vaughn. Two hits were registered with one error, and Cincinnati got a run. Toney went back in the last half and set three Cubs down in a row, thus winning the day and the honor of a no hit no run game.

Many times it has happened that a pitcher on one side has gained the honor of allowing no hits, but none of the old time fans can remember of seeing two pitchers fight for nine innings and neither one allow a hit. There wasn't even a fluke which might have been called a hit in the first nine rounds. Vaughn passed two batsmen and one Cincinnati man got to first when Rollie Zeider fumbled an easy grounder.

TONEY GIVES TWO WALKS
Toney walked two batsmen, but those two were the only men to reach first base. He was given perfect support by his mates, not a bobble being made behind him. The duel was so desperate that when the ninth inning was over and the honors were even the crowd cheered both men.

Vaughn really was the more brilliant of the two pitchers for nine innings. Only twenty-seven men faced him in that time, because each time he walked a man double plays occurred, clearing off the bases, and the one fellow who reached first on Zeider's fumble was pegged out trying to steal. Vaughn also fanned ten men in the nine innings, while Toney fanned only three all told, and two of the three strikeouts occurred in the last of the tenth, when the big Tennessee man called upon all the reserve power in his right arm to make sure of the honor of a no hit game.

It was a wonderful game for Toney to win and a tough one for Vaughn to lose. Had Vaughn been given the keen support that Toney had the Cubs might have prolonged the battle, and possibly connected with Toney's curves later on. But when the first hit was made in the tenth there was a general breakdown.

The first fellow to drive the ball to safe ground was Larry Kopf, the young shortstop of the Reds. One was out in the tenth when he came up, and he hit a liner to right field. Fred Merkle made a desperate lunge to his right with one hand stretched out, and perhaps came within a foot of the ball, but it was out of reach, and the terrible suspense was broken.

WILLIAMS DROPS BALL

That blow shouldn't have lost the ball game. Neale followed with a fly ball to Williams, and then Chase hit a line fly right at Williams. Cy scarcely had to move, but if he had advanced two steps he could have taken it in front of his belt buckle. Instead, he had to catch it at his ankles, and he muffed the ball. Kopf was on third and Chase safe at first.

Jim Thorpe, the athletic red skin, then bounced one into the earth in front of the plate. The ball rolled slowly toward third base, with Vaughn after it. It looked as if Vaughn figured he had lost a chance to get Thorpe at first base, and there seemed little hope of such a play, so in desperation he scooped the ball to Wilson standing on the plate, with Kopf tearing in. The ball hit Wilson on the shoulder about the same time that Kopf crashed into him, and the run was in.

Chase also tried to dash in when he saw the ball roll away, but Wilson recovered it in time to get Hal. There wasn't any need of Hal's run anyway, for one run was all that could be used.

41

Baseball Ruled Nonessential Occupation (1918)

SOURCE: *Washington Post*, July 20, 1918

The United States officially entered World War I on August 6, 1917, but the war effort did not appreciably affect professional baseball until the middle of the 1918 season. Secretary of War Newton Baker, in response to an appeal by Washington player Eddie Ainsmith, declared that baseball players were not exempt from military duty. Although baseball officials publicly pledged to support Baker's directive, they feared it would result in the collapse of the current season. However, a compromise was reached which allowed an abbreviated season, and the World Series.

BASEBALL PLAYERS MUST WORK OR FIGHT, BAKER RULES, DOOMING NATIONAL SPORT

Arguments That Regulations Will Ruin Business Interests, Work a Hardship on Players and Deprive Public of Needed Recreation Are Swept Aside by Secretary of War in Upholding Decision That Affects 90 Per Cent of Major Leaguers

By J. V. Fitz Gerald

Baseball was ruled to be a nonessential occupation by Secretary of War Baker yesterday and ball players must now obtain useful occupations or be drafted into the army. The decision was made on the appeal of Eddie Ainsmith, of the Nationals, from a ruling of his local and district boards taking his deferred classification from him under the work-or-fight regulations. Unless the government waives the enforcement of the regulations for the remainder of the season the national pastime will pass out within a few days for the duration of the war. Ninety per cent of the major league players are affected by the ruling, and not enough would be left to permit the clubs in the American and National leagues to finish the season.

Secretary Baker, in upholding the work or fight regulations in reference to baseball, and unqualifiedly putting the sport in the class of non-useful occupations, left no loopholes for the game that for so many years has been the most popular with Americans. The work-or-fight regulations went into effect on July 1, but baseball men, it is indicated, will ask that they be permitted to finish the season and that the ruling be not enforced until the fall.

All are willing to do whatever the government says. They may ask, however, that in view of the millions of dollars invested in the game that they be allowed an extension that will permit them some financial relief. It will be pointed out that certain players have obligated themselves to financial contracts that they cannot fulfill unless they are allowed to play through the season. . . .

UPHOLDS DECISIONS OF BOARDS

In passing upon the Ainsmith appeal, Secretary Baker said:

"The language of the regulation pertinent here occurs in paragraph C, of section 121-K, as follows:

" 'Persons, including ushers and other attendants engaged and occupied in and in connection with games, sports and amusements, &c.'

"Obviously, baseball players are persons occupied in a sport, so that the ruling of the local and district boards must be sustained as plainly correct.

"It is suggested, however, that the regulations ought to be changed to exclude baseball players from their operation, and this appeal is not really based upon any doubt as to the correctness of the determination made by the local and district boards, but is addressed to the wisdom of the regulations.

"The arguments in this behalf are three in number:

"That baseball is a business in which very large investments of money have been made, involving the erection of properties, useless and unprofitable unless permitted to be continued in the use for which they were erected; and that the application of the regulations to members of professional baseball teams would so far disorganize this business as to destroy it and render this property temporarily valueless.

"That the occupation of a professional baseball player requires a very high degree of specialized training and skill, procurable only by a substantially exclusive devotion of the time of persons aspiring to become professional players, so that there is not much likelihood of such players having any other available occupation, or fitness for any other occupation, at all adequate in its returns to maintain for themselves and their families the standard of living which has been established on the earnings in their professional occupations.

"That baseball has been accepted as the national sport of the people of the United States, that it affords wholesome outdoor recreation and enjoyment to large numbers of the American people, and is to many workers and business men of the United States almost the only opportunity for such recreation; so that to bring about the cessation of professional baseball would work a social and industrial harm far out of proportion to the military loss involved by the exemption of the limited number of players in question.

CONSIDERS EACH PLEA

"Upon each of these grounds separate comment is appropriate," his statement said.

"As to the first: The situation of professional baseball differs in no wise from other civilian peace-time business which by reason of the stress of war and its demands upon the industries and energy of the country must be content to bear whatever burden is imposed by temporary inactivity.

"While the number of men affected by the order may be sufficient to disorganize the business, many of the players are beyond the present draft age and it is by no means certain that complete disorganization of the business would follow adherence to the order as made.

"As to the second: Baseball players are men of unusual physical ability, dexterity and alertness. It has been necessary for us in this country to institute processes of rapid industrial training, and it is quite inconceivable that occupations cannot be found by these men which not only would relieve them from the onus of nonproductive employment, but would make them productive in some capacity highly useful to the nation. This change will be welcomed by the individuals involved, and its usefulness to the country, both direct and indirect, is obvious.

REALIZES VALUE OF RECREATION

"The third consideration is of course the serious one, and is the one which has brought about the present appeal to the President—the stress of intensive occupation in industry and commerce in America in normal times, such as to give the highest importance and social value to outdoor recreation. It may well be that all of the persons who attend such outdoor sports are not in need of them, but certainly a very large preponderance of the audiences in these great national exhibitions are helped, physically and mentally, and made more efficient, industrially and socially, by the relaxation that they there enjoy.

"But the times are not normal; the demands of the army and of the country are such that we must all make sacrifices, and the nonproductive employment of able-bodied persons useful in the national defense, either as military men or in the industry and commerce of our country, cannot be justified. The country will be best satisfied if the great selective process by which our army is recruited makes no discrimination among men, except those upon which depend the preservation of the business and industries of the country essential to the successful prosecution of the war.

"I am, therefore, of the opinion that the regulation in question should not be changed, but, rather, that the scope of its provisions should be so enlarged as to include other classes of persons whose professional occupation is solely that of entertaining.

"Our people will be resourceful enough to find other means of recreation and relaxation if there be not enough persons beyond the useful military or industrial age to perform such functions, and they will be wise and patriotic enough not to neglect the recreation necessary to maintain their efficiency merely because they are called upon, in the obvious public interest, to sacrifice a favorite form of amusement."

42

Baltimore FL Team Wins Lawsuit against Majors

(1919)

SOURCE: *Baltimore Sun*, April 13, 1919

Making good on a threat made following the dismissal of the Federal League lawsuit against organized baseball, the Baltimore FL club filed its own antitrust case in the District of Columbia Supreme Court on March 25, 1919. Barely two weeks later the court ruled in favor of Baltimore, awarding the club $80,000 in damages (trebled to $240,000 under the Sherman Antitrust Act)—less than one-third the sum sought by the victors, but a significant triumph nevertheless. The decision was immediately appealed by organized baseball, and was overturned on December 6, 1920. Following this setback Baltimore appealed the case to the Supreme Court, which issued its ruling in 1922.

For the best explanation of the legal complexities of baseball antitrust cases see G. Edward White, Creating the National Pastime: Baseball Transforms Itself, 1903–1953 (Princeton NJ: Princeton University Press, 1996).

JURY AWARDS FEDS $240,000

Terrapins Win Great Legal Victory Over Organized Baseball
SUM COVERS MONEY OF STOCKHOLDERS
Combination Of American And National Leagues Is Unlawful

[From the Sun Bureau]

Washington, April 12—Organized and monopolized baseball in this country received a staggering blow today, when a jury in the District Supreme Court awarded the Baltimore Federal League Club $240,000 damages inflicted upon it when the unlawful combination of the American and National Leaguers conspired to deprive Baltimore of major baseball.

The Baltimore Club had asked for $900,000; that is, it asked for $300,000 damages actually sustained by it, which amount, under the Sherman Antitrust law, would have been multiplied by three as a further measure of punishment. The jury awarded Baltimore on the face of the verdict $80,000, which multiplied by three makes $240,000, which the Baltimoreans will receive if there is no reversal upon appeal.

COVERS CLUB'S INVESTMENT

The award today exactly covers the investment made in the Baltimore Club including the money put up by stockholders. It does not include the value which the Baltimore interests placed upon their franchise. Evidently the jury did not feel that it would be the part of justice to compel Organized Ball to stand for the value of a franchise which might be regarded as in doubt.

Even so, Baltimore has won a tremendous victory. It has been the means of pronouncing Organized Ball to be an unlawful combination in restraint to trade. It has made a successful attack upon the oppressive practices of a combination which all the sporting world has known to be an airtight monopoly, but which the courts never before passed upon.

And the result, in the opinion of the Baltimore counsel in the case, is that Baltimore may now apply for and secure major league baseball at any time it may desire to do so. William L. Marbury, leading Baltimore lawyer for the Feds, gave this as his opinion just as soon as the jury had rendered its verdict late this afternoon.

OVERHAULING NOW IMPERATIVE

Moreover, today's decision of the court and jury makes it possible for other interests which have been outraged by Organized Ball to go into court and to demand damages. Should this case stand, it is not too much to say that professional baseball, as it is now organized, will have to undergo a complete overhauling. The magnates who have been here since the trial began are said by their friends to have a full realization of this fact.

Nor is it too much to expect that the Department of Justice may give consideration to the criminal phases of Organized Ball as developed during the trial of the Baltimore suit. Certainly this will be true if upon an appeal the Supreme Court of the United States sustains the findings and opinions of the lower courts based upon the decision of Justice Stafford that this combination is a bold attempt at monopoly and could therefore be sued for damages. If it can be sued as an unlawful combination, under the civil section of the Sherman law, it might be prosecuted as well under criminal sections of the same law.

43

Hugh Fullerton Alludes to World Series Scandal

(1919)

SOURCE: *Chicago Herald and Examiner*, October 10, 1919

Throughout the 1919 World Series between the Cincinnati Reds and the Chicago White Sox the public sensed, in the light of considerable circumstantial evidence, that something was amiss. Even suspicious reporters, following the "Gee Whiz" school of sportswriting, believed that publishing negative information violated their duty to both the national pastime and their readers. Others, like Damon Runyon and Hugh Fullerton, were more cynical and were willing to attack the game when appropriate.

This column appeared the day after the Series ended with a resounding 10–5 Reds win. Fullerton, while never naming names, explicitly stated his concerns about the honesty with which the Series was played, and predicted (the element of his columns for which he was best known) that seven White Sox players would be released because of their performances in the Series. Fullerton anonymously wrote an article in the New York Evening World *on December 15 in which he quoted Chicago manager Kid Gleason and others as saying he did not believe the Reds had won the Series honestly. Fullerton would be castigated by fellow baseball journalists for his breach of protocol.*

FULLERTON SAYS SEVEN MEMBERS OF THE WHITE SOX WILL BE MISSING NEXT SPRING

HUGH PREDICTS END OF WORLD'S SERIES AS WELL
Still the Mother Shipton of Baseball, Whose Prophecy Failed, Gives Reds Credit
By Hugh S. Fullerton

Cincinnati's Reds are champions of the world. The Reds turned yesterday and gave the dope the worst upsetting it has had during all this surprising and upsetting series. They slashed away at Claude Williams' pitching and before the big crowd had settled to see the contest, it was over. The knockout punch was landed by Duncan, the kid who is the hero of the series and Williams was driven to his retreat and elected to the office of false alarm of the series.

The close of the series was discouraging. Wednesday the dopesters all agreed that the Reds were on the run. The Cincinnati fans who have been canonizing a lot of mediocre athletes turned upon them and declared that they were dogs, yellow curs and German quitters. Yesterday these same Reds swarmed upon the cocky White Sox and battered them into the most humiliating defeat of any world's series.

There will be a great deal written and talked about this world's series. There will be a lot of inside stuff that never will be printed, but the truth will remain that the team which was the hardest working, which fought hardest, and which stuck together to the end won. The team which excelled in mechanical skill, which had the ability, individually, to win, was beaten.

EVERYTHING GOES BACKWARD

They spilled the dope terribly. Almost everything went backward, so much so that an evil minded person might believe the stories that have been circulated during the series. The fact is that this series was lost in the first game, and lost through over confidence. Forget the suspicious and evil minded yarns that may be circulated. The Reds are not the better club. They are not even the best club in their own league, but they play ball together, fight together and hustle together, and remember that a flivver that keeps running beats a Roll Royce that is missing on several cylinders. The Sox were missing on several. They played the game as a team only through one game, and part of another, and they deserved defeat.

It is not up to me to decide why they did such things. That all probably will come out in the wash. They were licked and licked good and proper, deserved it, and got it.

Yesterday's game in all probability is the last that ever will be played in any world's series. If the club owners and those who have the interests of the game at heart have listened during this series they will call off the annual inter-league contests. If they value the good name of the sport they will do so beyond doubt.

Yesterday's game also means the disruption of the Chicago White Sox as a ball club. There are seven men on the team who will not be there when the gong sounds next Spring and some of them will not be in either major league.

4

The Age of Ruth

One of the reasons for the enduring popularity of Babe Ruth is that he arrived just when baseball fans needed a reason to smile. Still, fans had to endure the trial of the Black Sox players, plus the tragic death of Ray Chapman, before daring to believe in their game again. The hiring of Kenesaw Mountain Landis as the first baseball commissioner created an impact on all levels of baseball, as he sought to stamp out all traces of gambling in the sport. In the meantime the Negro Leagues—sponsored in large part by African American gamblers—became the most successful black sports enterprise in American history. Baseball took advantage of the baptism of radio to broadcast the World Series to thousands of new fans, the youngest of whom were playing their own versions of baseball on local playgrounds and in schoolyards.

44

Yankees Sign Babe Ruth (1920)

SOURCE: *New York Herald*, January 6, 1920

The most celebrated—and despised—player transaction in American sports history occurred when Boston Red Sox owner Harry Frazee sold Babe Ruth to the New York Yankees on December 26. The deal was struck in Los Angeles, where, according to the Los Angeles Times, Ruth and Yankee manager Miller Huggins met on a golf course to sign the necessary paperwork. The article below, the first public acknowledgment of the deal, offers proof that New Yorkers knew that the deal would immediately transform the Yankees into a contender for years to come, and that Boston fans would never forgive Frazee.

YANKEES PURCHASE THE HOME RUN KING FROM RED SOX

Ruth at Once Signs Contract to Play with the Yankees
Star of American League Comes to New York for Record Price—
Deal Startles Fans

LOS ANGELES, Cal., Monday—Miller Huggins, manager of the New York Americans, tonight announced he had signed "Babe" Ruth, champion home run hitter, to play with the Yankees next season. Papers were exchanged here late today, Huggins said. He refused to state what salary Ruth was to receive.

COLONEL RUPPERT ANNOUNCES PURCHASE

Negotiations with Harry H. Frazee, owner of the Red Sox, for the purchase of George H. ("Babe") Ruth, noted pitcher, by the Yankees, were completed yesterday and it ended in a cash deal. What the figure was Colonel Ruppert refused to say, but he admitted that he knew Frazee had turned down an offer of $100,000 for the player recently, and from that admission it may be concluded that the New York club did not pay much less than that amount, if not more. It need scarcely be mentioned that the news will create a furor in major league baseball circles, that it will please Gotham fans mightily, and at the same time raise a storm of protest in the Hub, where fans never dreamed that Frazee would dare dispose of the star. Boston baseball followers will probably not permit the Red Sox owner to forget about it for some time, but in local circles it was suggested that the offer was undoubtedly too tempting to be refused. One thing that may be said with certainty is that the price was the greatest ever paid for a ball player.

From Boston Frazee sent word yesterday that he had disposed of Ruth because he thought it was an injustice to keep him with the Red Sox, who "were fast becoming a one man team." He added that he would use the money obtained from the New York club for the purchase of other players and would try to develop the team into winning combination.

The acquisition of Ruth will undoubtedly give the Yankees added strength as well as prestige. Just now, Ruth, who established a record of twenty-nine home runs last season, is the most talked of player in baseball, and he probably will continue to be for some time to come. Recently Babe returned his three year contract from Los Angeles, where he has been playing ball and posing for the films, with the ultimatum that unless his stipulated salary was increased from $10,000 to $20,000 he would refuse to play next season. He added, furthermore, that he would refuse to play with any other club but the Red Sox. The ultimatum is not worrying Colonel Ruppert, however, who declared that Ruth would have no cause to complain of the treatment the New York club would accord him if he showed any desire to be reasonable.

Frazee in League to Stay.

"Does this mean," Colonel Ruppert was asked, "that Frazee is about ready to get out of baseball?" "Nothing of the sort," was his reply, "Frazee is in the league stronger than ever." The Yankee club owner added that "we entered into negotiations for the player in pursuance of a policy to give the club's following in New York an aggressive, strong, well balanced team that would be in all respects worthy of the league's largest city."

Miller Huggins, the Yankees' manager, is out on the coast now trying to sign Duffy Lewis for next season, and will probably see the club's new batting ace before returning East, if he has not seen him already. Colonel Ruppert thought yesterday that Ruth would be played in right field, which he considered his natural position, but that question will be left for Huggins to decide.

In addition to beating a record for home runs that had withstood assaults for many years, Ruth led the league's outfielders with only two errors in 258 chances. His batting performance embraced in all 129 hits, seventy-five of which were for extra bases. In fact, he poled out more extra base hits than singles. He scored 103 runs, forced pitchers to walk him 101 times, and finished with a batting average of .422. He also pitched thirteen games, and proved his ability on the mound by winning eight of them. As a fielder he had 230 putouts and twenty-six assists, the latter figure indicating the excellence of his throwing arm.

Ruth came to the Red Sox in the closing month of the 1914 season from the Baltimore club along with Ernie Shore, now a member of the Yankee pitching staff, and Ben Egan, a catcher. Ruth immediately made good as a pitcher and won recognition as one of the best in the American League. His ability as a batsman came to light in 1915, and he was frequently called upon as a pinch hitter. In 1918 he batted extra base drives with such regularity that he was given a place in the outfield on days when he was not pitching. He came with a rush last season as a batsman, proving the sensation of the league and attracting crowds wherever he played.

45

"Freak Deliveries" Regulated (1920)

SOURCE: *Baseball Magazine*, February 1920

In spite of the promise of Babe Ruth, baseball officials were concerned about the low offensive output in the major leagues. They wanted not only to improve the game on the field but distract fans from rumors of a World Series fix by the Chicago White Sox the previous fall. The decision was to restrict use of the spitball and other "freak deliveries" to certain designated pitchers whose livelihood depended on these pitches. It is interesting that this editorial also mentioned the possibility of creating a "more elastic" baseball. No evidence exists that this step was actually taken, but many believe the Age of Ruth was made possible through the introduction of livelier baseballs. For a persuasive argument against the "lively ball" thesis see William Curran, Big Sticks: The Phenomenal Decade of Ruth, Gehrig, Cobb, and Hornsby (New York: William Morrow, 1990).

MORE BATTING

The problem of getting additional batting is one that is vexing the rule-makers this winter, just as it vexed them years ago, and will keep on vexing them. There will always be just that kind of a problem while the average pitcher is smarter than the average hitter. No matter what rules have been made, the pitchers have always found ways to overcome them, and you can't choke off the ingenuity of the pitchers without imposing such huge handicaps as to turn the game into farce comedy.

Reduction of the called balls to three has been advocated. It might have been a great idea up to 1919, but its value faded last season, because the pitchers gained such wonderful control that bases on balls became the exception, not the frequent incident. So skilful and accurate were the 1919 pitchers that they didn't need any three-ball rule to make them cut the corners—they stopped using "waste balls," shot everything inside the strike zone, made the batsmen hit desperately when they weren't ready, and thus cut down the hitting. They didn't cut down the actual batting nearly as much as they did the total number of men reaching first base, and the smaller number of base runners meant fewer runs. How, under such circumstances, with the pitchers steady as clocks, can there be better batting? . . .

Choking off freak deliveries wouldn't help much, because that stuff is mainly psychological—the batsmen are bluffed and imagine they see funny shoots when they don't. There's just one way by which batting can actually be boosted for the 1920 season—that's by making the ball a trifle more elastic. Not a tremendous addition of rubber or cork to the center of the ball—just a small percentage. Such an addition would result in giving the ball a "kick" that would carry dozens of hot ones sizzling just out of reach of the infielders. There is just one objection to such a scheme: Clubs playing in parks where the fences are too close would gain even a greater advantage than they possess at present. The Giants, with this bulge in their favor, might almost count the pennant cinched, and the annual flock of home runs at the Philadelphia Nationals' park would be almost doubled. Pittsburgh, the Braves, the Reds, and other clubs having large outfields would be handicapped more than under present conditions—and, say, when would Babe Ruth EVER get through hitting home runs?

Nevertheless, this would be the only way to increase the batting, unless by changing the material of the bats. Bats could be made that would massacre the ball, and I have never been able to understand why ingenious sluggers have never thought about getting them manufactured. Bats could be made of pressed wood, like that now used in bowling pins; such bats would be perfectly legal and almost unbreakable—and a ball squarely hit with one of those bats would hardly ever stop going.

More rubber in the ball, or pressed hardwood in the bats. One way or the other to increase the hitting—and those would be the only practicable methods. It can't be done by any written rules.

Legislation against freak deliveries, artificial pitching, was wildly demanded, but fizzled quite a lot when every magnate happened to think that he had at least one freak pitcher on his own staff. It looks, at this time of writing, as if the magnates would adopt a rule permitting the various pitchers to continue their deviltries for 1920, but to have them all discarded by 1921, such a rule, of course, giving the sinners time in which to practice "square shooting." Of course, such flagrant, wide-open violations as strips of emery paper or parafinned cloth on the trousers won't be allowed.

Legislation against tricky pitching isn't needed half as much as common sense among the batsmen. As often remarked, the pitcher is far craftier than the batsman, taking the general average. Pitchers can think up more tricks in ten minutes than batters can invent in six months. Mentality counts a whole lot, right there. The batsman is told that the pitcher has a new, terrible and unhittable delivery. When he faces said pitcher, said pitcher contorts himself like a flock of angleworms, makes hideous faces, gives the ball a rub on his pants, and lets go probably the same old stuff he has used for the past four years—and the batsman fishes frantically in the air. Clear case of "buffalo" or bluff. The pitcher hasn't actually thrown a blamed thing new, or any harder to hit than it used to be, but he has that batsman all full of frazzled nerves till a straight, tossed ball seems to take on a snaky curve.

Hod Eller is referred to as the trickiest of the 1919 pitchers and the master of the shine ball. Eller has often told me that he doesn't throw a blamed thing that is new—just uses the same old fast ones and jumping curves that he had in 1917 and 1918. But his mere rubbing of the ball on his trousers; the deliberation with which he does this, and the care with which he seems to hold the shined ball before letting it go, plus the publicity given the said shine ball, all bluff the batters, and they are beaten before he even starts his pitching. Yes—freak deliveries should be stopped, but a campaign of education for credulous batsmen would be the best way to stop them.

46

On Accusations of a Fixed World Series (1920)

SOURCE: *Baseball Magazine*, February and December 1920

In the wake of the 1919 World Series, rumors abounded that the White Sox had not given their best effort. However, no journalist directly addressed the issue until columnist Hugh Fullerton quoted gamblers saying that the Series had been fixed. Outraged, periodicals like Baseball Magazine *and* The Sporting News *chose to attack him rather than investigate his claims. According to Eliot Asinof in* Eight Men Out: The Black Sox and the 1919 World Series *(New York: Holt, Rinehart and Winston, 1963), these publications were more concerned with protecting the institution on which their existence depended than on exposing a potential scandal. In the excerpts below, taken before and after the fix became public knowledge, the editors of* Baseball Magazine *focused on attacking Fullerton.*

[FEBRUARY]

The sport world was recently greeted with a giddy screed from the facile pen of Hugh Fullerton.

The screed began with the sensational statement: "Baseball has reached a crisis. The major leagues, both owners and players, are on trial." To this we reply, very interesting if true. Who is to try them? Presumably, Mr. Fullerton. If so we tremble at the result, for we know of no one less competent by clear reasoning and fairness of vision to pass judgment on so broad a question.

Mr. Fullerton goes on to say that certain gamblers, whom he claims to know, have made repeated assertions that players on the White Sox team were in their pay. Can anything be more vague or unsubstantial than this?

"In the last world's series," continues Mr. Fullerton, "the charge was made that seven members of the White Sox team entered into a conspiracy with certain gamblers to throw the series. Some of the men whose names are used are my friends and men I would trust anywhere, yet the story is told openly with so much circumstantial evidence and with so many names, places and dates that one is bewildered."

Referring to these players, Fullerton says: "If these men are guilty they should be expelled. If they are innocent they should be allowed to prove it and the persons who are responsible for the charges should be driven out of the sport forever."

We agree with Mr. Fullerton. If he were driven out of the sport forever it would be a consummation devoutly to be wished. . . .

How much weight should be given to Mr. Fullerton's present assertions? How much weight does he give them himself? His statements are all of nameless gamblers. According to his own story, he told these gamblers to their faces that they were crooks. Why does he give so much weight to their stories now? He further asserts that seven plays during the series might have been the result of deliberate quitting on the part of players; but he hastens to add that they might equally have been caused by the accidents of the game. . . .

As for Mr. Fullerton's predictions particularly of world's series games, they have long been the joke of the whole baseball world. Fullerton, with his usual acumen, predicted that the White Sox would win. They failed to fulfill his prophecy. For this treachery they should, no doubt, be heavily punished. How much of Fullerton's activities now are a mean attempt at an alibi? Does Mr. Fullerton remember how the hooting of the fans drove him out of the press box at Chicago during the recent series? If he does, he will know about how much the public cares what he thinks or writes.

[DECEMBER]

Last fall, a baseball writer, Hugh Fullerton by name, published a number of sensational articles charging that the World's Series of 1919 was fixed. There was in those articles, not a scintilla of actual evidence. At that time no evidence was obtainable. He quoted various professional gamblers, but even they had no direct evidence to offer. The articles were founded entirely on rumors without tangible substance. In fact, Mr. Fullerton himself confessed that the players implicated were, some of them, his friends and he could not believe them guilty. We considered the articles in question as a triumph of muckraking journalism and took occasion to criticise them in our winter editorials.

In response, we assume, to these editorials, we were recently favored with the following communication from Mr. Fullerton:

Oct. 4, 1920
Editor Baseball Magazine,
Sir:

Several months ago you printed several scurrilous and entirely untrue (in detail) stories concerning me. In almost every statement made there were lies and part lies. For several reasons I ignored them chiefly because I knew such things hurt the writer more than they do the object of the attack.

In view of recent developments do you not think that it is up to you to print in an equally prominent space an apology and a retraction? I suggest this before proceeding further in the matter.

I desire most of all to know who inspired the attack, in plain English, what person in organized baseball ordered you to write it? I think that such a statement from you at this time may have bearing upon the case now before the Grand Jury in Chicago.

I will await your reply until the latter part of the present week. You may address me, etc.

(Signed) HUGH FULLERTON

We have no comments to make upon this letter. Nor would we waste time or space upon this particular individual were it not for the recent turn of events which makes it advisable to define our attitude toward the gambling rumors of last fall, which formed the basis of Mr. Fullerton's attacks. . . .

Events have played into Mr. Fullerton's hands in a manner which is probably very gratifying to him. We begrudge him none of his personal triumph. Baseball is essentially honest and no one knows it better than Mr. Fullerton. The Baseball Magazine has no personal feeling against Mr. Fullerton but it recognizes in him a man who has shown a dangerous tendency to pervert his acknowledged gifts as a writer to pure muckraking. Its attention was called to Mr. Fullerton's activities during the late war at which time he came out with a series of articles condemning and berating baseball in the very hour when it most needed the loyal support of every scribe. Mr. Fullerton's alacrity in running out on the game which had given him all the notoriety he ever possessed roused our resentment.

The Baseball Magazine is opposed to the publication of mere rumor simply because it is sensational and has a certain news value. And it is opposed to the professional muckraker on any grounds.

47

Gehrig Homers in High School Championship Game

(1920)

SOURCE: *Chicago Daily Tribune*, June 27, 1920

In 1920 promoters scheduled an unprecedented game between the high school champions of New York City and Chicago to be played in Cubs Park (later renamed Wrigley Field). The contest generated considerable publicity in the host city. When New York's High School of Commerce won the city title, a June 19 article in the Daily Tribune *observed that they "have a 17 year old boy of 190 pounds on first base who is a regular Babe Ruth. If he gets a high, fast one he'll slam it over the right wall at the Cubs' park." The first baseman was Lou Gehrig (misspelled "Gherig" throughout the article), whose ninth-inning grand slam clinched Commerce's 12–6 victory over Chicago's Lane Tech.*

NEW YORK PREPS DOWN LANE TECH IN HITFEST, 12–6

Gherig Swats Homer with the Bases Loaded

By James Crusinberry

New York City's High School of Commerce conquered the Lane Tech boys of Chicago yesterday at Cubs park in a baseball combat of thrills and heroic acts featured by a home run over the right wall by Louis Gherig, the New York lad known as the "Babe Ruth" of the high schools. The real Babe never poled one more thrilling, for the bases were filled, two were out, and it was the ninth inning. The four base drive settled all chances the Chicago lads had to pull the game out of the fire, the final count being 12 to 6.

That Chicago loves to see a real game played by "kids" was established by the fact that more than 6,600 followers of the national game assembled to see this contest. The size of the crowd makes it assured that such a game will be an annual affair which in time will become a classic event for the prep boys.

LANE PUTS UP FIGHT

Although decisively beaten, the Chicago boys put up a game and spirited fight all the way, and until the homer by young Gherig occurred in the ninth they were always within striking distance. In the first inning, the New Yorkers knocked in a cluster of three runs which would have discouraged most any team. Lane came forth with a gallant assault in the third and tied the count. New York scored once in the fourth and twice in the fifth, and from then on remained in front.

Perhaps Lane was playing in bad luck to some extent. Tom Walsh, who pitched the team to the championship of the Chicago public school league, labored only for five innings. He suffered so badly from a sore arm that he had to be removed from the game. Norris Ryrholm, the star of the Lane team, who has shifted from short to catcher, was compelled to take the slabbing job and, though he turned out some clever and steady work, he was wild.

In the ninth, he lost control after getting two men out and a couple of walks with an error filled the bases and made it possible for "Babe" Gehrig to come to bat once more. The husky New Yorker had been up five times and made nary a hit. He walked twice, but hadn't been able to get hold of the ball, and the crowd was wondering if the stories of his batting prowess were all myths. This time he made good.

Ryrholm didn't intend to give him one in the groove, but did, and the "Babe" landed on it. The ball sailed out high and far and cleared the right wall screen by many feet, finally landing in Sheffield avenue and bouncing on to a front porch across the street. It was a blow of which any big leaguer would have been proud and was walloped by a boy who hasn't yet started to shave. . . .

TWO BANDS FURNISH TREAT

Features outside of the game were enjoyed by the spectators. Before the contest began the Lane band in khaki suits marched across the field, followed by the ball players. In front of the flag the band and athletes halted, and the national anthem was rendered. All during the game Jack Bramhall's band reeled off jazz, and the three Lane cheer leaders were on the field continuously, doing stunts and leading the throng of students in the yells. Some song boosters sneaked in and megaphoned a couple of the latest to the crowd, and Frisco, the noted dancer, who came from New York on the same train with the team, took the field once and gave an exhibit of the latest moves of the "shimmy."

PRONOUNCE GAME GREAT SUCCESS

When the battle was over the New York faculty men and Superintendent of Schools Ettinger and his assistant, Mr. O'Shea, who came out here for the game, pronounced the affair an immense success, and said they hoped to see Chicago's champions of next year play in New York.

In the evening the players of both teams attended the play, "Poker Ranch," as guests of the Olympic theater management. The New York squad will start back for Gotham today.

48

On Ray Chapman (1920)

SOURCE: *Literary Digest*, September 18, 1920

The death of Ray Chapman on August 16 after being hit in the head by a Carl Mays pitch has been written about often, perhaps best by Mike Sowell in The Pitch That Killed: Carl Mays, Ray Chapman, and the Pennant Race of 1920 *(New York: Macmillan, 1989). Sowell reminded his readers that the incident occurred toward the end of a tight pennant race between the Indians, the Yankees, and the White Sox—who still benefitted from the play of Joe Jackson and the others implicated in throwing the previous year's*

World Series. After the beaning the Indians left New York in first place, then fell back to second before rallying to finally take the pennant with a one-game lead over Chicago and one-and-one-half game advantage over New York.

THE DEATH OF CHAPMAN, KILLED BY A PITCHED BALL

The death of Ray Chapman, star shortstop of the Cleveland American Baseball Club, who was killed by a ball thrown by Carl Mays, premier pitcher of the New York Yankees, cast gloom over the baseball world, but unfortunate as the occurrence admittedly was, a number of editors note that the fact that in comparison with the number of men who play the game there are few accidents in baseball and fewer fatalities. Grantland Rice, sports editor of the New York *Tribune*, says that the marvel of it is not that men are killed here and there in both baseball and football, but that in the major contests so few fatalities ever occur. "When you consider the number of big-league pitchers using the speed of a Johnson, a Walsh, or others, and the number of men who are hit," he writes, "the wonder grows that so few accidents result." The effect on a pitcher after hitting, and seriously injuring or killing, a batsman have been varied. He recalls that:

Some years ago Russ Ford beaned Roy Corhan, of the White Sox. Corhan was not expected to live. His condition was serious for several weeks. During this period Ford was so badly upset that he was of no further use to his club. He lost weight, lost effectiveness, and finally had to take a vacation to build up his shattered nervous system.

He was never the same effective pitcher after Corhan's narrow escape.

A short while after this accident Tom Rodgers, pitching for Nashville in the Southern League, killed Johnny Dodge, who for a time was with both Philadelphia and Cincinnati.

Dodge was killed with a fast ball which caught him squarely in the temple.

But the effect upon Rodgers seemed to be the exact opposite of Ford's case. As we recall the statistics, Rodgers then went in and won five consecutive shutout games, doing his finest work of the year. Rodgers's case was certainly more unusual than that of Russ Ford.

The ball that struck Chapman and fractured his skull has been variously described as a "submarine" ball and a "bean" ball, which is thrown near the head of the batsman in order to make him back away from the plate and then disconcert him. For a time after the game there was talk by other teams of having Mays disbarred; but he was held blameless for the accident. However, there is some agitation to have the "bean" ball banished as not only dangerous but lacking in sportsmanship. Ross Tenney, writing in the Cleveland *Press*, observes that there is a feeling that Chapman would not have been struck had not this particular type of ball been pitched. And he believes that baseball's lawmakers should meet in special midseason session and adopt a rule that would banish the "bean" ball from the game. "Penalize the ball thrown at the head of a batsman and all baserunners two bases each," he argues, "and you will see the last of the 'bean' ball. The 'bean' ball has never contributed anything to the science of baseball. And when 'bean' balls cost games pitchers will not throw them." But almost every baseball player of any experience has been "beaned" at one time or another, and once in a while somebody is killed, says the New York *Times*. However, players and sporting writers of long memories can not recall that any man was ever killed before in the major leagues. It is observed further:

In the average nine-inning game perhaps some two hundred balls are pitched. There are approximately twelve hundred major-league games in a year. Nearly a quarter of a million balls are pitched up to batters in the course of a big-league season, and this is the first time that a batter has been killed. All in all, baseball is a pretty safe game, despite the legs broken in sliding to base and the occasional blood-poisoning from a spike cut. For even when a batter is hit in the head by a pitched ball, usually he has been able to duck or dodge so that it strikes a glancing blow and at a point where the skull is not so thin. Chapman was hit squarely in a weak spot. The fact that most of the deaths from this cause in the game are in amateur and semi-professional circles is no doubt due to the inexperience of young players, who are unable to judge the break of a curve in time to move their heads out of line.

Much has been said of the danger to the Cleveland club's pennant chances from the loss of Chapman. Something might also be said of the disadvantage which the New York club may sustain from the reaction on Carl Mays, the pitcher who threw the ball. Indeed, it may be conjectured that for some time to come pitchers all through the league will be a little more careful not to graze a batter's head, and that will probably mean more batting.

Unlike football, baseball has never been regarded as a dangerous game. "It is the exceptional fatality, therefore, that proves the comparative safeness of baseball, says the Troy *Record*, and notes that—

Football, even under present rules, is brutal compared with it. Swimming on a pleasant Sunday or holiday has more fatalities than big-league baseball has in years. Compared with automobiling, baseball is as safe as a game of parlor croquet. . . .

For a short time after the accident, Detroit, St. Louis, Boston, and Washington players talked about a "strike" against the pitcher who had thrown the fatal ball, but later judgment of the occurrence was that it was a pure accident. Pitcher Mays himself "took great comfort," according to the New York *World*, "from the fact that when, Chapman regained consciousness in the club-house, before being removed to the hospital, he said to John Henry, the former Washington catcher, who was one of his closest friends: 'I'm all right. Tell Mays not to worry.' Mays himself is reported to have said at an interview some time later:

"Chapman was one of the hardest men to pitch to in the league. He was plucky, crouched over the plate, and the only way to get a ball over was to pitch it so low that there was a risk of it being called a ball. In the fifth inning on Monday I pitched him a straight ball inside, just above the waist. I expected that he would drop as Ruth does when the pitchers swing them in close to the big fellow to drive him away from the plate. Instead he ducked and the ball hit him. I found a rough place on the ball afterward and believe that made it sail in far more than I intended."

It was Chapman's loyalty to his team and his home town that caused him to play ball this season, for he had agreed with his bride that he should remain in business. But he had been feted and treated by Cleveland people, and he thought it his duty to help bring the pennant home as a reward for their kindness. The Providence *News* pays this tribute to him:

> His exemplary career carries a lesson for all. He was from first to last a hard-working, cheerful teammate. In the hope of accomplishment he made many an error, as most of us do. But he went after balls that most players would never attempt to get and sometimes turned "impossibility" into accomplishment. Personal records did not count with him where there was hope of achievement that would help as a whole.
>
> Chapman was second on his team's batting list—the sacrificer. It was his business to advance the other fellow, to hit himself out, but get the other player to second. He was the leading sacrifice-hitter of the league. Down through the years he team-worked for victory, never sulking, always optimistic, praising the other fellow. He was the gentleman of his profession, who sought no adornment but wished well the way of all.

49

Indians Make Baseball History in World Series (1920)

SOURCE: *Cleveland Plain Dealer*, October 11, 1920

The fifth game of the 1920 World Series was without a doubt the most thrilling 8–1 contest in major league history. Aside from giving the Indians a 3–2 edge in the Series over the Dodgers, Cleveland fans received additional thrills by witnessing three World Series firsts: Elmer Smith's first-inning grand slam, Jim Bagby's fourth-inning round-tripper (the first by a pitcher), and most dramatically, Bill Wambsganss's unassisted triple play in the fifth inning. After losing its 2–1 Series lead, Brooklyn dropped the final two games and Cleveland celebrated its first world's championship.

**ROUT RIVALS IN FIFTH GAME, DRIVING DODGERS'
STAR PITCHER FROM BOX**

**Unassisted Triple Play by Wambsganss and Home Runs by Bagby
and Smith Feature Triumph of Cleveland Clan; World Championship
Hopes of Indians Now at Fever Heat as Result of Third Victory**
By Richard T. F. Harding

When Elmer Smith hit the ball over the right field fence with the bases full in
the first inning of yesterday's game with Brooklyn at League Park, he not only
cinched the game for Cleveland but started a series of sensational hitting and
fielding plays, probably unparalleled in any previous world series game.

The Indians won 8 to 1, thereby making the series stand three games to two in
their favor.

Burleigh Grimes, Brooklyn's top hole pitcher, was driven from the field by the
onslaught of the Indians, and today baseball experts say Cleveland's chances of
winning the world's championship are just about twice as good as they were before
yesterday's game.

Of all the events of an eventful afternoon the most momentous was a triple play
by Wambsganss unassisted. With runners on first and second, Wambsganss leaped
high and grabbed, with his gloved hand, a line drive from Mitchell's bat, one that
looked as if it might fairly wind up by being a two-base hit. The runners, who had
started as Bagby began to deliver the ball, were far on their way, so far that it was
the work of but an instant for Wambsganss to step on second base, thus putting
out Kilduff, then turn and touch Miller, who had come so fast and so far that he
had no chance to turn back toward first.

FANS MOMENTARILY STUNNED

For a moment the crowd scarcely could realize what had happened. Everybody
got to his feet, drew a long breath and then figured the play for himself before
letting out a great yell.

As the Cleveland team walked off the field the cheering rose steadily in volume
and continued until Wambsganss stepped down into the Cleveland dugout.

Then everybody sat down and began to talk about what had happened, empha-
sizing his remarks, in many cases, by belaboring his neighbor, a total stranger, over
the back. It seemed that everybody knew the history of unassisted triple plays. It
was said this was the first time one ever was made in a world's series. But it took
time only for a second thought to raise a laugh at that, for the one made yesterday
is the second on record in big league baseball.

There were many present who saw Neal Ball, then playing shortstop for Cleveland, make the first of such plays against the Boston Red Sox at League park and
there were many speculations as to the date of that performance. The records say it
occurred July 19, 1909, and it is recalled that on that occasion the spectators
received it much as did those present yesterday, in the beginning seeming almost

stunned because it had seen the impossible performed, then bursting into a great cheer for the player who did it.

All this had postponed mention of the game's other big dramatic moment, when Jim Bagby hit a home run into the new right field stand, with two men on the bases. Not only did that raise Cleveland's total score to seven, and so make the game look more like a slaughter of Burleigh Grimes than a baseball contest, but it was as well a grim joke at the expense of Brooklyn's best pitcher.

Doc Johnston had reached third base and one man was out when O'Neill came to bat. This is the O'Neill who hit savagely in Brooklyn, and was so much respected Saturday that he was given two intentional passes. With him at bat Grimes saw but one thing to do—let him walk to first and play to get Bagby.

So he pitched to O'Neill four balls so wide that Otto Miller, the catcher, was jumping around like an acrobat to keep him from throwing to the grandstand. O'Neill ambled down to first base, and then Bagby came up and slammed the ball far and high into the end of the new stand.

It was a triumphal procession the three runners formed as they crossed the plate within a stride of one another. Johnston, with the dramatic instinct which is the ball player's, had dallied on his way from third until O'Neill and Bagby caught up with him to give the crowd the fullest and most impressive view of three runs being made at once. . . .

These three big features so far overshadowed in interest the rest of the game that it might be easy to forget that even without them the afternoon's play would stand as unusual.

Remember that Bagby pitched. Often as the records show, Bagby pitches winning games in which his opponents make many hits; but seldom does a team make thirteen hits off him and score but one run, as was the case yesterday.

That means there was a great deal of sharp fielding behind him, especially as Brooklyn made at least one hit in every inning but the sixth, when Joe Sewell made a jumping catch of a well intentioned line drive by Olson. . . .

Among the nearly 27,000 present there was a feeling of relief because the game began without formalities, except for the usual conference of managers and umpires. William Klem, who gives decisions in the National league through the regular season, presided at the plate.

Klem excited some interest by his gestures. He does not limit himself to the conventional jerk of the thumb over the right shoulder to indicate that the pitch he just observed was a strike.

He elaborates that movement by swinging his right arm across his body and leaning far to the left to indicate "strike one," and for "strike two" extends the arm to the right and leans far in that direction.

Further interest in Klem was aroused by another of his departures from the conventional, in that, to all appearances he wears no chest protector, but present[s] his bosom to the hurtling ball with nothing but the ordinary clothes of commerce to ward off its treacherous and sudden blows.

But it may be stated, on the authority of Henry P. Edwards, that beneath his blue umpirical vestments Mr. Klem wears a coat-of-mail not unlike that which graced the bowmen at Agincourt and even now keeps safe the ribs of careful members of the black hand.

For information as to who will pitch today consult the experts who make their announcements in other columns of this paper. Since in two days Cleveland has seen in action six of Brooklyn's seven pitchers it is more than possible that the seventh will join the parade today. The seventh is Sherrod Smith.

Whether he will fare as badly as those whom Cleveland had seen, only this afternoon can tell.

Brooklyn.	AB.	R.	H.	O.	A.	E.	Cleveland.	AB.	R.	H.	O.	A.	E.
Olson, ss.	4	0	2	3	5	0	Jamieson, lf.	4	1	2	0	1	0
Sheehan, 3b.	3	0	1	1	1	1	Graney, lf.	1	0	0	0	0	0
Griffith, rf.	4	0	0	0	0	0	Wamby, 2b.	5	1	1	7	2	0
Wheat, lf.	4	1	2	3	0	0	Speaker, cf.	3	2	1	1	0	0
Myers, cf.	4	0	2	0	0	0	E. Smith, rf.	4	1	3	0	0	0
Koney, 1b.	4	0	2	9	2	0	Gardner, 3b.	4	0	1	2	2	1
Kilduff, 2b.	4	0	1	5	6	0	W. J'nston, 1b.	3	1	2	9	1	0
Miller, c.	2	0	2	0	1	0	Sewell, ss.	3	0	0	2	4	0
Krueger, c.	2	0	1	2	1	0	O'Neill, c.	2	1	0	3	1	1
Grimes, p.	1	0	0	0	1	0	Thomas, c.	0	0	0	1	0	0
Mitchell, p.	2	0	0	1	0	0	Bagby, p.	4	1	2	0	2	0
Totals	34	1	13	24	17	1	Totals	33	8	12	27	13	2

Brooklyn . . . . .0 0 0 0 0 0 0 0 1—1
Cleveland . . . . .4 0 0 3 1 0 0 0 *—8

Three-base hits—Koney, E. Smith. Home runs—E. Smith, Bagby. Sacrifice hits—Sheehan, W. Johnston. Double plays—Olson to Kilduff to Koney; Jamieson to O'Neill; Gardner to Wamby to Johnston; Johnston to Sewell to Johnston. Triple play—Wamby unassisted. Left on bases—Brooklyn 7, Cleveland 6. Bases on balls—Off Grimes 1, off Mitchell 3. Hits—Off Grimes, 9 in 3 1/3 inning; off Mitchell, 3 in 4 2/3 innings. Struck out—By Bagby 3, by Mitchell 1. Wild pitch—Bagby. Passed ball—Miller. Losing pitcher—Grimes. Umpires—Klem, at the plate; Connolly, at first; O'Day at second; Dinneen at third. Time of game—1:49.

50

"Wireless Fans" Enjoy Historic Game (1920)

SOURCE: *Cleveland Press*, October 12, 1920

The first radio broadcast of a baseball game occurred on August 5, 1921, on station KDKA in Pittsburgh. Later that year the Westinghouse Network—which included KDKA and two other stations—attempted to broadcast the World Series, but only KDKA received Grantland Rice's account because the other stations lacked a direct link to the Polo

Grounds. Before radio firmly established itself as the premier broadcast medium for baseball, however, the telegraph had served as the means by which many fans enjoyed major league baseball. The following article describes a "wireless party" organized by the Press. Notice how the word listening *is always printed within quotation marks, and how the word* radio *is used almost interchangeably with* wireless.*

The best history of baseball broadcasting is Curt Smith, Voices of the Game *(rev. ed., New York: Fireside, 1992).*

WIRELESS FANS FAN AT PRESS SERIES PARTY

The whole wireless world is "listening in," on The Press' play-by-play account of the world series being played in Cleveland.

It is being relayed to every nook and cranny reached by wireless.

It is started within a radius of 750 miles thru courtesy of A. A. Penland, electrician in charge of the United States Naval Station in Cleveland, who uses a 600-meter wave length.

But it doesn't stop there. Hundreds of amateur radio operators pick it up from the edge of the 750-mile radius and carry it on.

From New York to San Francisco, down to the Gulf of Mexico and back north to the great Canadian northwest, they all get the play-by-play account furnished by The Press.

Letters of thanks for The Press' wireless party were coming in steadily Tuesday. Some by wireless, some thru the mails.

Penland estimates 600 amateur and professional wireless men within his own 750-mile radio zone are "listening in."

Many of these post the reports for others to read.

This is being done in Oberlin. The front of a store has been converted into a radio receiving station for the express purpose of receiving The Press' play-by-play account.

AT CONNEAUT

Two high school boys daily are hosts at informal Indian rooter parties at their home, 271 Whitney-rd., Conneaut.

The boys, Owen and Homer Barton, have a wireless apparatus. They follow the world series games in Cleveland play by play.

"It's the next best thing to seeing the games," they say.

The Barton home becomes the long-distance grandstand for the boys of the neighborhood as the game starts each afternoon.

Forty ardent baseball fans get the story of the World Series game at New Philadelphia every day.

The men are employed by the West-end Garage, which is equipped with wireless. Charles Furray is the operator.

The men say their only regret is that they can't stop work altogether and devote themselves entirely to the game.

N. R. Lamphier is a Painesville fan who "listens in."

Lamphier has a wireless apparatus at his home on South-st, Painesville.

Dr. J. W. Collins, a Steubensville baseball fan, is a member of The Press party whenever patients will give him time to devote to the wireless apparatus in his home.

"It's great service," he says.

Penland estimates that 150 operators in the vicinity immediately adjacent to Cleveland are "listening in"—in Lakewood, East Cleveland, Rocky River and many other suburbs and nearby townships.

The service started with the first game played in Cleveland. It will be continued until the series is over.

Hundreds of thousands of persons are benefitting by "seeing" the world series game as furnished by The Press' wireless party.

"Each day I am besieged with requests of wireless operators thruout the territory asking whether the service is to be maintained thru each game," said Penland.

"Fifteen regularly designated naval radio stations along the Great Lakes are receiving it and relaying it inshore to other points more densely populated.

"Fifty or 60 lake ships plying in all parts of the Great Lakes at the time are receiving The Press' story."

LETTERS OF THANKS

These are letters typical of the ones wireless operators receiving The Press' play-by-play account are sending in:

"In view of the wireless party, we amateurs wish to express our gratitude for the efforts of The Press to make such a party possible.

"The baseball reports come in fine.

"Being an amateur myself I know it feels 'grand and glorious' to announce the score and have your friends say 'Gee, by wireless!'

"Hooray for The Press wireless parties.

"Signed: 2204 TAMPA-AV."

51

Landis Is the "Supreme Ruler" (1920)

SOURCE: *Chicago Daily Tribune*, November 13, 1920

After the Black Sox scandal, in 1920 the sixteen team owners, desperate for ways to demonstrate to the public that they were serious about fixing baseball's tarnished image, unanimously elected federal judge Kenesaw Mountain Landis the first "chairman of the national pastime." Landis demanded, and received, near-absolute powers to regulate baseball as he saw fit, starting with the permanent expulsion of the eight White Sox players accused of throwing the 1919 World Series.

NEW ERA IN BASEBALL
By I. E. Sanborn

Judge Landis' acceptance of the chairmanship was a climax to nearly a month of "crucial" days and is believed to mark a new era in professional baseball. For the first time in the history of the sport the promoters of it have sought out and obtained a supreme ruler who has not and never expects to have any interest in the pastime other than that which is born in every red blooded American.

They have selected in Judge Landis a man in whom the men of all branches of sport, as well as business, have so great confidence that if one of his important decisions ever shall be questioned by a club owner, player, or fan, the questioner will be "in bad" with the public, and the burden of proof will rest with him. Hitherto when a club owner let out a yell about a verdict of the national commission, he was sure of the sympathy of at least the fans of his own home town. Now he will not get even that.

LONG DAY OF HARD WORK
The formality of reaching this settlement of all their differences occupied several hours yesterday, during which the sixteen club owners aired their varying views without the aid of league presidents or other intermediaries.

The magnates selected as their chairman President Baker of the Philadelphia Nationals, who was obliged to leave the meeting to catch a train east before the discussion was concluded. His successor in the chair was President William L. Veeck of the Chicago Cubs. After reaching an understanding informally, the meeting became formal long enough to pass the following resolution.

"That the chairman of the board of control shall be elected by a majority vote of the clubs composing the American and National leagues.

"That his successor be elected in the same manner, and that this shall be incorporated in the new national agreement.

"That upon all questions of an interleague nature or in any matter coming up at a joint meeting of the two major leagues the roll be called, and after voting by clubs of each league, if there be a division, then the American league shall cast one vote and the National league one vote. Should these two votes be at variance then the commissioner shall cast the deciding vote and there shall be no appeal therefrom.

"Further, that the commissioner shall preside at all joint meetings."

END SPLIT OF SEVERAL WEEKS
The foregoing means that the club owners reached a compromise on the chief point of difference which has kept them apart for weeks. That was the controversy over the right to vote by clubs or leagues. The National league contention that in the selection of a governing body the majority vote of the sixteen clubs should decide was conceded by the American league.

In all other matters it was conceded by the National league that interleague disputes should be decided by a vote of leagues, each having an equal voice, but if no agreement could be reached in this way, the commissioner [Judge Landis] should have the right to decide without appeal.

In disposing of the question of associate members of the commission to act with Judge Landis, no final action was taken, but it was provided that the president of the American league shall appear before the commissioner as a special pleader in case[s] involving the American league, and that the president of the National league shall be empowered to act in a similar capacity in cases involving the older circuit. And it was further understood that these men should appear only in cases in which their respective league or clubs were concerned.

If second and third members are chosen for the commission, it is virtually certain, according to club owners, that Judge Charles A. McDonald of Chicago will be one of them. Judge McDonald indirectly brought on the baseball war, for he started the baseball scandal investigation which brought about the proposals for reorganization of control of baseball. Judge McDonald is acceptable to the Johnson faction, and also is well thought of by the other eleven clubs.

SPECIAL PLEADER FOR MINORS

It was also stipulated that if the minor leagues decide to operate with the majors in the new arrangement, they shall appoint a special pleader to appear before the commissioner in all cases in which a minor league or a minor league club owner may be involved.

President Herrmann of the Cincinnati club introduced a resolution which was seconded by President Dunn of the Cleveland club, indorsing [sic] the Lasker plan without specifically mentioning its author. It follows:

"Resolved, That this meeting indorse the principles of ethical control of baseball proposed in the plan submitted to all professional league clubs by four major league club owners in October last, and instruct the drafting committee that the spirit contained therein be embodied in the new national agreement.

"That the unreviewable control of all ethical matters be invested in the chairman of the control board."

FURTHER DETAILS TO WORK OUT

Details of the new national agreement for the control and perpetuation of baseball will be worked out by a draft committee to be composed of twelve members equally divided between the majors and minors. The minors already have named their six. The National league had nominated a committee of four consisting of Herrmann, Ebbets, Dreyfuss, and Ruppert, but this will be reduced to three, and it is likely that President Heydler of the National league will be included on it.

Likewise it is believed the committee of three to be appointed by the American league will include President Johnson of that circuit and Clark Griffith of the Washington club, who is generally credited with having been the most efficacious factor in bringing about peace between the warring factors in the dispute.

The committees are to be appointed within thirty days, and after completing their work will report to the two major leagues and the National association for acceptance. It is expected the lines of the previous national agreement will be followed in many respects and that improvements will be made to the old document founded in the results of years of experience in operating under it.

Chicago will become the headquarters of the supreme court of baseball and arrangements will be made immediately for suitable offices for the commissioner and the secretarial staff which is to be selected after consultation with him to cooperate with him in the administration of the affairs of the national game.

52

Orioles Win Twenty-seventh Straight International League Game (1921)

SOURCE: *Baltimore Sun*, June 16, 1921

The Baltimore Orioles of the 1920s were perhaps the greatest minor league dynasty of all. They won seven consecutive International League pennants between 1919 and 1925, usually by substantial margins. Club owner Jack Dunn generated considerable profits for himself by discovering and developing talented players like Babe Ruth and Lefty Grove (whose name was usually spelled "Groves" early in his career), and then selling them to the highest bidder.

GROVES HURLS BIRDS INTO TIE FOR TOP MARK

Bisons Unable To Score Off Him Until The Final Frame
VISITORS BECOME WILD IN NIGHTCAP
Stop Champions Winning Streak At 27 Consecutive Victories
By Don Riley

Stopped at last by Buffalo in their mighty rush to make a new record in Organized Baseball, the Orioles yesterday dashed the hopes of one of the greatest crowds that has ever seen an International League game in Baltimore.

They made it 27 consecutive victories and tied the record—there is consolation in that—but the strain of the long and gallant race was too great, and just as they were to pass under the wire the [sic] broke.

By winning the first game from Buffalo, 4 to 2, the Orioles tied the figure set up by the Corsicana Club, of the Texas League in 1902. The count in the nightcap was 19 to 8. The final exhibition was a weird contest in every respect, four Oriole flingers being pounded to the confines of the park, with the champions hopelessly trailing at all times.

A triumph and a tragedy was enacted at Oriole Park the cheers of the fans ringing in their ears, Jack Dunn's new right-field bleachers filled to capacity for the first time, and the crowd urging Lefty Groves to new feats of effectiveness, a great outpouring exulted in the proud moments of supreme desire. . . .

The first match showed Lefty Groves at his best, with the whole club playing airtight ball. Lefty shot the balls over the plate like the proverbial pea, and he was not scored upon until the ninth.

Rogers, who opposed him, was going great guns and made Lefty hurl his finest to keep ahead.

BARNEY MAKES HOMER

In the final stanza Barney, always a terrific slugger, found him for a home run into the right-field bleacher, and McCarron repeated before the crowd had time to catch its breath. One was out when Barney hit his smash, and two when McCarron connected. Lefty showed Tragresser that he still had something on the ball by fanning him, while the Buffalo players pleaded with the pinch-hitter to "get another."

The air was surcharged with electricity when the Birds started on their quest for new honors, and the large crowd did not have long for its first thrill. Groves set down the opposition in regular order, but Snooks Dowd hit a clean two-bagger to left, with one down in the second. Dowd tried out Egan's arm attempting to purloin third, but Maisel put the ball on him after Ben's good throw. Keating then fanned.

A triple in the fourth by Gilhooley availed him not, for Groves cut loose like a house afire. He walked Barney, but Sheehan, Jacobs and Dowd punctured the atmosphere in their efforts to score the base-runners.

JAKE MAKES HOMER

Baltimore fans exulted in the Orioles' turn at bat in this inning, when Lawry beat out a roller to Sheehan. They raised a mighty anthem of praise for Jacobsen a moment later when he hit the ball into the right-field bleacher for the first scores of the match.

The Orioles made two more in the eighth stanza, and, as it turned out, they were needed for the victory. Jacobsen and Holden went down in order, but Bentley smashed a safe one to right. He advanced when Max Bishop was safe on Keating's error, and then Boley tallied them with a triple to the flag pole. Boley attempted to stretch his wallop into a homer and was thrown out at the plate. He protested the decision, and the crowd cheered him on as he argued with Umpire McGowan.

With victory in sight, Lefty Groves eased up, and Barney and McCarron made their ninth-inning circuit clouts. Stung to desperation, the Bisons landed on the pellet with determination, but Groves remained master of the situation, and the crowd roared its delight when he fanned Tragresser.

53

Ruth Suspended, Fined by Landis (1921)

SOURCE: *The Sporting News*, December 15, 1921

In the early twentieth century baseball players often supplemented their meager salaries by forming their own teams and touring, or "barnstorming," the country during the off-season. Top stars could earn several times their annual salary in just a few months. However, due to a rule intended to preserve the integrity of the World Series (now an important consideration), players who appeared in the Series were prohibited from touring. This did not prevent Babe Ruth and several of his Yankee teammates from starting their own tour following their loss to the Giants in the 1921 Series. Ruth publicly declared that the rule was unfair and that he could not be prevented from barnstorming.

Commissioner Landis thought otherwise. He allowed the tour to proceed, and watched it end prematurely due to poor attendance. After receiving Ruth's response to a questionnaire on the tour, Landis acted on December 5. He fined Ruth, Bob Meusel, and Bill Piercy the amount of their World Series winnings, and suspended them for the first month of the 1922 season. Landis demonstrated that he, not Babe Ruth, was the most powerful figure in baseball.

NEW YORK, N.Y., Dec. 12.—The big magnates are drifting into town for the annual meetings of the National and American Leagues, their separate sessions of Tuesday and Wednesday, to be followed by the joint session presided over by Commissioner Landis on Thursday. The minor league moguls will be around, too, waiting to hear what may happen. Baseball fans, meanwhile, are not so much interested in the politics of the game as in the players, which is shown in the columns published regarding the punishment of Babe Ruth and the acquisition of Heinie Groh by the Giants.

Commissioner Landis surely has thrown a monkey wrench into the machinery of the American League. In fining Ruth, Meusel and Piercy of the Yankees their World's Series spoils, and suspending them until May 20, 1922, when they must apply for reinstatement within 10 days thereafter, the Commissioner possibly has wrecked the pennant chances of the New York Americans, and also has deprived the whole American League circuit of a huge sum in gate receipts.

Yet what other course could the eminent Chicago jurist have pursued? Ruth grossly insulted Commissioner Landis in the Yankees' dressing room when told that he could not be granted permission to go barnstorming. Ruth openly violated the rules and then refused to send an apology to the Commissioner. He ignored the wishes of his employers and deliberately jeopardized their interests and welfare.

If Commissioner Landis had fined Ruth $10,000 with no suspension, would the player have been forced to pay the money out of his own pocket? Probably not, for he would have refused to sign a contract unless the Yankee owners made good the full amount. But in suspending Ruth for 35 or 40 playing days next year, the Commissioner hit him hard, because the big fellow, under those conditions, will lose a $20,000 bonus for failing to break his home run record.

So in order to make Ruth realize that he isn't bigger than the national game, the Commissioner has been compelled to inflict a penalty that must necessarily limit the owners of the Yankees, in addition to the Home Run King who struck out eight times in the World's Series.

Deprived of Ruth and Meusel, the Yankees are tremendously handicapped in their battle with the world champion Giants for the patronage of the public. Right now the wise men are counting the Yankees out of next year's American League race, explaining that so much ground will be lost by the Hugmen before Ruth and Meusel are reinstated that the Cleveland Indians, St. Louis Browns and Washingtons cannot be overtaken.

If the Yankees, minus their star hitters, drop among the also rans during the first month of the 1922 campaign, Huggins will be confronted with a tremendous undertaking, to make up for early defeats. Goodness knows that the Yankees were lucky to win the pennant this year by a comparatively narrow margin. The Clevelands were the better ball team, but accidents beat them out of the World's Series.

It is my impression that the entire American League is burning up over the Ruth-Meusel, Piercy case, but what can be done? The magnates, who didn't want Ban Johnson and Garry Herrmann, practical baseball men, to rule the game, selected Judge Landis, engaged him for seven years at $42,500 year, and put their names to an iron-clad agreement in which they pledged themselves to accept all rulings, whether right or wrong in their opinion.

THEY MUST EAT THEIR PUDDING

If the American League men, therefore, openly take issue with the Commissioner in the Ruth matter, they will stultify themselves in the estimation of the public and also will offend the chairman of the Advisory Council instead of appealing to the courts, as in the celebrated case of Carl Mays, the American League magnates, therefore, must accept the Landis edict just as it reads.

54

President Harding Attends Army-Navy Game (1922)

SOURCE: *Baltimore Sun*, May 30, 1922

Early in the twentieth century the "Army-Navy game" did not necessarily focus on football. The baseball game described below, played during the Naval Academy's June Week, attracted 18,000 fans, including President Warren G. Harding—who presided over the dedication of the Lincoln Memorial the following day—and Secretary of War John Weeks. The two men sat behind the Army dugout, even though Weeks was a graduate of the Academy. The Navy club, a decided underdog, ignored this slight and defeated its rival 8–6. Even though the reporter noted that "the game's the thing," he almost ignored the contest, concentrating instead on the atmosphere in which the game was played.

Interestingly, this article dominated the front page, while the announcement of the Supreme Court decision affirming major league baseball's antitrust exemption, and therefore denying the claims of the Baltimore Federal League club, was relegated to the back page.

HARDING SEES MIDDIES DEFEAT WEST POINTERS

Navy's Baseball Team Auspiciously Opens June Week
18,000 PEOPLE WITNESS GAME
Annual Influx of Girls In Love And Proud Parents Begins
By Raymond S. Tompkins, Staff Correspondent of The Sun

Annapolis, May 29—Navy beat the Army at baseball, 8 to 6, this afternoon, right in front of the President of the United States and the Secretary of War, both of whom sat on the Army side of the field all the time and turned out to be jinxes instead of swastikas.

It looked unfair at first, considering that the West Pointers had won 13 games and the Midshipmen only 5 and that men who can't be happy until they have put up a little money were offering 2 to 1 on the Army. People thought President Harding and Secretary of War Weeks should have sat on the Navy side to sort of trim the ship.

NAVY SUPPLIES TRIMMING
But the Army stands were the shady stands—under the trees—and had backs to the seats like the expensive sections at the circus; and the Navy ball team took care of all the necessary trimming anyway, trimming the metaphorical ship, the Army ball team, and three West Point pitchers. This was piling it on rather thick for a branch of the nation's fighting service that is seldom spoken of nowadays except in connection with junk piles and "scrapping" programs, especially when Navy won the football game last fall, too.

They were suggesting in the Navy stands that "hoodles" was the Army game; a more or less apt allusion based upon the theory that the Army's fingers were mostly thumbs. This theory gathered many supporters as the game went on with West Point fielders handling the ball at times as though it were a hand-grenade with a loose spring.

JUNE WEEK BEGINS PERFECTLY
Thus June Week at Annapolis, America's own revival of the tournament fetes of the Middle Ages, when lords and ladies gathered for parading and jousting, started out beautifully. Weather, ball game, ladies and lords all synchronized perfectly, and from now until President Harding comes back to hand out the diplomas, Annapolis-on-the-Severn will be a midsummer night's dream-town, full of brave boys in blue, wondering when to eat; sweet girls in love, wondering what to wear; and proud families of first classmen, wondering where to sleep.

You knew it was June Week just riding through the town before the game and looking at the quaint old doorways. Call Annapolis "old-fashioned" or what you will, the men who built those houses and doorways either knew what they were doing or else some power they wotted not of put it into their heads to build perfect frames and backgrounds for the sweethearts of midshipmen waiting to be taken to ball games. Of course they couldn't figure on the smell of cooking which is bound to come out of an open door, even if the Queen of Sheba is standing in it, and spoil the illusion a little. But no queens know better how to counteract that than the queens of Annapolis at the opening of June Week.

About 18,000 people saw the game. They filled grandstands and bleachers completely skirting the field on all four sides, the field being so arranged that the batters would bat in a direction away from the Presidential yacht Mayflower, riding at anchor in the river, her smokestack and Executive stateroom windows within reasonable reach of a centerfield home run.

HARDINGS UPSET PLANS

President and Mrs. Harding arrived at 2.20 o'clock, 10 minutes before the game was to start. They had been expected to come in behind the backstop and to walk part of the way down the field to their seats. Instead they gave the quaint impression of climbing in over the back of the grandstand, making their way from the top row down toward the bottom, to sit protectingly over the Army team's dugout. The President wore white flannel trousers and a blue coat and looked like a yachtsman. Mrs. Harding's hat and gown made a brilliant dab of henna or the new "rust" color, or something highly visible.

It was all so sudden that the mighty Navy cheer the leaders had been preparing the Navy cheer section for during the preceding 15 minutes was a bit feeble. The Naval Academy goat came in a few minutes later, and they cheered him with much more fervor. But then they knew he was coming. He walked out and showed himself on the way to the post as the President had been expected to do and didn't. However, as between a goat and a President there isn't much to choose at an Army-Navy ball game. The game's the thing.

55

"Casual Comment" on Baseball
Antitrust Case (1922)

SOURCE: *The Sporting News*, June 8, 1922

Although Sporting Life, *the sporting periodical he founded in 1883, had stopped publication, baseball journalist Francis Richter kept busy by editing the annual* Reach Guides *and contributing columns to his onetime rival publication,* The Sporting News. *Richter earned a reputation as a passionate chronicler of baseball who championed the rights of players and minor leagues to counter the dominance of the major leagues. Nevertheless, Richter accepted the common wisdom that the National and American Leagues had to act collectively for the greater good of baseball. It is not surprising, therefore, to read that Richter was pleased with the Supreme Court decision that validated baseball's antitrust exemption.*

CASUAL COMMENT

By Francis C. Richter

At last the long-pending and extremely vexatious damage suit by the Baltimore Club of the Federal League against Organized Ball has been definitely settled by the highest court in the land, and Organized Ball has emerged triumphantly from the ordeal in which its very existence, at least as now constituted, was threatened.

The suit under the Sherman anti-trust law was originally won in the lower court by the Baltimore Club and Organized Ball has mulcted in heavy damages, which, however, was of less importance than the fact that Organized Ball had in effect been declared an illegal combination in restraint of trade. The district court of appeals at Washington gave Organized Ball a breathing spell by reversing the verdict, and then appeal to the United States supreme court followed.

Before this court of last resort counsel for both sides in the momentous case made their final arguments, and after the customary delay the supreme court has handed down a decision which dismisses all of the Baltimore Club's contentions, leaves it virtually empty-handed, sustaining Organized Ball on every point, and therefore definitely fixes its status before the law—a consummation all baseball men have hoped for in a long period covering over a quarter of a century, but never daring to bring the question to an issue, until it was finally forced by the Baltimore Federal League club.

In effect the decision affirms that Organized Ball is not in any way a trust within the meaning of the law, that baseball, though played for money, is not trade or commerce, that it is a game entirely of personal effort, not related to production, and therefore not a subject of commerce, that baseball clubs are state affairs, and that traveling between states to play their schedules does not mean commerce between the states; and the contracts of players do not make them chattel slaves and are not an interference with commerce.

Now Organized Baseball knows definitely where it stands, and the baseball magnates, as well as the millions of fans, may well give thanks for this wonderful decision, which obviates once and for all any change in the system which time and experience have amply proven as the only system under which professional baseball can be successfully conducted, and under which it had grown steadily and mightily as a national institution.

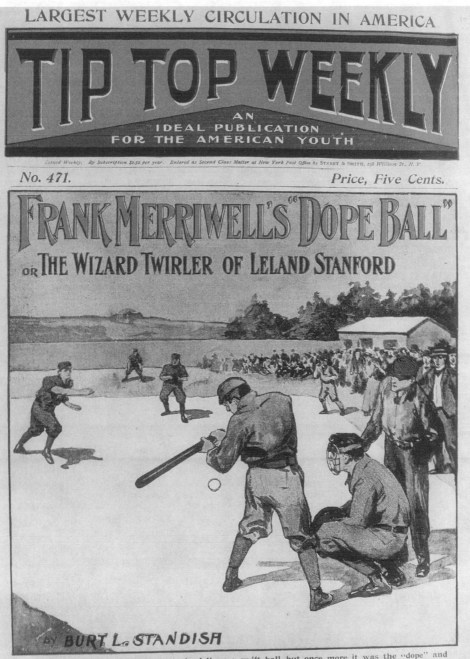

Cover of the April 22, 1905, edition of *Tip Top Weekly*, a popular weekly featuring
the serialized adventures of Frank Merriwell, American hero.

Team photo of the Chippewa Falls, Minnesota, semipro team, 1905. Notice the presence of George Wilson, one of the nation's best African-American pitchers, on this otherwise white club. Courtesy of the Library of Congress.

The Waseda University baseball club, shown here in an undated photo, frequently toured the western United States in the early twentieth century. Courtesy of the National Baseball Library and Archive, Cooperstown NY.

This enchanting picture of a boy on his way to a baseball game was taken by a fourteen-year-old girl in 1911 for the monthly photo contest in *St. Nicholas*, an illustrated magazine for youth that often published stories and articles on sports.

In this 1910 action photo we see the beginning of a close play at third, with the runner, third baseman, umpire, and ''coacher'' all in the proper position.

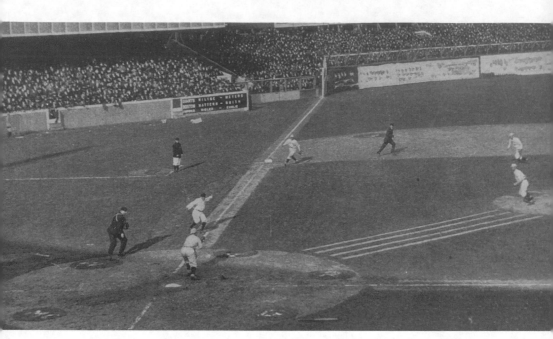

A rundown is in progress at the Polo Grounds during a 1910 game between the Giants and the Braves. The third base coach appears to be John McGraw.

This panoramic shot of Washington Park in Brooklyn was originally published in the July 2, 1910, edition of the *New York Saturday Evening Mail*. The overflow crowd indicates the need for a larger park, which would be built three years later.

In this picture of the 1920 Commerce Tech (New York City) baseball team, Lou Gehrig is positioned ninth from the left. He would lead his club to a well-publicized victory over Chicago's top prep team with a grand slam home run at Cubs Park (later renamed Wrigley Field). Courtesy of the Library of Congress.

A photographer captured this dramatically lit picture of a half-empty Ebbets Field on Opening Day, April 2, 1913. Courtesy of the National Baseball Library and Archive.

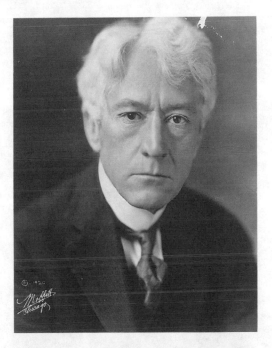

Picture of Judge Kenesaw Mountain Landis taken in 1920, the same year he assumed leadership over organized baseball as the game's first commissioner. Courtesy of the National Baseball Library and Archive.

In this undated photo a young-looking Ban Johnson does not yet show evidence of the strain of his job as the first American League president and as rival to Commissioner Landis. Courtesy of the National Baseball Library and Archive.

Baseball fans gather at a Los Angeles railroad station to experience the 1926 World Series through a telegraphic reenactment. Such scenes, once common, would soon become rare with the rapid acceptance of radio broadcasts in the 1920s and 1930s. Courtesy of the National Baseball Library and Archive.

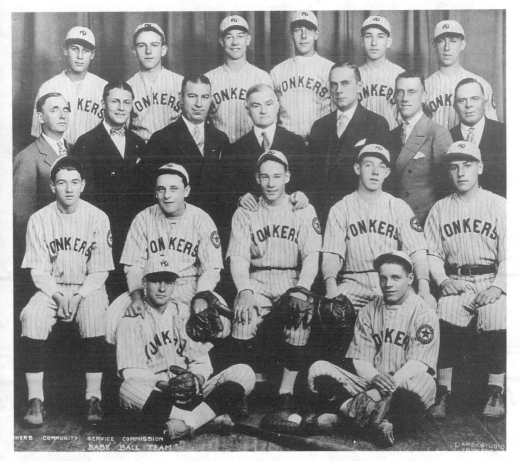

The Yonkers Base Ball team in 1926, the year they won the first American Legion national championship. Courtesy of the National Baseball Library and Archive.

Margaret Gisolo, fourteen-year-old star of the Blanford, Indiana, American Legion team, getting a hit in the 1928 state championship game, won by Blanford. They would lose the next game in regional competition, but Gisolo would be remembered as the last girl to play in the tournament until the 1970s. Courtesy of the *Indianapolis Star/News*. Photograph from the Library of Congress.

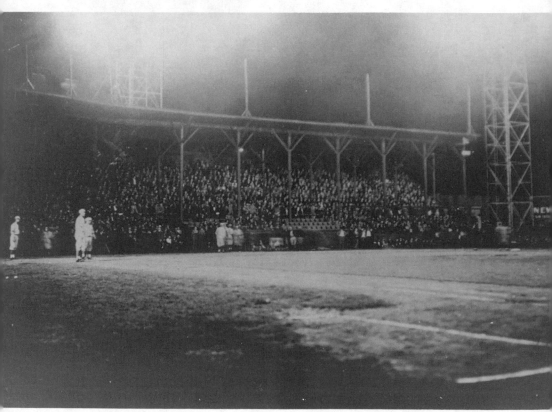

Photo of the first night game ever played by the Des Moines, Iowa, minor league team. The success of this 1930 game helped popularize the notion of night baseball within the minor leagues. The novelty of night games helped these clubs survive the onset of the Depression. Courtesy of the National Baseball Library and Archive.

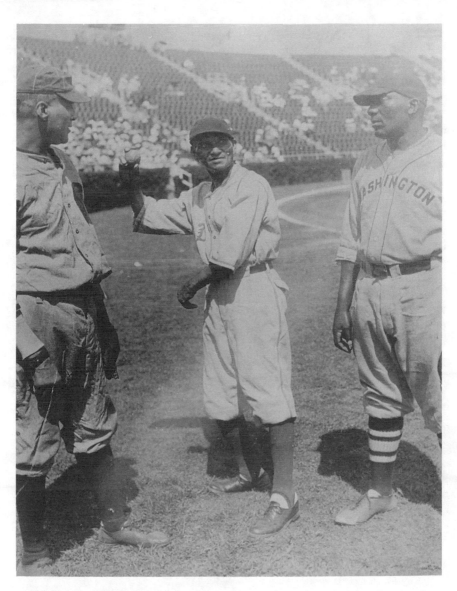

Sol White, black baseball pioneer, flanked by two legendary pitchers, Smokey Joe Williams (right) and Cannonball Dick Redding, in an undated picture. Courtesy of the National Baseball Library and Archive.

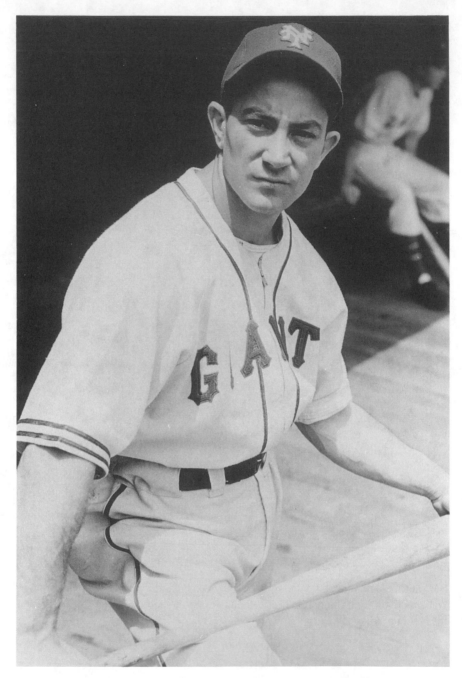

New York Giant Danny Gardella, shortly before he stunned the baseball world by jumping to the Mexican League in 1946. Courtesy of the National Baseball Library and Archive, Cooperstown NY.

56

Ban Johnson Awards Cobb Third .400 Season (1922)

SOURCE: *New York Times*, December 9, 1922

On December 4, when the official American League statistics were published, fans were surprised to learn that Ty Cobb's average had been increased from .398 to .401, allowing Cobb to join Jesse Burkett as the only men to surpass the magic .400 figure three times in their careers. Newspapers revealed that the discrepancy occurred on May 15, when the official scorer determined that Cobb had reached base against the Yankees on an error, while the Associated Press scorer, BBWAA president Fred Lieb, credited Cobb with a hit. American League President Ban Johnson, noting Lieb's experience, rejected previous practice and ignored the official account of this play. Ironically, the rookie scorer, John Kieran, became one of the best known sportswriters in the nation through his "Sports of the Times" columns in the New York Times, and his regular participation on the popular "Information Please" radio quiz show.

Lieb stated in the article below that Johnson made the wrong decision by accepting the unofficial (Lieb's) statistic. He described the event in greater detail in his memoir Baseball As I Have Known It *(New York: Tempo Star, 1977; rpt., Lincoln: University of Nebraska Press, 1996).*

TY COBB CALLS FOR SCORING CLEAN-UP

Alleges Discrimination Against Him Here— Lieb Deplores Official Hit Change

AUGUSTA, Ga., Dec. 8—Ty Cobb in a statement today on the disputed hit in a game at New York last May, which had just been awarded him by President Ban Johnson of the American League, declared that "the several baseball writers who have so interested themselves in the disputed hit also should turn their attention to what happened on my last trip to New York in the 1921 season.

"Let them tell me and the public why it was three safe hits were taken from me during that series and two times at bat added," he said. "I would also like an explanation as to why the official score in the disputed hit game of last May was not authenticated," he continued.

Cobb declared this to be the first time he had anything to say regarding the scoring at New York during the last series with Detroit in 1921. "I have tried to let it pass by," he stated, "but since they are raising such a commotion in New York over the disputed hit, let them investigate this matter also.

"Of course the public understands that I had nothing to do with the fact that President Johnson awarded me the hit in question," Cobb concluded, "but since the aforementioned baseball writers are reported to have threatened to protest this action, I would like to have the scoring in that last series at New York in 1921 cleared up."

Frederick G. Lieb, President of the Baseball Writers' Association and the scorer who credited Ty Cobb with a doubtful hit in The Associated Press box score of May 15, issued the following statement here yesterday:

The American League had no authority to accept the unofficial score of the Detroit-Yankee game played in New York on May 15, 1922, in preference to the official score.

My failure to agree with the official scorer in the disputed play was due to the fact that it was a rainy afternoon, and Mr. Kieran, the official scorer, left the press stand for the covered section of the grandstand. Had Mr. Kieran been in the press stand The Associated Press score compiled by me would have agreed with the official score.

Obviously when there was a difference of opinion between the two scores, the official and not the unofficial score would have been accepted.

There would be no further need for members of the Baseball Writers' Association serving as official scorers, if their scores were relegated to a secondary position whenever they failed to agree with unofficial averages.

No member of the New York Chapter of the Baseball Writers' Association begrudges Cobb a .400 batting average, but the use of baseball records will be undermined when records are deliberately tampered with in order to favor any batsman, whether he be a star or a mediocre player.

57

Joe McGinnity, 52, Throws Shutout (1923)

SOURCE: *Dubuque Times-Journal*, June 4, 1923

When the subject of pitching endurance is raised, the name of Iron Joe McGinnity usually comes up. McGinnity, a star with the New York Giants in the early 1900s, was famed for pitching entire doubleheaders. After his major league career ended in 1908, McGinnity continued pitching in the minor leagues with success. In the game below he teamed with his old battery mate, the forty-three-year-old catcher John "Chief" Meyers, to record yet another shutout.

IRONMEN WIN ANOTHER GAME FROM WATERLOO

McGinnity Sets New Record; Hurls Game in 1:07

The total receipts in the Mississippi Valley league for Memorial day were nearly twice the amount of last year, according to the figures of M. H. Sexton, president of the league. Last Wednesday the gate receipts amounted to $2441.55 making the pool $406.92 for each club. Last year the best holiday pool during the entire season was only $219.74.

The Ironmen won a 2 to 0 victory over Waterloo in the third game of the series here Sunday.

That makes it three straight wins for Dubuque over the Waterloo club. It also makes eight consecutive games that the followers of McGinnity have won since coming home from their trip on the road.

Their win Saturday made them 16 won and 16 lost, or a percentage of .500. Sunday's game gives them 17 won and 16 lost. In other words, instead of being at the bottom of the list they are rising as rapidly as possible toward the top.

While on the road they signed up Mann for center field, and the way that worthy has been covering his territory brings dismay to the batter who sees the pill he has just walloped arching high out into this Mann's country.

Since arriving at the home diamond they have taken on Jackson, shortstop, and "Chief" Meyers, catcher, who have aided materially in strengthening the team. The way "Jack" scoops up grounders causes the batter to want to clout the ball in some other direction, while "Chief's" whip to second is the terror of the base runner.

They are also handy with the stick. May 31 Meyers batted 1.000, getting four hits in four times up from the Ottumwa hurler. In the first game with Waterloo Mann got four hits. Jackson got two doubles in the first game here with Marshalltown.

However, they are not the only players on the team. Armstrong glued onto three hits and four runs in the opening game with Rock Island and Delaney got a home run in the final game with that team. Hyde made a home run in Saturday's game with Waterloo. The rest of the boys have all being doing their work consistently.

McGinnity hurled Sunday's game in one hour and seven minutes, beating his record made at Marshalltown by one minute.

In the go here Sunday Mann and Armstrong, Dubuque's first men up, scored in the first inning. These two were the only counters made. The game was close and well played. Several times the visitors threatened to score. In the third, Storm, Waterloo pitcher, traveled to within four feet of the plate and a score, but just at this moment "Chief" Meyers received the ball from the field and carried it, football fashion, into the abdomen of the runner. He somersaulted onto the plate, but not until after the "Umps" had called "out."

Waterloo got five hits to Dubuque's six, but the fast work of the local lads kept them from scoring.

58

"Nondiscrimination" in Baseball (1923)

SOURCE: *The Sporting News*, December 6, 1923

This remarkable editorial condemns the idea that baseball could ever discriminate against any racial or ethnic group—with the exception of blacks—and simultaneously demonstrates the prejudices of the era. The writer casually—and ironically?—uses what we today would consider gross ethnic slurs to applaud baseball's "progress."

A NEW DIVISION IN BASEBALL

It is a pity that in a democratic, catholic, real American game like baseball—we call it our "national" game—there ever should arise that hideous monster of racial or religious prejudice that has made martyrs of millions, brought out all the hate that is in humanity and caused woe through the centuries. Yet, sad to say there are evidences of it.

In Organized Baseball there has been no distinction raised except tacit understanding that a player of Ethiopian descent is ineligible—the wisdom of which we will not discuss except to say that by such a rule some of the greatest players the game has ever known have been denied their opportunity. No player of any other "race" has been barred. We have had Indians, Chinese and Japanese playing ball and if a Malay should appear who could field and hit he probably would be welcomed. All shades from lightest blonds to darkest brunette have been admitted, with the one exception of the woolly-haired race.

And as to the matter of a man's religious belief, education or his preferences never has a question been raised. He may be Catholic, Methodist, Mohammedan or a believer in no god at all—or willing to admit gods are many—and his contract is the same. He is on a level in that respect.

But there have been cases of prejudice and ostracism, the history of the game tells us, despite the fact that players of whatever division subscribe to the same contract and agree to deliver the best they have at all times.

When one scans a box score or a reserve list and notes from what pools of our polyglot population baseball players are drawn, it is amazing that any question ever should be raised as to a man's antecedents, or the particular form of his worship of the one Great God. But sometimes the players themselves have raised it.

Not so with the fan, who is himself as cosmopolitan as the player. It matters not what branch of mankind the player sprang from, with the fan, if he can deliver the goods. The Mick, the Sheeney, the Wop, the Dutch and the Chink, the Cuban, the Indian, the Jap or the so-called Anglo-Saxon—his "nationality" is never a matter of moment if he can pitch, or hit, or field. Nor does the fan who makes the game go care whether he worships this form of god or that.

It is not then the fan who is to blame for prejudices and factions that arise from differences indicated; the players themselves are responsible. There was a story of a great ball club disrupted because of the religious prejudice of the manager—a story that may or may not have had any truth in it. Now we have stories of discord on clubs today because of the same sort of prejudices.

Now it's that newly-arisen Ku Klux movement that is alleged to be causing disturbance. The incident of Robert Keller Hasty, a Georgian who is a member of the Philadelphia Athletics' pitching staff, being implicated in a "flogging" case in his native state, is seemingly the basis for "disclosures" that during the past season players who were alleged to belong to the K.K.K. did not get along well with players, non-members or "ineligible" to take the Klux oath.

Alarmists are predicting we are likely to have quite a row in baseball for some time to come—until the Klux wave subsides and we Americans, who always must have some sort of mob "revival," have returned to a degree of normalcy. And that we will do, as indicated by our history, for haven't we had Knownothingism, Billy Sundayism, the A.P.A., free silver and even prohibition numbered among our spasms?

We are not so pessimistic; here and there a fanatic may appear among the playing fraternity, but he won't be able to do much harm. The normalcy of fandom itself will serve to suppress him. And above all the 100 per cent of real Americanism that makes baseball what it is discourages factionalism and tends toward that tolerance and democracy that is the great care for these boils that now and then, here and there, break out in our body politic.

And in passing it might be remarked also that a "national" game that has its hold in Canada, Cuba, Japan and other points East, West, North and South can't be damaged much by any ivory-headed obsession that one man made in God's image is any better than any other made in the same image, within the limitations that seem to fit the conditions of the day, yet may be in the discard tomorrow.

59

Negro National League Is Chartered (1924)

SOURCE: Corporate File, box 1779, no. 12478, Dissolved Domestic Corporation Charters (RS.103.112), Illinois State Archives

The Negro National League was chartered with $2500 in common stock at $25 a share. The shares belonged to the five directors: Willie Foster, Russell Thompson, Rube Foster, Walter M. Farmer and J. L. Wilkinson. The first three men lived at the same address in Chicago, which also served as the principal office of the NNL. Farmer also lived in Chicago, while Wilkinson—the only white owner in the league—resided in Kansas City. In 1925 the number of directors was increased from five to eight to reflect the eight clubs in the league. The NNL was officially dissolved on June 5, 1929.

Reprinted below are the terms of the incorporation and the stated objectives of the league.

To LOUIS L. EMMERSON, Secretary of State:

We, the undersigned, adult citizens of the United States, at least one of whom is a citizen of Illinois,

Willie Foster   3342–44 Indiana Ave., Chicago, Illinois.
Russell Thompson   3342–44 Indiana Ave., Chicago, Illinois.
Walter M. Farmer   184 W. Washington St., Chicago, Illinois.

propose to form a corporation under an Act of the General Assembly of the State of Illinois, entitled, "An Act in relation to corporations for pecuniary profit," approved June 28, 1919, in force July 1, 1919; and all Acts amendatory thereof; and, for the purpose of such organization, we hereby state as follows, to-wit:

1. The name of such corporation is THE NEGRO NATIONAL LEAGUE OF PRO-FESSIONAL BASEBALL CLUBS.

2. The object for which it is formed is:

Section 1. This organization has for its objects, the organizing, equipping and maintaining Baseball Clubs, composed of Colored Professional baseball players, sufficient to constitute and form a Circuit for the playing of championship games among the clubs belonging to THE NEGRO NATIONAL LEAGUE OF PROFESSIONAL BASEBALL CLUBS.

Its further object shall be to protect and promote the mutual interests of Colored professional baseball clubs belonging to THE NEGRO NATIONAL LEAGUE OF PROFESSIONAL BASEBALL CLUBS as well as Colored Professional Baseball Players.

Section 2. To establish and regulate professional baseball championship games under the supervision of the Board of Control of THE NEGRO NATIONAL LEAGUE OF PROFESSIONAL BASEBALL CLUBS.

Section 3. To maintain and own by purchase, gift or otherwise, amusement parks or buildings for the carrying out of the objects and purposes of THE NEGRO NATIONAL LEAGUE OF PROFESSIONAL BASEBALL CLUBS.

3. The duration of the corporation is Fifty (50) years

4. The location of the principal office is 3342–44 Indiana Avenue, City of Chicago, County of Cook and State of Illinois.

5. The total authorized capital stock is Common $2500.00.

7. The number of shares having a par value is One hundred (100). . . .

9. The name and address of the subscribers to the capital stock, and the amount subscribed and paid in by each, are as follows:

NAME	ADDRESS NUMBER STREET CITY STATE	NUMBER OF SHARES	AMOUNT SUB-SCRIBED	AMOUNT PAID IN
Willie Foster	3342 Indiana Ave., Chicago, Ill.	40	$1000.00	$1000.00
Russell Thompson	3342 Indiana Ave., Chicago, Ill.	15	$375.	$375.00
Walter M. Farmer	184 W. Washington St., Chicago, Ill.	5	125.	125.00
Andrew R. Foster	3342 Indiana Ave., Chicago, Ill.	20	500.	500.00
J. L. Wilkinson	4118 Agness St., Kansas City, Mo.	20	500.	500.00

60

National League Celebrates "Golden Jubilee" (1926)

SOURCE: *New York Sun*, February 3, 1926

After weathering the Black Sox scandal and a variety of other controversies, the owners and fans of the National League were no doubt thrilled to be able to celebrate the league's fiftieth anniversary. The gala attracted figures from baseball's past as well as important politicians and other celebrities.

NATIONAL LEAGUERS BANQUET

Fancy Horsehide Souvenirs, Speeches, Spotlights, and So Forth, Feature Astor Blowout

By Will Wedge

The National League is $20,000 poorer—and fifty years richer. The twenty "grand" was blown last night for a banquet. The fifty years have been blown into the echoing alcoves of time. The answering reverberation came in the grand ball room of Mr. Astor's Hotel, adjoining a prominent excavation on Broadway. It was a banquet. Everyone knows how this banquet craze has grown. The National League put in on high stilts last night. Everything was splendidly elegant. It was one of the best banquets since the Actors Equity threw their last party. One thousand persons pried into the grand ball room and emerged with souvenirs.

The souvenirs were in a gilt box. They were a pair of National League baseballs. One was for the kiddies and one was for the wife who waited up for the belated banqueter. Some of these banqueters probably still are coming home. Those who are already home and are standing regimental inspection before their wives will find they drew as souvenirs one blank baseball and one covered with the photographic likenesses of the eight presidents of the National League from the era of Morgan G. Bulkeley to John A. Heydler. . . .

COL. MILLS AND MAX CAREY

The first speaker introduced by Toastmaster Heydler was Col. A. G. Mills of New York, one of the oldest surviving members. Col. Mills said a few things on his own behalf and then came a copy of his remarks to President Heydler to read for him. President Heydler's rendition of the remarks was practically perfect.

Next on the program came Max Carey, captain of the Pittsburg Corsairs, who beat the Senators for the world championship last October. Max made the boys get out their handkerchiefs. He pointed out the big obligation of baseball to the small boy. This is the part of the business that is usually characterized as "applesauce." Carey, a theologian of one of the denominations probably prominent in Pittsburgh, played on the heartstrings of his hearers and had this reporter crying in less than no time. The Rev. Carey—he is a Lutheran—feels thankful that baseball has given him the chance to be called "one of its own"—"his life," says the Rev. Carey, is not in vain, if he feels that one little boy has been kept on the straight and narrow path by his efforts.

With their handkerchiefs still within reach the patrons of the fiesta were next treated to a prolonged introduction of old stars. The spotlight was turned on these gents for a few minutes, but they were not called upon to speak. There were a dozen veterans of 1876. Tommy Bond of the first underhand delivery. Pitcher George Washington Bradley of St. Louis, who pitched and won the first game in the National League, April 23, 1876. Alonzo Knight of Philadelphia, who pitched and lost for Philadelphia, the first National League game. John Morrill of Boston, first to sign a National League contract. Deacon Jim White of the old Detroit "Big Four" of Brouthers, Rowe, Richardson and White. Tom York, who has been employed at the Polo Grounds press box in recent years. Ren Mulford of Cincinnati, the famous old scorer, and Bill McLean, first umpire, who despite all the threats of the fans to kill the umpire is still alive and healthy, aged 94—94, can you beat it?—older than some of the wrestlers under contract to Jack Curley.

GOV. PINCHOT

After all the old players had been introduced Toastmaster Heydler called upon Gov. Gifford Pinchot, who dwelled fondly upon the fact that he came from Pittsburgh, which seems to have taken a great national importance of late since New York has followed its example of using soft coal for smoky fuel.

From Mr. Pinchot Toastmaster Heydler directed the spotlight to Rogers Hornsby, one of the real gentlemen of the game, who batted .403 last season, which is a coincidence, as this was the figure attained by Ross Barnes of the National League some fifty years ago. Which probably proves something. . . .

Along about this time in came Jimmy Walker. You couldn't keep that chap out at a Republican mass meeting. The Honorable James announced that he got more mileage out of a dress shirt than any other dinerout in the town. No one disputed him. He said he had been farmed out to Albany for sixteen years and when Tammany exercised its option on him the thrill he received was that of one finally landing in the big leagues. When he was inaugurated a month ago he said it was like going to bat with the City Hall full.

After Mayor Walker everything seems like an anticlimax, but not so. Senator George Wharton Pepper, who wrote the present rules of baseball and waxed very eloquent, was next. The best thing he said was that he brought the greeting from Nicholas Longworth, Speaker of the House, and Gen. Dawes, muffler of the Senate. He also said that the Congressional Record was sorry reading as a substitute for the baseball scores.

61

Cobb, Speaker Named in Gambling Scandal (1926)

SOURCE: *The Sporting News*, December 30, 1926

In November of 1926 Ty Cobb and Tris Speaker stunned the baseball world by announcing their retirements. It was not until late December that the reason for their decision was revealed. They, along with several other players, had been accused by pitcher Dutch Leonard of fixing a game in 1919. Even though seven years had passed since the Black Sox scandal, the specter of gambling in baseball was still present, and the thought that men such as Cobb and Speaker might be involved in throwing or betting on games was frightening. Since Leonard failed to face the players (allegedly because he feared a thrashing from Cobb), and since no further evidence surfaced, Commissioner Landis dropped the case. Cobb and Speaker resumed their careers, but both retired (for good) following their stint with the Philadelphia Athletics in 1928. For further details see Charles C. Alexander, Ty Cobb (New York: Oxford University Press, 1984).

LANDIS TOOK WISE COURSE, SAYS RICE

COVERING UP OF SCANDAL WOULD HAVE HAD BAD EFFECT
Writer-Lawyer Says Press Was About to "Pop" Story and
This Might Have Proved K. O. for Game

BROOKLYN, N.Y., Dec. 27—Was Judge Kenesaw Mountain Landis justified in making public his investigation into the charge that Tyrus Cobb, Tris Speaker, Joe Wood and Hubert B. (Dutch) Leonard engaged in some sort of conspiracy to bet, with foreknowledge of the outcome, on the game which Detroit won from Cleveland by 9 to 5 in Detroit on September 25, 1919? In this writer's mind Judge Landis had no other course than to make his investigation public.

Considerable evidence is at hand to indicate that a large number of persons knew of the alleged transaction, and it is a dead moral certainty that the circle of those who had the tip would grow. It is equally certain that eventually a newspaper or a newspaper syndicate would have had sufficient leads upon which to publish the story in a more or less garbled form. In fact, one newspaper service claims that it already had the information.

Judge Landis is now being accused in many quarters of giving out the story in order to advertise his own virtues and to gain cheap publicity. The accusations are coming from the very sort of people who would have accused him with the utmost virulence of attempting to smother a scandal and whitewash accused men, if the story had received its first publication through the private initiative of a newspaper or of a newspaper syndicate.

IT WAS UP TO THE JUDGE

If a newspaper had originally sprung the story, the same cry would have been raised that used to be raised every time a scandal arose in the past and was spread before the fans by other than the baseball authorities. That cry was that the baseball authorities were afraid to denounce men in high places, that they winked at moral offenses against the sporting code for fear of injuring the game in which they had their money invested. That cry, or charge, has appeared in hundreds of columns of newspaper space in the past. It would have appeared in thousands of more columns of space if a newspaper had beaten Judge Landis to the punch in the matter of Cobb, Wood and Leonard.

In the light of events which have developed up to this writing, if Judge Landis had held his hand, and a newspaper had published the story, he would have been accused of having refrained from doing his duty because he feared to imperil the seven-year job to which he was re-elected this month at a salary raised to $65,000 per year.

Moreover, since it is now plain that officials in both major leagues, and other men whose incomes are dependent upon baseball, were aware of the scandal, or alleged scandal, they would have been charged with having acted in concert with Judge Landis in failing to expose men of the standing of Speaker and Cobb, from fear of possibly injury to the enormous financial investments in baseball.

Having had 30 years' experience as a newspaper man, and having been a member of the bar for more than 27 years, I may say without boasting that I have learned to analyze both sides of a question. . . .

Judge Landis, in my opinion, practically saved baseball by being first in the field with the expose, and at one stroke earned the $455,000 he is to receive for seven years' work as High Commissioner of Baseball. That may not sound good or reasonable to those who have for various reasons been opposed to the Judge or his policies, but baseball men who have grown from boyhood to middle age in the sport will appreciate that my conclusion is well founded, remembering that if Judge Landis had not laid the story before the fans other persons would have done so.

CHASE VERDICT RECALLED

As an illustration of how some writers and fans react, take the first charges made against Hal Chase when he was a member of the Cincinnati team. Those charges were fully investigated by President Heydler of the National League. He returned something in the nature of a Scotch verdict of "guilty, but not proved," and he did not expel Chase, or recommend that he be expelled.

Immediately, Heydler was virulently assailed. He and the National League were accused of being so much afraid of the consequences of demonstrated crookedness that they dared not expel Chase. Now, it so happened that Heydler turned over all the papers in that case to me, after his decision had been given, with a request that I express an opinion upon his course. Thorough examination of the evidence convinced me that Heydler could have come to no other public decision than that which he published without having laid himself and the National League open to a huge libel suit that any fledgling lawyer could have won for Chase. Heydler consenting, I published my opinion at length in The Sporting News and in the Brooklyn Daily Eagle.

With Judge Landis, it was a case of "I'll be damned if I do, and I'll be damned if I don't," in the matter of Cobb, Speaker, Wood and Leonard, but the damning would have been inestimably more severe and disastrous, if he had not published the expose before its inescapable publication by outsiders.

Darn the whole mess. It has had the same effect as if a lifelong friend had suddenly died.

THOMAS S. RICE

62

Ruth Breaks Own Home Run Record (1927)

SOURCE: *New York Herald-Tribune*, October 2, 1927

On October 1, 1927, Babe Ruth slugged his sixtieth home run of the season, off Washington Senators pitcher Tom Zachary. The feat, which broke his 1921 mark of 59, awed even the least romantic sportswriter of the era, W. O. McGeehan. McGeehan was a no-nonsense writer who refused to see athletes as heroes or sports as sacrosanct. McGeehan lived up to his reputation in this column, focusing on Ruth's economic worth and his role in helping to save baseball after the Black Sox scandal.

At the end of the column McGeehan noted that Ban Johnson was no longer involved in baseball. Johnson had taken medical leave early in 1927, and retired several weeks after the publication of the column. McGeehan did not comment on another Johnson, Walter Johnson, who made his final major league appearance (as a pinch-hitter) in this game.

DOWN THE LINE WITH W. O. MCGEEHAN

The Babe Breaks Through

In his particular field of endeavor Babe Ruth stands alone. There was no record for the Babe to break but his own, no mark to shoot at but the mark that he had set himself. He broke his own record and he set a new mark at which he may aim next year.

The performance of the Babe rather seems to dwarf the impending world series. The baseball season ended in a way when the Babe drove his sixtieth home run out in the Yankee Stadium. Witnesses of this act in the drama say that it was only six inches fair. It was not one of those magnificent home runs, banged out against the dim horizon, perhaps, but it was a home run, nevertheless, and the sixtieth.

The record that was smashed by that vehement sweep of a left-handed bat was Mr. Ruth's own, a record of fifty-nine home runs batted out in various parks, some with short right fields and some with long. The record which Mr. Ruth smashed the other day marked what the boys might call an epoch in baseball.

It came immediately after the revelations of the Black Sox scandal when the customers were shocked to learn that baseball games, even games in a world series, might be fixed. There was much popular indignation and a readjustment of the executive department of the business of professional baseball. The old National Commission was scrapped and Kenesaw Mountain Landis was coaxed from a Federal bench to be the overlord of professional baseball.

But still it seemed that the customers were skeptical. I read through bales of letters denouncing the National Pastime and all its works. Then Babe Ruth started to do his stuff, as the boys say, which was banging home runs against the far horizons. He banged them from New York to St. Louis. He banged them to the number of fifty-nine, which was a greater number of home runs scored within the knowledge of any of the recognized statisticians. This made Babe Ruth the Home Run King, the Colossus of Swat, or what have you?

The assurance of the magnates that anything of the nature of a fixed world series would not and could not happen again did not convince the skeptical customers. But there was no doubt as to the fact that Babe Ruth was hitting home runs. The interest returned to the National Pastime. Instead of losing customers, it gained customers, and new ones. They were coming to see Babe Ruth.

It was all very well to make the change in the executive department of the National Pastime, but if that had been the only change the customers might have remained unconvinced. The shock of learning that the one professional game in which there was no absolute faith could be corrupted left them still bewildered.

Then Mr. Ruth, as they say, started to do his stuff. Prior to his acquisition by the Yankees he had been a pitcher and made only occasional trips to the bat, but he had made more home runs than any pitcher before him. When he came to the Yankees they made him an outfielder and the Babe started to find himself.

In the season of 1921, which was a very critical one for gentlemen who had their money interested in professional baseball, the Babe started to set the new record. The swing of his bat was so sincere, whether it met the ball or not, that the customers started to renew their faith in the National Pastime. Instead of facing vacant stands and deficits in the box offices the magnates began to take heart and to talk about the immortality of the great American game.

They agreed that it could survive any shock, even a shock of the force of the Black Sox scandal. Possibly. But it always has been my contention that Babe Ruth with his bat pounded baseball back into popularity. There is no doubt as to the sincerity of Babe Ruth at bat. He swings with the utmost sincerity. When he hits the ball goes into the wide-open spaces. When he misses with vehement sincerity.

THE BABE EARNS HIS SALARY

It seems only a few months ago that there was some discussion as to the propriety of Colonel Jacob Ruppert, owner of the New York Yankees, paying the Babe $210,000 for a period of three years. Colonel Ruppert to-day is very willing to admit that he has earned the first annual installment.

But when the Colonel was considering the matter of the Babe's salary in the seclusion of his brewery, it was brought to his attention that after all, ivory in the baseball sense was a decidedly perishable commodity. Also he was reminded that Babe Ruth was subject to fits of stomach-ache and of temperament that would come upon him at most inopportune moments. Also he was reminded that Babe had, on occasions, thumbed his nose at his manager, at the Baseball Commissioner and at the baseball universe in general. He might do it again.

In spite of this the Colonel was willing to take the chance of guaranteeing the Babe a salary of $70,000 a year for a term of three years. The Colonel might have been moved to do this because the prospective customers, taking several straw votes, agreed that Ruth should receive anything from $100,000 to $200,000 a year.

But the offer of $70,000 a year was agreeable to the Babe and seemed agreeable to the customers in general.

Naturally the Colonel expected the Babe to knock out a reasonable number of home runs, but he did not expect that he would set about making new records. But when Mr. Columbia Lou Gehrig started to match the Babe home run for home run during the season, Mr. Ruth insisted upon showing that the home run record was his own particular property, and in doing so increased the patronage at the Yankee Stadium.

Colonel Ruppert will testify to the fact that the Babe has earned his first year's salary and a little more.

BY HELP OF THE BABE

It was Ruth with his bat who brought the American League out of trouble at the end just as he brought all professional baseball out of trouble in 1921.

The tail end of the American League season found the Yankees so far ahead of the other clubs that the scheduled games were almost perfunctory. Then Mr. Columbia Lou Gehrig started to menace the home run supremacy of Babe Ruth. When the newcomer from Columbia tied and then passed Ruth there was a reawakening of interest—not in the American League race, but in the race between the two home run hitters.

Perhaps it was in the stimulus of this competition rather than the desire to break his own home run record that made Babe Ruth establish the new one. But at any rate the Babe has set up the new one for Gehrig or any other batter to shoot at.

If the competition should be keen again next year I think that Mr. Ruth may shoot at it himself.

ANOTHER SHOW-DOWN LOOMS

It seems that the annual trouble in the administration of organized baseball has started even before the opening of the world series. I read that Mr. Ban Johnson, president of the American League, is highly dissatisfied with the administration of Commissioner Landis. This is nothing new. Mr. Johnson always has been dissatisfied with the administration of Commissioner Landis.

But somehow, I thought that Mr. Johnson was read out of the National Pastime some months ago. I recall that there was the positively last show-down between the commissioner and Mr. Johnson. It would seem not. After the world series, the commissioner and Mr. Johnson will have another show-down as usual, a bigger and better show-down than they ever have had before. But as to its finality, who can say? All show-downs but this have been final. But the Landis-Johnson show-down goes on forever.

63

Radio Pioneer Graham McNamee Critiqued (1927)

SOURCE: *New York Sun*, October 5, 1927

In the midst of its comprehensive coverage of the performance of the Yankees in the 1927 World Series, the New York Sun *complained about the performance of Graham McNamee, the first man to announce a baseball game (and other sporting events) on the radio. Later in the Series the* Sun *published another article stating that McNamee had improved considerably. McNamee added his own perspective on announcing the 1927 Series in "My Adventures in Broadcasting Sporting Events,"* American Magazine *106 (July 1928).*

M'NAMEE'S EYE NOT ON THE BALL

Radio Announcer Mixes Up World Series Fans

Graham McNamee, announcing the world series game between the Yankees and the Pirates this afternoon to radio listeners from New York to California, struggled unhappily through base hits and double plays and interrupted himself to demand, in the end a little plaintively: "You know what I mean?" And from most of those tuned in there went up a despairing negative, which he happily could not hear.

He mixed players and innings and teams in his often interrupted story. He told of the spectacle about him while players hit safely or retired to dugouts. He made right handed batters left handed and announced triumphantly on occasion that the Giants were leading—which must have been rather a surprise to McGraw. He put players on bases where they weren't and left them off of bases where they were. The radio audience, most certainly, didn't know what he meant.

OFTENER WRONG THAN RIGHT

Firmly, early in the game, he announced that Dugan and Traynor were left handed, which neither is. He interrupted his ball by ball account of Waite Hoyt's trip to the plate in an early inning to announce that One Eyed Connolly had at last appeared. At the moment Hoyt had two strikes and three balls—when the thrill of Connolly's arrival had passed the Yankee pitcher had gone out on an infield play.

Harris of the Pirates hit into a double play in the last half of the second and McNamee hit into a blind alley. He announced both men safe, he grew excited, he discovered that everything was confused. He divigated for several minutes, while everybody hung breathless. Suddenly, apologetically, he discovered that there had been a double play. He was still almost too apologetic for coherence a moment later when Smith grounded to Gehrig. . . .

The first half of the third went along easily enough until there was a man on second and another on first. The announcer explained that this was the world series being broadcast by the National Broadcasting Company. Suddenly he interrupted himself to exclaim, excitedly: "They missed it!" Some time later it developed that Smith had let a throw from Traynor by and Lazzeri had advanced a base. Mr. McNamee then announced the score as 4 to 1 in favor of Pittsburgh. The Yanks were leading at the time. . . .

He got a number of telegrams at the start of the seventh inning and began to read them. He read a letter and interrupted himself to announce that Combs had struck out. He explained that his watch was not in the pocket he thought but in another pocket, forgetting altogether the position of the diamond. But he improved as he went on, interrupting himself now and then to demand whether "that was plain enough." Finally it was.

"You know what I mean?"

64

No-Hitter in Negro World Series (1927)

SOURCE: *Chicago Defender*, October 15, 1927

The first Negro World Series, featuring the champions of the Negro National League (based in the Midwest) and the Eastern Colored League, was staged in 1924. Two years later the Chicago American Giants faced the Bacharach Giants, of Atlantic City, in the Series and won five games to three. One of the victories by the Bacharach Giants was a no-hitter by Red Grier. The sequence repeated itself in 1927, except that the no-hitter was thrown by Luther Farrell. Notable players in this series included pitcher Willie Foster, third basemen Dave Malarcher and Oliver Marcelle, and shortstop Dick Lundy. The American Giants could not defend their title in 1928 because of the collapse of the Eastern Colored League. The Negro World Series did not resume until 1942, and lasted through the 1948 season.

The writer of this article, Frank A. "Fay" Young, enjoyed a fifty-year career with the Defender, *beginning in 1907. A selection of his articles appears in* Black Writers/Black Baseball: An Anthology of Articles from Black Sportswriters Who Covered the Negro Leagues, *ed. Jim Reisler (Jefferson NC: McFarland, 1994).*

CHICAGO STILL ONE GAME FROM TITLE

Atlantic City Nine Comes to Life and Wins Two Games; Monday's Game Ended in Tie
By Frank A. Young

Atlantic City, N.J., Oct. 11.—(Special)—The American Giants of Chicago came East last Friday needing one more game to win the little world series and at sundown tonight the Chicago club is still one game away, although they are leading the Bacharachs, four games to two.

The Bees, as the Seashore team is popularly known, have just found their stinger and they are going along in fine shape.

With their pitching staff shot to pieces because of sore arms they are making a last stand much greater than the stand made by the Pittsburgh Pirates in the big series against the New York Yankees.

All the games here have been witnessed by the higher-ups in Atlantic City politics. Former Mayor Harry Bacharach and his brother, Ike Bacharach, now U.S. congressman; Mayor Anthony Ruffu, Postmaster Alford, and Enoch Johnson, the county leader, have been regular guests in the box behind home plate. Attorney Isaac Nutter, president of the Eastern league; Judge W. C. Hueston of Gary, Ind., president of the Negro National league; Baseball Commissioner W. J. Gilmore of Kansas City, Mo., and Lloyd Thompson, secretary of the Eastern league, are looking after the game.

Saturday's game went to the Bacharachs, 3 to 2. The game being called after Chicago had taken their bat in the seventh because of darkness. Bunched hits off Foster in the second frame gave the Atlantic City boys three runs and enough to win the game. Things broke bad for Willie because all the four hits he allowed in the game came in that one frame. From then on and before that nary a semblance of a hit was brought forth by the home boys.

Jones' error which was a wild, hurried peg to Marcell to try to get Davis at third went to the outfield and Davis romped home with the first Chicago run here of the series.

In the fifth Larry Brown scored when J. Brown was safe on Wagner's fumble. Chicago failed to get a hit off Farrell in the seven frames. . . .

Saturday's game hadn't been called but a few minutes when the heavens let loose a shower that developed into an all night rain and at game time, 3 o'clock on Sunday, it was still coming down, forcing Sunday's game to be called off and thus disappointing thousands of folks who came over from New York, Cape May, Wilmington, Baltimore, Philadelphia and nearby towns. The baseball men, Commissioner W. J. Gilmore, Judge Wm. C. Hueston, Lloyd Thompson, secretary of the Eastern league, and the Defender representative were the guests of Attorney Isaac Nutter, president of the Eastern league, at his palatial home in Douglas Park, a suburb.

Saturday's Game

AMERICAN GIANTS

	AB.	R.	H.	P.O.	A.
J. Brown 1b.	3	0	0	10	0
Malarcher 3b.	1	0	0	1	2
Davis rf.	3	1	0	0	0
Russ ss.	3	0	0	0	1
Sweatt lf.	2	0	0	2	0
Jackson cf.	3	0	0	0	0
L. Brown c.	2	1	0	3	0
Williams 2b.	1	0	0	2	1
Foster p.	2	0	0	0	5
Totals	20	2	0	18	9

	AB.	R.	H.	P.O.	A.	
Reid lf.	3	0	1	1	0	
Marcell 3b.	2	0	0	0	1	
White cf.	3	0	0	1	0	
Lewis 1b.	3	1	1	8	0	
Lundy ss.	3	0	0	2	3	
Smith rf.	1	1	1	2	1	
Jones c.	2	1	1	3	2	
Wagner 2b.	3	0	0	3	4	
Farrell p.	2	0	0	1	1	
Totals	22	3	4	21	12	
American Giants 0	0	0	1	1	0	0—2
Atlantic City 0	3	0	0	0	0	*—3

Errors—Jones, Wagner, Marcell, Farrell, Russ. Two-base hit—Smith. Stolen bases—Davis (2). Struck out—By Foster, 3; by Farrell, 5. Bases on balls—Off Foster, 3; off Farrell, 5. Double plays—Wagner to Lewis; Lundy to Wagner to Lewis. Umpires—McDevitt and Magee.

65

Margaret Gisolo, Baseball Star (1928)

SOURCE: *Indianapolis News*, July 26, 1928

In the third year of its existence, the American Legion baseball program encountered a difficulty. In the latter stages of its annual national tournament it became known that one of the best players of the Blanford, Indiana, club was a girl. A club that lost to Blanford in the state finals protested to the Legion, but the director of the Legion's Americanism division, which administered the baseball program, reaffirmed the eligibility of Margaret Gisolo. Her Blanford Cubs won the Indiana title but lost a week later in regional competition. The following year the American Legion banned girls from playing on its teams.

Gisolo did not stop participating in sports, however. She earned a degree in physical education, enjoyed a long career as a university professor, and in the 1990s was still a nationally ranked tennis player in her age group. For details on Gisolo see Gai Ingham Berlage, Women in Baseball: The Forgotten History *(Westport CT: Praeger, 1994).*

GIRL BASEBALL PLAYER AIDS IN WINNING LEGION TOURNAMENT

"She helps her mother every morning with the housework, but as soon as she lays down the broom she picks up the baseball bat, and is out on the diamond the rest of the day."

Thus a friend described Margaret Gisolo, age fourteen, second baseman for the Blanford Cubs, which team defeated the St. Philip's Boys' Club, of Indianapolis,

Thursday forenoon in the finals of the state American Legion junior baseball tournament at Riverside park.

Margaret was the object of all eyes as she took her place at second base. The foregoing picture shows her just as she hit the first ball pitched to her in the third inning in which she was first "man" up. The hit was too hot for the third baseman. She went to second base on a sacrifice, to third on a fielder's choice and scored on a hit.

Margaret, who weighs 106 pounds, knows baseball. When her little girl friends in Blanford played with dolls and painted tin dishes, she was learning how to throw a curve. She was constantly encouraged by her brothers, one of whom, Tony, is now coach for the Blanford team and a player on the New Goshen team.

Margaret is recognized as a good base stealer, pitcher and batter. Pitching Wednesday at the Terre Haute sectional, she struck out a pinch hitter. She was wearing the shoes given her by Tony a few weeks ago when she got the single in the twelfth inning that gave Blanford the game in the county championship.

Clinton, defeated team, protested against her eligibility because she was not a boy. A decision in favor of Blanford was handed down by Dan Sowers, national director of the Americanism division for the Legion, and Margaret was ruled eligible to remain in the tournament.

66

NL **President Suggests Designated Hitter** (1929)

SOURCE: *Spalding's Official Baseball Guide 1929*

Editor John B. Foster started this edition of the Guide *with his "Editorial Comment," a series of brief, disconnected articles. The second of these noted a suggestion by John Heydler that a tenth man be allowed to bat for the pitcher. Foster observed that "conservatives" would prevent the plan from being instituted, but that current trends in American sports allowed for such specialization.*

PRESIDENT HEYDLER'S SUGGESTION

At the annual winter meeting of the National League, held in New York City, President John A. Heydler suggested to the owners who were present the advisability of having a player, to be named before a game began, act as batter for the pitcher, throughout. He called attention to the fact that however novel the proposal might seem to be, it would only be carrying a little farther a custom that has already made itself manifest in Base Ball by the substitution of pinch hitters.

The suggestion was received with approval by some of the managers and owners and with hesitation by others. Any plan of that character necessarily would meet with a plea by some for further consideration.

Conservatives hold back on the plan on the ground that it would make Base Ball a ten-man game. That is not exactly true, because it would be a game both of nine men and ten men. The policy of substitution has become so common in sports of the United States that the old notion of continued team work and an intact team which is to fight through all the periods of a contest, is not as prevalent as it was.

67

Disaster in Yankee Stadium (1929)

SOURCE: *New York Herald-Tribune*, May 20, 1929

Prior to 1900 many baseball parks were constructed entirely of wood, and they frequently burned to the ground or collapsed within a few years of their construction. Due to architectural advances, incidents of this nature were rare by 1929. So the shock after a section of the right-field bleachers in Yankee Stadium—a six-year-old, state-of-the-art facility—collapsed was considerable. Fans had congregated in the bleachers to see Babe Ruth. A severe rainstorm struck and, in their haste to escape the rain, they rushed for the closest exit, stampeding others in the process. Yankees owner Jacob Ruppert declared the incident to be an "act of God," and noted that "the persons who reacted to the mob stimulus were to blame. I am intensely grieved, but do not think the corporation is to blame or liable for damage suits. Our employees did their duty."

**2 DIE, 100 HURT IN PANIC AT YANKEE STADIUM
AS RAIN STAMPEDES 5,000**

**Girl and Man Trampled to Death as Bleacher Crowds Rush for
Exits to Escape Heavy Downpour
Scores Fall Into Pit Near Narrow Chute
Physicians at Game Treat Victims in Clubhouse;
Tragedy Unseen by Majority of 50,000 in Park**

By Thomas Compere

A crash of thunder followed instantly by a deluge of rain, caused a panic among 5,000 persons crowded into the right field bleachers of the Yankee Stadium yesterday and started a stampede for exits which resulted in the death of a young woman student at Hunter College and a man and the injury of nearly 100 other persons. Eighteen were hurt so seriously that they remained in Lincoln Hospital last night.

The crowd surged almost as one person for the three exits, two of which lead from the lower tier of seats in the center of the section and the other from the left top rear.

The confusion broke as 50,000 persons were watching the Yankees and the Boston Red Sox play the thirteenth home game of the season. The score was 3 to 0 in favor of the Yankees in the first half of the fifth inning in which the game halted.

TRAMPLE ON GIRL STUDENT

Miss Eleanor Price, seventeen years old, of 1848 Loring Place, the Bronx, a student in Hunter College, was one of the first to reach the main lower exit. A surge of the crowd sent her sprawling down the wooden steps. Half a dozen boys tripped over her.

Miss Price, who is the daughter of Dr. Maxwell Price, who is head of the Union Health Center Clinic, 222 Fourth Avenue, was found unconscious. Near her was Joseph Carter, sixty years old, truckman's assistant, of 218 East 128th Street. Both of them died a few minutes later, "Babe" Ruth, the idol of baseball, holding the girl as she passed.

The panic-driven crowd had gone over the victims, trampling the boys underfoot and knocking down three men who attempted to stem the mad rush.

Those who attempted to aid Miss Price and the youths were crushed to the runway and stamped by those forced ahead by the crushing tide of people who were fighting to get out of the rain.

The force from the rear was irresistible. Thousands from above pushed those in front over the prostrate young woman and boys, and the crowd milling from the top exit crashed into those charging from the main lower exit on the ground where the runways converge immediately under the center of the stands. A dozen men and boys went down at the first impact.

POLICEMAN SHOUTS WARNING

Patrolman Louis Baer, of the Baskett Avenue Police station, who was on duty at the intersection, shouted for the crowd to halt. They came on, trampling the fallen men and boys underfoot. He drew his pistol and threatened to shoot. Several men backed up and tried to check the crowd.

The combined stream of stamping humanity swept over them, knocking the patrolman down and stepping on his revolver. . . .

The first indication that something was amiss was given those in the grandstands when Elias Gottlieb, a probationary patrolman, ran out on to the field carrying Morris Lerner, fourteen years old, of 893 Trinity Avenue, calling for a physician.

Babe Ruth ran from the Yankees' dugout and asked what the trouble was. He then shouted for a physician. Dr. Edward S. Cowles, the well known neurologist and psychiatrist, of 591 Park Avenue, ran from the stands and took the boy into the club's dressing room. Then Ruth called for other physicians, and a half dozen of them made their way to the scene of the catastrophe.

Police inspector Joseph F. Thompson rallied reserves from four police stations in the Bronx. Hundreds of them responded and held the crowd in check.

VICTIMS TAKEN TO CLUBHOUSE

Forty of the injured were taken into the Yankees' dressing room. They were placed on tables and the floor, while calls for aid were sent to the Fordham, Lincoln and Harlem Hospitals. A dozen physicians attempted to give first aid, but none of them had any medical kits, and the small supply in the clubhouse did not begin to go around.

The majority of the injured were boys. Most of them were unconscious. They suffered from broken bones, internal injuries, fractured skulls and exposure. Five ambulances responded, but they were insufficient. Two large buses were rolled near the bleacher entrance and loaded with the injured. They were taken to Lincoln Hospital.

Gottlieb, after carrying young Lerner to the field and summoning aid, returned to the stands and assisted in carrying fifteen of the injured into the dressing rooms. Louise Underwood, a Negro woman, of 318 West Forty-first Street, took charge of a small emergency room, and aided a number of those until the ambulances arrived.

There was a shortage of stretchers, and the injured were carried from the dressing room to the ambulances and buses. Nearly all the injured were drenched by the rain and their clothes were torn to shreds. . . .

5

Lights, Action, History

The most significant development in baseball during the years of the Depression was the introduction of artificial illumination. It was first popularized by the Kansas City Monarchs, who played many games under their portable lighting system, including a memorable loss to Smokey Joe Williams and the Pittsburgh (later Homestead) Grays in 1930. The innovation was adopted by numerous minor league clubs, who credited the ability to play night games with saving their industry. Later in the decade some major league clubs installed lights with great success, but fans of the Chicago Cubs—who resisted the trend—were grateful that one of the greatest moments in their history, Gabby Hartnett's pennant-winning home run in the gloaming, was made possible by the absence of artificial light.

History was on the minds of others in baseball, as Cooperstown, New York boosters took steps to commemorate the game's greats in a Hall of Fame. Both the major leagues and the Negro Leagues started playing annual All-Star games, which enabled them to commemorate current stars. Two of those stars, Babe Ruth and Dizzy Dean, ended their careers after falling victim to age and injury, but the seemingly invincible Lou Gehrig ended his historic consecutive game streak only after developing a fatal disease that later was named for him. In the meantime Commissioner Landis continued to make history of his own, but for the most part his efforts were overshadowed by the explosion of scoring that made the 1930s one of the most exciting decades in baseball history.

68

Early Minor League Night Game (1930)

SOURCE: *Des Moines Register*, May 3, 1930

Following the lead of the Kansas City Monarchs, several minor league clubs, desperate for spectators in the early stages of the Depression, installed lights and started to play night games. One of the first was played in Des Moines, Iowa. Officials, umpires, and players quoted in the newspaper the following day all expressed support for the idea, saying that the lighting was remarkably good. Photographs of this and other of the first night games appear to indicate otherwise, but they may be more indicative of the primitive cameras of the day.

OFFICIALS ALL PLEASED WITH NIGHT CONTEST

Omaha and Decatur to Get Equipment at Once

By Bert M'Grane

"Within a year every class A and class B ball park in the country will be equipped with lights. That's my prediction after watching the game tonight."

This convincing boost for night baseball at its inauguration here Friday night by C. C. Slapnicka, veteran scout of the Cleveland club of the American league, coupled with the announcement that the Omaha club of the Western league will install a lighting system within the next three weeks and that the Decatur club of the Three-I league signed a contract for lighting equipment here Friday, put the stamp of success on the venture of Lee Keyser, president of the Des Moines Western league club in introducing night baseball into league competition.

Without a dissenting opinion baseball officials and prominent fans who saw the game were convinced that night baseball not only is practical from a playing standpoint but that it provides the solution of the attendance problem in the minor leagues.

SALVATION FOR MINORS

Slapnicka, the Cleveland scout, was one of the many diamond notables who watched the game from the standpoint of the player.

"I did not see a man flinch from any ball either batted or thrown. The playing of both teams indicates that everything can be done under artificial light that can be done in daylight games. I believe that night baseball will spread over the entire country and that it will prove to be the salvation of the minor leagues," said Slapnicka.

Les Nunamaker, the old Boston Red Sox catcher who is now managing the Lincoln club of the Nebraska State league, was another who expressed himself enthusiastically in favor of the night game.

"We already have illuminated our field and are ready for league games right now. I am thoroughly convinced and I feel that the attendance problem in the minor leagues is solved," he said.

OMAHA FOLLOWS SUIT

Barney Burch, owner of the Omaha Western league team, said: "This demonstration has convinced me. We will have lights in our park just as soon as they can be installed."

J. D. Barnhart, president of the Decatur club of the Three-I league, after witnessing a demonstration in Lincoln Thursday night and the inaugural game last night, signed a contract for the installation of lights in the Decatur park, to be ready for the opening game May 14.

Opinions in favor of the lights were virtually unanimous and few if any of the spectators were inclined to blame any misplays in the game on the lights. They felt that the same miscues would have been made in daylight games.

69

James A. Michener on Sandlot Baseball (1930)

SOURCE: *Literary Digest*, July 12, 1930

Seventeen years before he published his first book, James Michener was a twenty-three-year-old schoolteacher and coach in Pennsylvania. He recorded his impressions on the popularity of baseball among young boys, which he felt was declining because of competition from sports like tennis and golf, as well as from the movies. Michener later wrote a lengthy book, Sports in America *(New York: Random House, 1976), in which he placed much of the blame for the sad shape of children's sports on the parents—and coaches— who placed too much emphasis on winning and too little on spontaneous play.*

IS THE AMERICAN BOY QUITTING BASEBALL?

According to some observers, American boys are turning away from baseball to tennis, golf, track, swimming. If this is true, whence will come to-morrow's players and fans? Among those who see a decline of baseball interest is a man who should know what he is talking about—James A. Michener, coach and teacher at the Hill School, in Pottstown, Pennsylvania. In a copyrighted article in the Philadelphia *Public Ledger*, he states his belief and gives reasons for it, based on personal experience, statistics, and interviews with others in touch with the situation.

We wonder if our readers will agree with Mr. Michener's conclusions, quoted from *The Public Ledger*:

Baseball rose to great popularity, and from the sand-lot came many of the game's outstanding stars.

Sporting pages of the last fifteen years have been very careful to point out, at every possible turn, the sand-lot derivation of the home team's stars, and the records of the big leagues show that a fine training place for aspiring youngsters was the old corner-lot ball game, in which the whole of the small town might take part.

This state of affairs began to change about nine or ten years ago. The distracting influence appeared in a multitude of shapes. Many have laid the blame to golf or to the movies or the revived interest in swimming or football or any other of a number of things.

Whatever the reason, in the early years of the last decade baseball, as a nationwide diversion, went into a devastating decline from which it has not yet emerged and which, if present indications are correct, it can not hope to overcome.

This does not mean that baseball will die. Big-league parks will be filled just as surely ten years from now as they are to-day, but the small-corner games, the alley ball, the "movin's up," and the famous catch during recess have grown old and died a natural death in many sections of the country, and will probably do so in many more within the next few years.

This may sound like a broad generalization to the baseball addict, but to any one connected with the intramural or playground recreation of boys, it is a proved fact. Baseball has, as a sport for schoolboys, passed its period of greatest interest, and is now being supplanted by several other forms of athletic and social entertainment.

Before observing what these substitutes are, "it may be of interest to produce some proof of the contention that baseball is on the wane as far as the young mind is concerned," the writer says as he proceeds:

First of all, the most significant fact is that the big-league magnates are aware of the fact that interest on the part of the younger generation is decidedly below what it used to be. Consequently, this year three ball-parks are thrown open to youngsters "in an effort to build up an interest in the game."

There is still, and there always will be, the scrambling horde of boys about the ball-park gates, but the other boys, the ones who used to play their game unobtrusively in the alleys, have put aside their bats and balls; it is to them that the gates are thrown open.

Whether they heed the invitation or not, the magnates have done their share.

The second proof comes in the form of reports from playground centers, which find that year after year more boys are playing tennis and fewer baseball. In some sections this is true to such an extent that ball-fields have been made over into tennis-courts in order to utilize the ground for a greater number of interested boys.

Play supervisors find that boys are more and more awkward in the handling of the baseball implements, while they become more and more adept in the other sports.

Ball games, too, are organized with much more difficulty than the more personal games, such as tennis and golf.

The third place to look for this information is in the sporting-goods stores.

As one proprietor observed: "The boys buy gloves, but not as many, and they don't bother much about the game. Now when I was a kid. . . ."

I doubt if there has been an appreciable decline in actual sales, for baseball is a disease which all boys undergo at a certain stage in growing.

The difference is that to-day recovery from the once-virulent sickness is alarmingly rapid. This results in a quick change from one sport to another, with baseball almost always the discarded game.

What is supplanting the game? asks Mr. Michener. A variety of sports, we learn as we read on:

Two are immediately suggested, as of the two—golf and tennis—either seems at present to hold more interest for the young boy than baseball.

First of all, each of the two sports is intensely personal; there is always some individual action taking place.

Secondly, personal excitement is continually at a high pitch, for every stroke in tennis means just as much as another, and the same is true of golf.

There are no long waits in either game.

The most noticeable thing, however, is that golf and tennis, each in its own way, are quite tiring, and when one has shot eighteen holes of golf or played three sets of tennis, one is aware of a workout; but time after time, when baseball practise is over or when a game has ended, the boys run onto the track and take a couple of stiff laps about the quarter-mile in an effort to supply the physical exhaustion which baseball does not produce.

70

Smokey Joe Williams Fans Twenty-seven Players

(1930)

SOURCE: *Kansas City American*, August 7, 1930

In a 1952 poll conducted by the Pittsburgh Courier, *one of the nation's best black newspapers, Joe Williams was chosen over Satchel Paige as the top pitcher. He earned his reputation with a blazing fast ball and a variety of other pitches which made his fast ball appear even more unhittable. He maintained much of his speed well into his forties, but by that time he also regularly used an emery board to cut the ball—a common tactic in Negro League contests. With these two weapons, coupled with the famous—but inadequate—Kansas City Monarch lighting system, the (at least) forty-four-year-old Williams produced one of his greatest performances. Hurling for the Pittsburgh (later Homestead) Grays in the second of a three-game weekend series, Williams fanned an incredible twenty-seven Monarchs in a twelve-inning, one-hit, 1–0 victory over the Monarchs and twenty-three-year-old Chet Brewer, who chalked up 19 strikeouts of his own in a losing effort. For more details on this game see Larry Lester, "Smokey and the Bandit," in* National Pastime *14 (1994).*

HOMESTEADS TAKE THREE FROM KAY SEE

"Smokey Joe" Williams is Too Much for Local Aggregation Cudahy Rex Defeats K.C. Allies 20 to 3

SATURDAY NIGHT GAME

The Pittsburgh Grays, with their pitching "ace," Smokey Joe Williams, mowing down Monarch batters about as fast as they appeared at the plate, won their second straight night game from the 1929 Negro National League champions last night at Muehlebach Field, 1 to 0, in a great pitchers' duel.

"Smokey Joe" had everything except a blacksmith's file. Chet Brewer, the Monarch mound entry was about as effective but a fluke 2-base hit by White, Pittsburgh center fielder, with the walking Charleston on second, sent the Monarchs down to defeat in the twelfth.

The opposing pitchers were cheating without question of a doubt. An emery ball in daylight is very deceptive but at night it is about as easy to see as an insect in the sky.

"Smokey Joe" struck out twenty-seven and allowed only one hit, a double by Newton Joseph, Monarch third baseman in the eighth. For seven innings the Monarchs just as well have remained on the bench [sic] with their trainer. They didn't get a hit. In the eighth, however, "Smokey Joe" threw one in the center, and "Newt" got his double. Turner, Monarch first baseman, followed with a fly ball which looked like a sure Texas leaguer, but Stephens, Pittsburgh shortstop, went back and made a spectacular catch to rob the Monarchs of a possible victory.

Brewer gave a remarkable exhibition of emery ball pitching. Starting with the seventh inning, he fanned ten straight men, retiring the side on strikes in the seventh, eighth and ninth and getting the first man up in the tenth. All told Brewer fanned nineteen.

Pittsburgh . . . . .0 0 0 0 0 0 0 0 0 0 0 1—1
Monarchs . . . . .0 0 0 0 0 0 0 0 0 0 0 0—0

The summary: Errors—Pittsburgh 1 (Gibson); Monarchs 1 (Mothel). Left on bases—Stephens—Pittsburgh 6, Monarchs, 3. Stolen bases—Stephens, Evans 2, Williams, Taylor, Joseph. Two-base hits—White, Joseph. Double play—Allen to Mothel to Turner. Struck out—By Williams 27, (Taylor 5, Mothel 3, Allen 4, Livingston 2, Redus 3, Joseph 2, Young 4, Turner, Brewer 3); by Brewer 19, (Stephens 2, Harris 4, Charleston, Johnson 3, Scales, White, Evans 3, Gibson 2, Williams 2). Bases on balls—Off Williams 1 (Redus); off Brewer 5, (Harris, Charleston, Scales 2, White). Passed ball—Young. Time—2:00. Umpires Gholston and Hawkins.

71

President Hoover Booed (Perhaps) at World Series Game (1931)

SOURCE: *Editor and Publisher*, October 10, 1931

The following article illustrates the difficulty of interpreting the coverage of a sports event, or any news story for that matter. During the World Series game between the St. Louis Cardinals and the Philadelphia Athletics on October 5, 1931, when President Herbert Hoover took his seat prior to the game some reporters, including prominent sports writers Paul Gallico and Joe Williams, clearly heard the Philadelphia crowd boo him. Other writers, including Westbrook Pegler, felt the booing was not directed at the president, and another writer observed that Hoover was well-received by the crowd.

REPORTERS SPLIT ON WHETHER FANS BOOED HOOVER AT SERIES GAME

Some Reported Definitely That the President Was Object of Derision on Two Occasions at Monday's Contest—Others Carried No Mention—A.P. Men Heard No Booing

Exactly what the reaction of baseball fans was toward presence of President Hoover at the Monday World Series game in Philadelphia, seems to be a matter of doubt. Some of the writers covering the game say that unmistakeable boos from the throng were directed at the President on two separate occasions. Others say that they heard and saw no demonstration, or at least inferred as much by omitting any references to it in their dispatches.

Those who reported the alleged booing included the United Press, and Joe Williams and Paul Gallico, sports editors respectively of the *New York World Telegram* and the *New York Daily News*. Reporters for the Associated Press, International News Service and others were among those who saw and heard no booing.

The Associated Press, on receiving queries from editors in regard to the fans' supposed impoliteness, checked with its staff covering the game, who reported that if there was any booing they could not hear it in the press box, EDITOR & PUBLISHER was informed.

Robert J. Bender, vice-president and general news manager of the United Press, who attended Monday's game, told EDITOR & PUBLISHER this:

"Replying to your inquiry, yes, there was booing in the bleacher sections on two occasions at least during President Hoover's presence at the World Series game in Philadelphia last Monday. When he entered the ball park with his party to take his seat his arrival was greeted by sustained applause in the grand stands mixed with short-lived but perfectly audible booing in the bleacher section.

"Again when the announcer through loud speakers installed in the park asked that all remain seated until the President and his party left the grounds, there was booing in the same sections as before.

"In a little box story we handled the news incident as among those coming under the broad category of 'interesting but not important.'"

Barry Faris, International News Service editor, said I. N. S. dispatches from Philadelphia Monday said there was a small "We Want Beer!" demonstration, but that nothing was mentioned of any booing. He had had no queries from editors regarding the alleged booing, Mr. Faris said.

A special dispatch to the *New York Herald Tribune* said: "The President was given a rousing farewell and he waved his hat back to the packed stands. . ."

Mr. Gallico put it this way: "Mr. H. entered the ball park yesterday to the low snarling rumble of popular disapproval. . . . Customers in the rear seats first heard the Bronx cheer rising from the bleachers, and then, craning their necks to see who was being awarded the berry, spied the Presidential party marching in between rows of police. The most determined and violent booing occurred immediately after the mechanical speakers asked the audiences to remain seated until the President had left the field. And finally, when the Hoover party left, there was an undercurrent of growling against the polite pattering of applause."

Mr. Gallico was amazed that none of this appeared in the papers. "I do not know," he said, "why anyone should be squeamish at publishing such news, or why there were no reports that the populace began to snarl at the Presidential party outside the gates when the motorcycle escort charged through the crowd of citizens who, tickets in their hands, were trying to get in the ballyard."

Bill Corum wrote for the *New York Evening Journal* "Mr. Hoover was enthusiastically received as he marched to the flag-draped guest of honor's box through a double line of policemen."

Joe Williams, after describing the entrance of the President and his party, said:

"Out of the first spontaneous break of polite applause there comes an unmistakeable note of derision, and as this note seems to hang in mid-air, sullen and challenging, it is taken up by more timid souls, until ultimately it becomes a vigorous, full-rounded melody of disparagement.

"You say to yourself: 'This isn't right. This man is the President of the United States. He is here to see a ball game.' . . .

"But the strange vocal babble continues. . . .

"Mr. Hoover's humiliation did not end, I regret to report, with the pregame demonstration. . . . Taking it by and large it was not an altogether pleasant afternoon for Mr. Hoover, and I am afraid it will be a long time before any political friend gets him to another ball game."

A special to the *New York Times* pictured the President "smiling frequently at the applause of the throng." "The President obviously enjoyed every moment of the game," the dispatch said. "All in all, it was a great day for the President."

The United Press, the only press association to carry an account of the supposed booing, sent out this dispatch the morning following the game:

"Philadelphia, Oct. 6.—Some fans here gave vent to their political feelings yesterday during President Hoover's visit to the world's series game.

"While strong applause from the grandstands greeted his entrance and departure, boos arose from the bleachers as he entered and again when the announcer asked that all remain seated until the President and his party had left their places and the grounds."

Westbrook Pegler, sports columnist for the *Chicago Tribune* Syndicate, told EDITOR & PUBLISHER he had carried nothing of the booing, although he had heard it distinctly, because the booing of the President at Philadelphia baseball games was "a matter of routine."

"Last year during the series," he said, "the President was booed in Philadelphia and I wrote a column on it. I didn't write it this year because it would have been repetitious."

The incident was considered by Philadelphia newspapermen to be the usual outburst of expression by baseball fans and to have had no political aspect.

It was generally disregarded in the Philadelphia papers.

"I heard booing plainly," said James Gantz, sports editor of the Record.

"Baseball fans are prone to boo anyone and everybody on the least provocation. In this case I do not think they meant any disrespect to the President but were merely shouting disapproval at some suggestion that was being made to them."

72

First Negro League All-Star Game (1933)

SOURCE: *Chicago Defender*, September 16, 1933

Both the major leagues and the Negro Leagues introduced all-star games in Chicago's Comiskey Park in 1933. The major league game, inspired by Chicago Tribune *sports editor Arch Ward, was announced on May 18 and was played on July 6. The Negro League version was conceived in 1932 by Pittsburgh Crawford owner Gus Greenlee, who with much effort organized the contest that was finally staged on September 10. Unlike the major league contest, whose players were selected by the team managers, black papers like the* Pittsburgh Courier *and the* Defender *provided their readers with ballots to choose their favorites, and the running totals were printed weekly.*

WEST WALLOPS EAST, 11–7

Losers Get 7 Hits; Homer for Suttles

The big bludgeons of Mule Suttles, Radcliffe, Stearns, Larry Brown, Davis and Wells overcame the handicap of ineffective pitching in the early rounds by Willie Foster and the erratic play of Morney at second base, and the West tarnished the East in the game of games, played at Comiskey park in Chicago last Sunday, 11 to 7, before a crowd 20,000. The East employed a trio of flingers, Streeter, Hunter, and Britt, in that order, and only the starting flinger was anything like a puzzle to the West's sluggers.

Foster pitched the entire game for the West, allowing seven hits and as many runs. Streeter, on the other hand, went only six frames before being replaced by Hunter, who was followed by Britt. Streeter left in the sixth after the West had solved his left-handed slants for runs enough to lead, 4 to 3.

For the first two innings neither pitcher gave up anything that looked like a hit. Then in the first of the third Wilson singled to left for East's first hit and the first bingle of the game. Mackey had struck out to start the frame and Jud was easily wiped out in a fast double-play, when Lundy hit to Wells, who tossed to Morney, who relayed to Suttles to clear the sacks and end the frame.

WEST SCORES

The Wilson bingle gave West an idea, although an error had to show up to permit them to take advantage of the idea, to the tune of a run. Bankhead sent a slow bounder to Lundy and East's great short stop threw wildly to first, pulling Charleston off the bag. Brown then sacrificed and Turkey Stearns did the rest with a screaming drive to right, to send Bankhead home.

Then to start the third, Foster started to show the effects of a left arm that is over-worked, and the result was three runs for East. He failed to find the plate on Dixon in four pitches and the big fellow walked. Then he sent a screw ball into the ribs of Oscar Charleston and there were two on and no one out. At this point, Willie settled down to get Mackey on strikes, but the final pitch made quite a hit with East, as it was slow enough to permit the runners to negotiate a double steal. Radcliffe might have drawn an error for dropping the ball, only it is doubtful if he would have gotten his man, even if he had held onto the ball. Wilson then hit to Suttles, who tagged first and failed to see Dixon streaking for home with the run that tied up the score.

Foster then walked Lundy, who went to second as Charleston scored when Morney threw wild on Harris' tap. East then worked a squeeze play when Russell bunted toward first and beat it out for a hit while Wilson was scoring.

WEST GOES AHEAD

West got sweet revenge in the next frame when they scored thrice to take the lead, 4 to 3. Wells and Davis doubled to produce a run. Then Suttles caught one of Streeter's pitches squarely on the nose and lifted it into the upper deck of the left field stands for the only homer of the day. The drive scored Radcliffe and put Foster one run to the good.

East went to the front in the first of the fifth on solid smacks and Charleston's second plunk in the side. Wells tossed out Bell to start this frame, but Dixon walked and Charleston was hit in the ribs. Mackey then singled to score Dixon and Charleston registered on Wilson's hit. They would have had another run on a sacrifice fly, had Mackey not left third before the drive was in the hands of Davis. West's half of the fifth failed to produce a tied score because Jim Brown sent Larry Brown all the way home on his three-base drive over Bell's head. Bell went back for the ball and threw to Lundy, whose toss to Mackey caught the runner as he tried to stretch the triple into a home run. The sixth produced no action at all in the first half, but West got busy and put the game on ice.

Wells opened with a single to right center and moved up on Davis' sacrifice. Radcliffe then scored him with a long double to center. This drive removed Streeter from the game and Hunter went in. He was greeted with a single from the bat of Suttles and Radcliffe counted. Morney then singled and Larry followed suit, to count Suttles.

East did not score in the next frame, but West added three more, to make the margin 10 to 5. Willie Foster opened with a hit off Hunter and the showers beckoned him out. Britt came in to pitch and Stearns showed his appreciation by doubling to left center. Wells then flied out to center, but Davis doubled to left center and two runs were home. He scored on Radcliffe's single.

East got no runs in the eighth, but gave the fans a scare. Gibson, who had replaced Mackey behind the plate, and Johnson in for Wilson, both singled to put two on and none out. The next three men, including Fats Jenkins, who batted for Harris, were easy, however, and the runners got no place.

West added their last run to bring the total up to 11 in their half. Bankhead opened with a single, stole second when Gibson's throw went through to center field, and came home as the eastern players played tag with the ball. It was a bit of marvelous base-running on the part of the Nashville player.

The ninth frame was anything but comforting to the western fans, because Morney put on his act of "shim-shim-shimmie" baseball again. Britt opened with a single and, when Morney messed up Bell's grounder and threw wild, both men advanced. Two sacrifice flies sent the men across the platter, but Gibson also flied out, and the game was over.

EAST

	AB.	R.	H.	2b.	3b.	HR.	BB.	PO.	SO.	A.	SB.	E.	HB.
Bell, cf.	5	1	0	0	0	0	0	3	1	1	0	0	0
Dixon, rf.	4	2	1	0	0	0	1	1	0	0	1	0	0
Charleston, 1b.	3	2	0	0	0	0	0	6	0	0	1	0	2
Mackey, c.	3	0	1	0	0	0	0	7	2	0	0	0	0
Gibson, c.	2	0	1	0	0	0	0	1	0	1	0	1	0
Wilson, 3b.	3	1	2	0	0	0	0	1	0	1	0	0	0
Johnson, 3b.	1	0	1	0	0	0	0	0	0	1	0	0	0
Lundy, ss.	3	0	0	0	0	0	1	1	0	6	0	1	0
Harris, lf.	2	0	0	0	0	0	1	0	0	1	0	1	0
Jenkins, lf.	2	0	0	0	0	0	0	1	0	0	0	0	0
Russell, 2b.	3	0	0	0	0	0	0	3	0	2	0	0	0
Streeter, p.	3	0	0	0	0	0	0	0	1	0	0	0	0
Hunter, p.	0	0	0	0	0	0	0	0	0	0	0	0	0
Britt, p.	1	1	1	0	0	0	0	0	0	0	0	0	0
Totals	35	7	7	0	0	0	3	24	4	13	2	3	2

	AB.	R.	H.	2b.	3b.	HR.	BB.	PO.	SO.	A.	SB.	E.	HB.
Stearnes, cf.	5	1	2	1	0	0	0	2	1	0	0	0	0
Wells, ss.	4	2	2	1	0	0	0	4	1	3	0	0	0
Davis, lf.	3	2	2	2	0	0	0	5	0	0	0	0	0
Radcliffe, 3b.	4	1	2	1	0	0	0	0	0	1	0	0	0
Suttles, 1b.	4	2	2	0	0	1	0	8	1	1	0	0	0
Morney, 2b.	4	0	1	0	0	0	0	1	1	2	0	3	0
Bankhead, rf.	4	2	1	0	0	0	0	1	0	0	1	0	0
Brown, c.	4	0	2	0	1	0	0	6	0	0	0	0	0
Foster, p.	4	1	1	0	0	0	0	0	1	2	0	0	0
Totals	36	11	15	5	1	1	0	27	5	9	1	3	0

EAST ....0 0 0 3 2 0 0 0 2—7

WEST ....0 0 1 3 0 3 3 1 *—11

Sacrifices—Dixon, Gibson, Russell. Struck out—By Foster, 4; by Streeter, 4; by Britt, 1. Bases on balls—Off Foster, 3. Double plays—Wells to Morney to Suttles; Bankhead to Radcliffe. Hits—Off Streeter, 7 in 5⅓ innings; off Hunter, 4 in ⅔ inning; off Britt, 4 in 2 innings. Hit by pitcher—By Foster, 2. Losing pitcher—Streeter.

73

Bill Terry Insults Dodgers (1934)

SOURCE: *New York Herald-Tribune*, January 25, 1934

The 1934 National League season, starring Dizzy Dean and his Gashouse Gang, is memorable also for a remark by Giants manager Bill Terry that would come back to haunt him. Although his snide dismissal of the Dodgers was validated by their poor performance throughout most of the season, the Bums and manager Casey Stengel struck back by defeating the Giants in several crucial late-season matches. Terry's comments were said to have inspired the Dodgers to defeat their rivals.

TERRY PREDICTS GIANTS FINISH AMONG FIRST 3

Declares Pirates, Cards and Cubs Are the Teams to Beat; Schumacher Signs

By Rud Rennie

Colonel William Terry, member of the military staff of the Governor of Tennessee and manager of the world champion Giants, breezed into town yesterday to bet a few hats with the writers on the success of the Giants.

"I'll start with the same team that won the pennant," he said, "and we'll finish one-two-three."

"You mean," he was asked, "you are going to start with the team we picked for sixth place last year?"

Terry laughed. "The same team," he said. "Anybody want to get a hat?"

No one wanted to bet a hat.

Terry announced that he had made a working agreement with the Nashville and Evansville clubs.

"Understand," he said, "we have not put up any money into either club. I think it is a good thing to have these two clubs in different classifications where we can send young players for development."

HERE ON OIL BUSINESS

Terry happened to be in the city on business for the oil company by which he is employed in the off-season.

Hal Schumacher, one of the right-handed pitchers who helped pitch the Giants up to the top, also was in the office. He signed his contract. He is the tenth player to sign.

Hal sat silent during the meeting. Only when the boys were discussing Schulte's home run in the world series and Terry said: "I thought that ball was well-hit. What did you think, Hal?" He replied: "I wasn't thinking just then."

"Pittsburgh, St. Louis and Chicago will be the teams we'll have to beat."

"Do you fear the Dodgers?" he was asked.

"I was just wondering," said Terry, "whether they were still in the league."

BELIEVES CUBS STRONGER

Terry thinks the Cubs have been strengthened, and that the Pirates weakened themselves by letting Piet go, and by taking on Red Lucas.

"How about that lively ball, Bill?"

"I think there will be more hitting," he said. "I imagine it will add about fifteen points to my last years' batting average. I think it will help Ott more than any one on our team, because he is a pull hitter.

"You won't see infielders playing in as close as they did last year. The scores will be bigger. The style of play will change in that teams won't start off playing for one run. With our pitching staff last year, we could play for one run and win. This year it will be different."

Terry plans to start Joe Moore in left field and keep him there regardless of right or left-handed pitching. George Davis will be in center and Ott in right, Terry will be on first base, Critz at second, Ryan at short, and Vergez at third. If Jackson, who played third rather snappily in the World Series, can oust Vergez, Jackson will be the third baseman.

Fresco Thompson and George Grantham will be retained as infield reserves. O'Doul will be kept for pinch hitting purposes. "Frank can't field and he can't throw," said Terry, "but he is a handy man with the stick."

Al Smith, a lefthander who was carried as a coach last year, and Johnny Salveson, a righthander, will get a lot of work in the exhibition games; so will Danning and Richards, catchers.

74

Dizzy Predicts Forty Wins for Dean Brothers (1934)

SOURCE: *St. Louis Globe-Democrat*, March 12, 1934

The following article marked the first of many times in the 1934 preseason that Dizzy Dean predicted a large number of victories for himself and younger brother Paul. Unlike Bill Terry, Dizzy would have no reason to regret his outspokenness, as the Deans concluded the season with a combined total of 49 wins.

The article also chronicled the routine of spring training, including the players' off-field activities. The "St. Louis boy" mentioned in the final sentence, Johnny Keane, never made the majors but later managed the Cardinals to a World Series title in 1964.

DEANS TALK TO BREADON AND PAUL SIGNS CONTRACT

Amount of Pay Not Disclosed, but Youngster Had Balked at $3000 Offer—Brothers Promise 40 to 45 Victories

By Martin J. Haley

BRADENTON, FLA., March 11.—Paul (Harpo) Dean signed his 1934 contract with the Cardinals here today. Branch Rickey was out of town, but the Deans sought out Sam Breadon. Dizzy had Paul in tow. They pitched camp in the club president's hotel rooms, and he batted back contract adjectives as quickly as they were pitched. The game progressed for an hour or so before reaching a decision. Both sides declared they were perfectly satisfied.

Salary terms were not disclosed. Paul had been holding out for better than the $3000 proffered. If he got any more, he's not saying. In fact, he doesn't go in much for words. He lets Dizzy pinch-hit for him, and you know Diz.

STRAIGHT MAN TO DIZ

We tried out Harpo, but he wouldn't budge, save to nod his curly head up and down as the straight-haired Diz unwound.

"We're going to win between us forty or forty-five games this year," Dizzy said modestly.

"How many will Paul win?" we managed to break in.

"I don't know," was the comeback, "but I guess he'll win more than me. You know Paul's a great pitcher, got lots of stuff, haven't you, Paul?" (Harpo nodded.)

42 VICTORIES FOR PAIR

Last year Diz won twenty games and lost eighteen for the Cardinals. Paul checked in twenty-two victories and lost seven for Columbus. If they should ring the bell as often with the Birds this year, world series peanuts may be on sale at Sportsmans Park again next October.

Paul, however, must still prove that he can win a job with the Birds. He'll start his training tomorrow alongside of other pitchers also highly rated and trying to hold major league berths.

That's the way Breadon sized it up, even after hearing Dizzy shove in this final phrase: "If we don't win forty or forty-five games between us, we'll give the money back to you, Mr. Breadon. Won't we, Paul?"

Harpo was a bit slow on that nod. Of course, we're pulling for the Dean boys, but returning the money certainly would make a good piece for the paper.

It was a good story to break on a Sunday that made us feel as if we were in Philadelphia before they bounced the Sabbath blue laws. Manager Frisch had planned a seven-inning practice game today, but yesterday's rainstorm carried in a cold spell which spent the night here, liked and [sic] place and lingered.

Thermometers dropped to 50 or lower, steam heat went on and out came the overcoats. 'Twas a bad day for the Florida C. of C.s and Cardinal training. Frisch did sally out to the ballfield, got an earful of the wind blowing hard across the diamond, took a feel of the cold clubhouse and sallied back to the hotel, thinking of his ice skates up at Lake Placid.

DAY OF REST IN ORDER

However, the players probably welcomed the day of rest, if not the cold. They've been laboring hard under a terrific sun, these down-trodden athletes, and a little Florida golf, fishing and sightseeing fit like a glove after the week's wear and tear on the diamond. By the looks of the sun that came back on the job late this afternoon, there's another hard week in store for the boys.

Paul Dean's signing reduces the Cards' holdout squad to Orsatti, Rhem and Watkins. Orsatti, who has been in camp for several days, is said to be weakening, but he didn't betray as much in the dining room today.

Scout Charlie Barrett of the Cardinals drove into town from St. Louis this afternoon, bringing with him a young shortstop, Johnny Keane, a St. Louis boy who belongs to Columbus.

75

Monk Walks Out of Babe Ruth's Past (1935)

SOURCE: *Boston Evening Transcript*, February 28, 1935

After a spectacular fifteen-year career with the New York Yankees, Babe Ruth was placed on waivers prior to the 1935 season. Desperate for a boost on the field and in the stands, the Boston Braves signed him on February 26. Local reporters scrambled to cover Ruth's return to Boston from as many angles as possible, but Evening Transcript *reporter Thomas Shehan scored the greatest scoop by landing the only known print interview with Ruth's mentor at St. Mary's School in Baltimore, Brother Matthias. Brother Matthias had nothing but fond memories of Ruth's boyhood, and expressed disbelief at reports of Ruth's wilder exploits. An interesting detail is Shehan's conclusion that Ruth may even have copied his distinctive walk from Brother Matthias.*

BROTHER MATTHIAS TALKS OF "GEORGE"

The "Boss" Recalls Ruth's Early Days at St. Mary's School in Baltimore

By Thomas Shehan

Danvers, Feb. 28—Baseball's No. 1 artillery piece, Babe Ruth, comes back this evening on his old proving grounds—Boston. Here, where he saw the first flush of the light of greatness that was to be his, he is to spend the twilight of his career in the game.

What could be more appropriate than that he should write finis to the final chapter of his career with the man who gave him his start in the national pastime at his side. Brother Matthias, C.F.X., has been at once the idol, father, counsellor, coach and "big brother" of Ruth. Yet through all these twenty-odd years that Babe has been under the "big tent" the good brother has managed to avoid the publicity that comes with reflected glory.

Brother Matthias, originally an East Boston boy and product of the old Adams School, is spending his final years in the quiet cloisters of a monk's retreat at St. John's Prep in Danvers just twenty miles down the pike. In his late sixties, Brother Matthias still has the remarkable framework of a real athlete. It's only two years ago that he stopped playing ball, and confined his exercises to good long walks and the chores that are his part of a holy monk's life.

He's the "Boss" to the Babe and even now he has the bearing of a kindly martinet. Broad shouldered, with a shuttling gait that makes one realize where the "Sultan of Swat" got his peculiar stride, he still is a fine looking man. Well over six feet in height and with the broad shoulders and frame of an athlete he is a pleasant faced old gentleman with steel gray hair receding just a bit at the temples into a "widow's peak." When he talks in his modulated throaty voice he invokes a warm feeling of friendliness in return. His favorite subject is "George."

"I'm glad he's coming back to Boston. The fans here like him and he'll awaken new interest in the Braves. There never was a better boy at St. Mary's School in Baltimore than 'George.' I was stationed there thirty-eight years and there were better ball players, but never a better boy. Why, he was so loyal, always thinking of the school, the Xaverian brothers and the boys that went to school with him. I can't believe some of this talk I have heard about him. He couldn't do a mean thing if he had to. He was above all that. And did he like the young kiddoes. They idolized him when he was just a boy himself. He seems to have some magic touch with them.

WITH "RED SOX" AT SCHOOL

"He came under me when he was eight years old and played ball for me until he signed with the Baltimore team. We used to have a league of teams named after the big leagues out there. Funny thing, Babe played with the 'Red Sox' in that league. Afterward, when he played with the real Red Sox he used to remark to me about playing on the school 'Red Sox' without dreaming that he was going to sign with the real team.

"Brother Paul, now stationed in the Mother House, Bruges, Belgium, was in charge of St. Mary's while Babe was there. Many of the things that have been written about Babe are just myths. He never ran away from the school. He loved the place and for years after, always came back and visited. He never forgot what the school did for him.

"Once the school needed money for something or other and Babe made arrangements for the fifty-piece school band to travel the circuit. Why we came back with $20,000, all donated by fans who took an interest in the Babe's alma mater.

"He gave me an $8000 Cadillac car to ride around in when I was at Baltimore. In addition he took me to the World Series every year but last year since he has been in the majors. Oh, he's a generous boy. I used to speak to him about giving so much to the hangers-on and he would say, 'Brother, you don't know what it is to be down and out. God has been good to me.'

"He never forgets and he's always the same. The time he made his sixtieth home run, he called me up that night and shouted over the phone, 'I got my sixtieth today, Brother,' just as proud and as happy as when he was a kiddo at the school.

A "PIED PIPER" OF BASEBALL

"I think that eventually George will be the game's chief ambassador. It is my opinion that he could sell the game back to the youth of today better than any other individual in the world. Despite the fact that he is the game's greatest, the boys and girls don't feel awe stricken when with him. He warms them up with his smile and they would move the world for him.

"On a trip around the world instructing boys and girls everywhere in the fine points, he would be the 'Pied Piper' of baseball, and the youngsters would flock to him. He's the right man for that job, for while the baseball writers say they never saw him pull a 'boner' since he has been in the majors, I never saw him make a mistake as a kid. The first time he went after a ball he fielded it like a 'leaguer' and that was when he was eight years old.

"Ruth was never a trouble maker. He could take a jest with anyone. He did have the 'fight' in him, however, and were he convinced that somebody wasn't straight with him he would take pretty good care of them. He could handle his fists pretty well too.

"There's a funny story connected with how I happened to make a pitcher out of him. He always used to catch and one day he was standing on the side lines during a game among the younger boys. One of the lads was trying to pitch and only succeeding in making himself ridiculous. George thought it very funny and laughed and laughed. Just to show him up a little bit I ordered him to go in and pitch. He mowed everything down and I concentrated on his pitching from that day on. Yes, yes, I think he'll do well in Boston and wish him every luck for me."

With that the good brother was gone for the Chapel bell was ringing.

76

Baseball Hall of Fame Planned (1935)

SOURCE: *New York Herald-Tribune*, August 16, 1935

As America and baseball struggled to escape from the Depression, entrepreneurs from one small village in upstate New York worked to help both. Acting on the dubious conclusions of a special commission in 1908, which declared that the inventor of baseball was Cooperstown resident Abner Doubleday, village leaders announced plans to build a National Baseball Museum. One of the featured attractions of the museum was to be a hall of fame, which would forever commemorate the accomplishments of the game's greatest performers.

BASEBALL VOTES TO PICK 10 FOR "HALL OF FAME"

5 Oldtimers, 5 Modern Stars Will Be Honored in Cooperstown "Shrine"

By the Associated Press

An all-star "Big Ten," consisting of a galaxy of five major league stars from the nineteenth century and as many more from modern times, will form the foundation for an official baseball Hall of Fame in the National Baseball Museum, now located at Cooperstown, N.Y., the game's birthplace.

The National and American Leagues jointly will sponsor the plan to commemorate the game's greatest playing figures in co-operation with Cooperstown, which already has established a sporting shrine on the spot where Major General Abner Doubleday introduced baseball in 1839.

Details were discussed and a general program agreed upon yesterday at a conference of baseball men with Arthur [Alexander] Cleland, representing Cooperstown, at the offices of Ford C. Frick, president of the National League.

BASEBALL WRITERS TO DECIDE

Development of the Hall of Fame will be a preliminary to the elaborate program planned in observance of baseball's centennial at Cooperstown in 1939. Its exclusive membership will be determined by a nation-wide vote among sports writers and editors, with final decisions resting with the Baseball Writers' Association of America.

The Hall of Fame will be limited temporarily to ten players. Others among the game's stars will be picked from year to year. It will be determined later whether the tribute to the most famous players will take the form of plaques, photographs or statues.

Selection of the first ten all-stars promises to develop brisk argument. Legendary are many of the feats of the game's earlier heroes and the record books are embellished by the achievements of such renowned figures as A. G. Spalding, ace hurler of the 1870s, and Charles (Old Hoss) Radbourne, who pitched Providence to a National League pennant in 1884 by pitching twenty-seven consecutive games, winning twenty-six of them; Adrian C. (Pop) Anson, captain, first baseman and hitting champion of the old Chicago White Stockings; Denton (Cy) Young, whose pitching exploits extended from the gay nineties well in the new century; George Wright, shortstop and all-around ace of the Boston Nationals in the game's earliest big league days; Charlie Bennett, king-pin of the old-time backstops; as well as Mike Kelley, Ed Delehanty, Roger Connor, Buck Ewing, Hugh Duffy, Dan Brouthers and Willie Keeler.

FIVE GREATEST HARD TO NAME

Picking the outstanding five since 1900 may prove no easier. It would be difficult to leave off Christy Mathewson, Ty Cobb, Babe Ruth, Honus Wagner or Walter Johnson in determining the list, but the names of other favorites are certain to figure prominently in any national balloting. To mention just a few there are Tris Speaker, Eddie Collins, Ed Walsh, Nap Lajoie, Mordecai Brown, Grover Alexander, Hal Chase, George Sisler and Bob Grove.

77

Satchel Paige Pitches Bismarck to Semipro Title (1935)

SOURCE: *Wichita Eagle,* August 28, 1935

Semipro baseball, a longtime baseball institution, found its largest audience during the Depression, as young men were motivated to play for a few dollars and fans were happy to attend games with small or nonexistent admission charges. Two national semipro tournaments were organized in the 1930s. Perhaps the best known of the two, the Denver Post tournament, was held in late July. Another tournament, the National Baseball Congress, debuted in the city of Wichita, Kansas, in mid-August 1931. Both tournaments attracted the best semipro teams in the country, which paid handsomely to lure former major and minor leaguers and Negro Leaguers to their clubs. As a result these tournaments featured the most prominent integrated clubs in the nation and provided a national showcase for the best black players.

Satchel Paige was well known even to white fans in the mid-1930s. He participated in and dominated the Denver Post tournament in 1934, and with the help of fellow Negro League pitcher Chet Brewer and center fielder Quincy Trouppe led the Bismarck, North Dakota, team to the title in Wichita, beating a number of other black and integrated clubs as well as all-white clubs. In thirty-nine innings Paige struck out sixty-six men and allowed only twenty-nine hits.

SATCHEL HITS AND PITCHES TEAM TO NATIONAL HONORS

Great Negro Hurler Has Another Fine Night as
North Dakota Club Is Winner
SCORE IS 5 TO 2

North Dakota can today claim the country's semi-pro baseball
championship. Bismarck, capital of the state, can build a monument to
Leroy "Satchel" Paige, elongated, skinny, gangling and gawky pride of the
colored race.

It was Satchel whose marvelous pitching kept the battling Duncan Cementers at
bay until his mates had earned a lead in the traditional lucky seventh. And it was
Satchel himself in person who delivered the blow which brought an end to Duncan's last lingering hopes, a ringing, well hit single over second which brought in
two mates and gave the great hurler a three run lead to last the next two innings.
Bismarck won out 5 to 2.

If there were any doubts existing in the minds of the 9,000 fans who watched
the game and the thousands who got it off the air about the pitching ability of one
Satchel Paige, these doubts can be put to rest once and forever. For Satchel last
night faced as strong a ball club as was ever organized in independent ranks, a club
which played inspiring ball until late in the game when the Bismarck lead was too
great to be shaken.

SEVENTH IS FATAL

Duncan must be given due credit for its game fight. It battled Satchel and
company even up for six long innings. It looked like the better ball club for those
six innings. But its veteran southpaw, Lefty Johns who had hurled clever, brainy
ball for those six innings skidded in the seventh, was hit hard and before John Paul
Jones could submarine ball the Bismarcks out, the game was gone.

Duncan played almost errorless ball and Bismarck made but one mistake, for an
exhibition that was really of major league class. Each team got nine hits and made
one error. Satchel, however, fanned 14 men and thereby had the big advantage.

Satchel put on a final show for the fans in the ninth when Duncan put on a final
futile effort to gain one run and put two more on the sacks. Hits by Brown and
Coleman got two on and then Lowry scored Brown with a single to center.

Another long hit and the score might be tied. But then Satchel became Satchel.
Adair, a pinch hitter, came up first and was mowed down, and then the slugging
Lowell fanned to end it.

Bismarck won the toss and was the home club as a result. Satchel Paige tossed
a ball for Lowell on the first pitch. Working the count 2 and 2 Lowell singled
sharply to left. Holley popped to Desiderato. Hassler fanned on three pitches. Jones
punched a long fly to right which Smith could barely reach at the fence and it went
for a triple, scoring Lowell. Gulledge rolled out to first, Satchel making the putout.

Bismarck tied the score in the last of the same inning when with two out Trouppe doubled to the scoreboard reaching third but being called back on ground rules. He counted on Smith's single to center.

Bismarck had a chance in the third when Lowell singled and was bunted to second but Hassler fanned and Jones followed suit. Brown reached second in the fourth on a single and steal but he was out stealing third to waste a chance.

Bismarck did not get a man to second after the first for several innings. Haley singled in the fourth but there were two out and he soon expired on first.

Holley reached first on Haley's error in the sixth but again Hassler fanned. Jones also fanned. Gulledge singled to center but Brown hoisted a high one to Oberholzer for the third out.

Oberholzer beat out a hit over second in the sixth. Leary bunted him to second. The hard-hitting Trouppe, however, hoisted to left and Lowell made a fine running catch of a foul by Smith to pull Johns out of trouble.

HOW SATCHEL WON

Haley started the lucky seventh with a sharp single to center. Radcliff sacrificed, Holley making a fine jumping catch to get the out at first. Hancock walked. Desiderato drove a long drive to right which Lowry jumped up and knocked down off the boards but could not make the catch. Haley hesitated about running and when the ball fell to the ground he rounded third and dashed for the plate. A good relay would probably have nailed him but the throw was wide and Haley scored easily, Desiderato going to second and Hancock to third on the throw home. Long John Paul Jones relieved Johns at this point. Satchel Paige slapped a single over Jones' head and two runs came in. Paige was run down, but he had done the damage to the Duncan cause. Oberholzer grounded out to end the inning. . . .

DUNCAN, OKLA.	AB	R	H	O	A	BISMARCK, N.D.	AB	R	H	O	A
Lowell 1b	4	1	3	11	0	Ob'rh'z'r 2b	4	0	1	2	2
Holley 2b	3	0	0	4	2	Leary ss	3	0	1	2	0
Hassler ss	4	0	0	0	1	Troupe cf	4	1	1	0	0
S Jones cf	4	0	1	3	0	Smith rf	4	1	2	0	0
G'ledge 3b	4	0	1	0	2	Haley 1b	4	1	3	6	1
Brown lf	3	1	2	1	0	Radcliff c	3	0	0	13	3
Lowery rf	4	0	1	1	0	Hancock lf	2	1	0	1	0
Colem'n c	4	0	1	3	1	D's'r'to 3b	3	1	1	2	0
Johns p	2	0	0	0	1	Paige p	3	0	1	1	0
J P Jones p	0	0	0	0	1						
x—Adair	1	0	0	0	0						
Totals	33	2	9	24	8	Totals	30	5	9	27	6

x—Adair hit for Jones in 9th.

Score by innings:

										R	H	E
Duncan, Okla. 1	0	0	0	0	0	0	0	1—2		9	1
Bismarck, N.D. 1	0	0	0	0	0	3	1	x—5		9	1

SUMMARY: Two base hits—Troupe. Three base hit—S. Jones. Stolen base—Brown. Runs batted in—S. Jones, Smith, Paige 2, Coleman. Sacrifices—Holley, Leary, Radcliff. Left on bases—Duncan 5, Bismarck 5. Bases on balls—off: Paige 1, Johns 1. Struck out, by—Paige 14, Johns 1, Jones 1. Runs and hits—off: Johns in 7⅓ innings 4 and 6. Passed balls—Coleman. Winning pitcher—Paige. Losing pitcher—Johns. Umpires—Fair, Reynolds, Bloomer and Wilbeck.

78

Profile of a Young Umpire (1935)

SOURCE: *The Sporting News*, August 29, 1935

Umpires have always been baseball's anonymous men. Usually their names come to public attention only after making a mistake. On occasion, however, hard work and competence earns umpires some positive recognition. The following piece, a respectful profile of National League umpire John "Ziggy" Sears (1934–45), is an example of the latter. Author Fred Lieb was one of the best-known and most prolific baseball reporters in the business. This article appeared in the same year as one of the first books written by an umpire, Harry "Steamboat" Johnson's Standing the Gaff: The Life and Hard Times of a Minor League Umpire *(1935; rpt., Lincoln: University of Nebraska Press, 1994).*

FIRED AS "WASHED-UP" PLAYER IN MINORS, ZIGGY SEARS BECOMES ALL-STAR UMPIRE HIS FIRST YEAR IN MAJORS

Given Nickname by Veteran Jake Atz When He Joined Fort Worth Club; Let Out as Performer, Became Arbiter Next Day in Texas League
By Frederick G. Lieb

When an umpire made the World's Series after he had been four or five years in the league, it used to be considered quite a feather in his cap. Other older umpires shook their heads and solemnly remarked: "Well, maybe John Heydler is right, but it looks as though he is moving this young fellow along a little too fast. These kids are likely to get all puffed up if you make them too important. Still Joe Glutz is a pretty good young umpire; maybe he'll be lucky, not have any tough ones and get away with it."

What arching of eye-brows there must have been among the big league umps last month when they read the names of the arbiters who were assigned to the All-Star game in Cleveland on July 8. George Magerkurth and John (Ziggy) Sears for the National League and Harry Geisel and Emmett Ormsby for the American were the choices of Presidents Frick and Harridge.

"But this guy, Sears, hasn't been in the league a year," must have been the amazed comment of brother umpires.

Sure, that's right! This Ford Frick is a pretty young fellow himself, holding down the presidency of the National League at the age of 40. He believes youth should be served. It didn't take him five years to make up his mind that Ziggy is a good umpire, one who could be depended upon to maintain the interests of the 60-year old National League. So Ziggy got the call.

Of course, when an older umpire speaks of a newcomer as "a kid," or a man "still wet behind the ears," it hasn't exactly the same meaning as when applied to a kid ball player. A kid umpire is much in the same boat as a kid United States Senator. A chap who has spent a busy career as a ball player in the minors, one who has seen a generation of players come and go, still is referred to as a novice umpire until big league fans, players and writers get accustomed to seeing his name in the box score.

John A. Heydler did not exactly rob the cradle when he picked Ziggy out of the Texas League and put him to work in the National on July 22, 1934, as one of his last important official acts as league executive. Incidentally, none other than the late Hank O'Day, former National League scout of umpires, turned in a favorable report on Ziggy. Sears is 40 years old and has been around. Born in Central City, Kentucky, on January 10, 1895, he now is a Texan. He made his home in Fort Worth after a long and meritorious career as a Fort Worth Wildcat. . . .

Sears was a rough and tumble, knockdown ball player, who became an umpire, when, in 1929, the fact was brought home to him that he no longer had any value as a ball player. He received an unexpected release. It hurt like blazes when it came, yet it opened for Sears his biggest career in baseball. Like every other minor league player, he was ambitious to play in the big leagues. He fought hard whenever he played, and he knew there was a top above such leagues with which he had played, the Kitty, the Southern, the Texas, the Central Association. But, like a mirage in a desert, it always was a jump ahead. He never quite caught up with it. . . .

In 1918, Charlie Barrett, the St. Louis Cardinals' scout, but at the time scouting for the Tigers, placed him with the Fort Worth club, where he acquired his nickname of Ziggy and his greatest fame as a minor league player. And it was in Texas that eventually he turned umpire and started up the road which led to the magic major league fields and the All-Star game in his first year as a big leaguer.

But, we'll let Ziggy tell that part of it. "I was fired as a player one day and hired as a Texas League umpire the next," Sears relates. "Being let out was a stiff blow. I knew I was slipping, as I was being shifted from team to team. Perhaps I had about two years of minor league ball left. But that broken leg of 1916 had slowed me up before my time and perhaps prevented me from getting a real major league trial. During the off-season I had devoted a lot of time to officiating at football and basket ball games. I had the reputation of being one of the best men on basket ball in the Southwest. So the thought came. Why not try umpiring? And so I went to my good friend, Doak Roberts, who was president of the Texas League and since has passed on. I told him I wanted to be an umpire. He said: 'You can have a job whenever you are ready to start.' I replied I was ready then, so I started the 1929 season with him as one of his umpires. I didn't like the new job at first. It was like being in a different world, but all the players were my friends and that made it easier. Honestly, some of those tough birds that I had fought in the Texas League were pulling for me to make good. Ball players, of course, always will complain of decisions. I know, for I was a pretty good umpire-baiter myself, but I found early that if an umpire is on the job and on top of the play, no serious trouble can develop. So, I've made it a point ever since to be there when things happen."

"BILL BRANDT OF UMPIRES," WEIGHS OVER 200 POUNDS

That's Ziggy! Like Dolly Stark, another disappointed minor league player who reached the big leagues by perfecting himself as an umpire, Sears believes in being on top of things. He is hefty and stocky, weighs a bit over 200 pounds, and they call him "the Bill Brandt of the Umpires," but he still can move fast. He moves down to second with the runner and if he doesn't beat him to the bag he isn't far behind. In another period of the game, it used to be a habit of ball players to challenge new umpires to meet them under the grandstand. That handsome young fellow from Cornell, Billy Evans, had to prove his right to stay in the American League with his fists on more than one occasion. Were this practice still in vogue today, it is likely that the boys would stop, look and listen before sending Ziggy any challenges. He can take it and he can give it.

79

Olympic Baseball Trials Open in Baltimore (1936)

SOURCE: *Baltimore Sun*, July 1, 1936

Although baseball did not become an official medal sport in the Olympic Games until 1984, several exhibition games were staged in Berlin as a part of the 1936 Olympics. The following article describes the first stage of tryouts. None of the twelve Olympic candidates played in the major leagues.

TRIALS TO OPEN IN BASEBALL

Pick of Country To Be Banded Together For Exhibitions At Olympics

Amateur baseball stars from all sections of the country are invading Baltimore for the final tests for the teams which will invade Berlin to give exhibitions during the Olympic Games.

The Amateur Baseball Congress, with Les Mann, ex-big leaguer, as the leader, for several months has been holding eliminations throughout the country. Each section of the nation has selected the cream of its amateur tossers, and at an early hour last night fourteen ambitious youngsters had reported to Executive Vice-President Mann.

Included in the group already registered are:

Tom Downey, University of Southern California.

Ralph Hanna, Stanford.

Clarence Keegan, University of Maine.

Henry Goldberg, Brooklyn College.

Edwin Mumma, Sharpsburg, Md.

Bert Herringer, Stanford.

Vincent Fite, University of California.

Eldred Britson, Wren, Iowa.

Paul Amen, University of Nebraska.

Herb Shaw, Bowdoin College.

Don Hibbard, Western State Teachers.

Dow Wilson, Dow City, Iowa.

Leo McNeece, Fort Lauderdale, Fla.

The Penn A.C., of Philadelphia, has been granted extra days before sending a squad of twelve here. This group is working as a unit and will play an exhibition game with the Philadelphia American League club as a means of raising funds to aid the Olympic fund.

FIRST TEST SATURDAY

Commissioner Mann announced last night that the boys will be allowed informal practice at Gibbons Field, Irvington, until Thursday or Friday. Then a team will be selected and given its first test as a unit against the Pimlico All-Stars at the Pimlico field on Saturday.

Mann also said that all positions were still open and local talent stands a good chance of earning places.

After 12 days of tryouts and training here, two teams will be named to sail with the American Olympic party July 15.

PRACTICE GAMES SLATED

Practice games have been arranged with the United States Marines, at Griffith Stadium, next Tuesday, and with the Baltimore Police nine at Bugle Field next Wednesday.

Jackson Hyames, director of athletics at Western State Teachers' college and head coach, arrived here early last night. He also is a member of the final selection and training committee, members of which include Harry Walter, director of baseball at Stanford; Linn Wells, Bowdoin College baseball coach, and George Laing, Penn A.C.

80

Radio Broadcaster Contest (1936)

SOURCE: *The Sporting News*, August 27, 1936

Even during the Depression the majority of Americans owned radios, on which they enjoyed free broadcasts of the concerts, plays and ballgames they could not afford to attend. The Sporting News recognized the significance of radio by instituting a regular column on radio, "On the Air." Starting in 1933 it sponsored an annual contest in which readers were asked to name their favorite broadcaster and answer two questions: "Do you prefer radio accounts to attending games in person?" and "Do you think broadcasts tend to lessen attendance at games?" Answers to these questions were sought eagerly not only by The Sporting News *editors but by major league executives, who were only beginning to understand the effects of radio coverage. Some clubs restricted the number of broadcasts, or limited them to road games, while farsighted executives like Cincinnati's Larry MacPhail believed that full radio coverage could only benefit baseball.*

The results of this poll were noted briefly in the November 12 issue, in the caption to the photograph of the two winners. MacPhail's radio announcer, Red Barber, did not win.

VOTE FOR YOUR FAVORITE BROADCASTER IN MAJORS OR MINORS; WIN CASH PRIZES

Radio broadcasts of baseball games now blanket the country until there is scarcely a city with a station in any part of the United States which does not devote some time to the game. In many instances, the stations give accounts of both major league contests and the games played by their local minor league club and many cities without representation in Organized Ball receive play-by-play descriptions. As a result, announcers reach out far beyond their normal territory and their names and voices are as familiar at the cross-roads as they are in the metropolitan centers.

Four years ago, THE SPORTING NEWS conducted a contest to ascertain which of these announcers had the greatest following and what type of announcing was the most popular. The result of the balloting was illuminating and showed not only interesting, but definite trends on the part of listeners' preferences.

With the triple purpose of finding out whom the fans like best among the announcers, what type of broadcasts they favor and to obtain their reactions regarding threatened curbs on the airing of games, THE SPORTING NEWS this week is initiating another combination ballot-letter contest to ascertain certain facts of radio coverage that should prove of interest to the game's and radio's officials, as well as the fans themselves.

Each week, beginning with this issue and continuing until that of October 1, THE SPORTING NEWS will print a ballot which its readers are asked to fill out and mail to the Radio Editor, giving the name of their favorite announcer, his station, their names and addresses and a statement as to whether they favor the continuation of the broadcasts and whether the broadcasting tends to prevent them from attending the games in person.

As an added incentive to participation in this poll and to make it interesting for our readers, the publishers of THE SPORTING NEWS are offering cash prizes for entries in the contest accompanying the balloting. Entrants are asked to write a letter of not more than 300 words on whether they believe the broadcasts should be continued, what changes, if any, they would have made in them and what type of announcing they prefer, straight reporting of the games or dramatic portrayals.

Prizes totaling $65 will be distributed as follows: $25 for the best letter submitted; $15, second; $10, third, and three $5 prizes to the next three best. The editor of this paper shall be considered the final arbiter as to the eligibility of all entries and the decision of the judges shall be final. Awards will be based on neatness, soundness of reasons given and originality of the ideas presented. The contest is open to everyone, except employes of THE SPORTING NEWS and their families. Letters must be written on only one side of the paper and should be addressed to the Radio Editor, THE SPORTING NEWS, Tenth and Olive streets, St. Louis, Mo., fully prepaid. None will be returned.

The last ballot will be printed in the October 1 issue and both the contest and the balloting will close October 4, after which no letters will be eligible or votes counted. Ballots and letters may be sent separately and it is not necessary that voters enter the contest, if they do not care to do so. Names and addresses of senders, however, must be plainly affixed to both. As many letters or ballots may be sent as desired, but only one prize will be awarded to any one contestant.

In addition to learning what announcers are preferred by the majority of fans, it is hoped to gain their reactions to broadcasting as a whole. There is a considerable difference of opinion among the club owners and league officials as to the desirability of continuing the present widespread privilege of airing the games, so much so, that serious consideration will be given during this winter's meetings to placing a decided curb on them. How drastic this action will be is not certain at the present time. Probably, it will depend upon the protest of the fans themselves and they are hereby afforded an opportunity to register their demands in this poll.

The fans are given a chance to state whether they believe the present plan of broadcasting should be continued and they can by the force of their arguments and reasons given prove to the club owners that it is to their interest to put no bars in the path of the announcers. Radio station owners, undoubtedly, are interested, too, in the reaction of the fans to the broadcasts and the announcers. There are several types of air reporters; some of them confine themselves to a matter-of-fact account of the games; others attempt to dramatize the situation and put color into their reporting. Some give numerous details concerning the players; others have pre-game interviews and accounts from the field; some furnish no sidelights; a number lean strongly to advertising announcements. What do the fans expect and want when they tune in? They can give their suggestions in the letters they are asked to write.

Two awards will be made to announcers: One to the broadcaster in the major league city getting the largest number of votes, and another to the microphone man outside of the 11 big league cities gaining the largest support. A handsome plaque will be each winner's token of his popularity. Two awards are made in fairness to the broadcaster who is handicapped by the limited confines of his territory and the smaller range of his station.

To win either award should be a pleasing distinction for any announcer and his listeners can help him achieve this honor by casting their ballots. This is your chance to crown your favorite announcer as the outstanding broadcaster of the year and also air your views on radio reporting and the place it should have in the game. Cast your ballots early and write your letter giving your views in your own language. VOTE.

81

The Business of Promoting Baseball (1937)

SOURCE: *American Mercury* 41 (May 1937)

During the Depression all businesses scrambled for scarce consumer dollars. Baseball responded by scheduling night games, an innovation embraced far more enthusiastically by the minor leagues than by the majors, and by broadcasting games on the radio. All organized baseball clubs, however, recognized the wisdom of hiring "press agents" and "publicity directors" to curry favor with sportswriters and bolster attendance. The following article sarcastically described some of the methods employed by teams to achieve these goals. It also contrasted the attitude of two major league managers, Rogers Hornsby and Bill Terry, toward the press.

BASEBALL AND BALLYHOO
By Gerald Holland

The job of major league press agent was invented a few years ago by a St. Louis reporter named Gene Karst, later publicity director for the Cincinnati Reds. At the time, the Cardinals were beginning to add "farms" in the minor leagues and it was Mr. Karst's idea that complete records of ball players throughout the circuit should be kept on file at St. Louis headquarters for the convenience of sports writers. To clinch his job, he suggested that stories about the Cardinals be mailed to newspapers of nearby Missouri and Illinois towns. The idea, after considerable reception-room waiting, was accepted by Branch Rickey, vice president of the Cardinals, and Mr. Karst was given a desk. The publicity project began to enlarge, until at present the dwindling number of old-time baseball men regard the whole business of ballyhoo as a Frankenstein that will some day throttle the game itself to the din of a thousand fife-and-drum corps.

Yet the ballyhoo idea seems to be taking an unbreakable hold. After Mr. Karst first got his Vision, he himself was hired away from the Cardinals to work under the ablest of the baseball showmen, Lawrence McPhail at Cincinnati. The St. Louis Browns long ago bought a mimeograph machine and established a free beer depot for writers and radio announcers, yet since the sale of the club last Fall, they now not only retain a publicity man but a theatrical exploitation agency and a ticket-selling expert. The Pittsburgh Pirates pay a press representative. The Chicago Cubs have added a promotion department, publish a miniature newspaper for fans, and pay for radio time to re-enact each day's game after supper. The Cardinals, deprived of their Mr. Karst, have hired four men to replace him.

Ford Frick, youthful president of the National League, has advised every club to add what is technically known as an Information Department. He has indorsed night baseball and Summer suits for umpires; he has forbidden rival players to fraternize on the field lest spectators suspect that they do not hate each other adequately; he was quoted as saying of a postgame fist fight between Leon [sic] Durocher of the Cardinals and Casey Stengel of Brooklyn: "Good! I'd like to see more of that!" Mr. Frick, however, is not in sympathy with out-and-out circus methods; he believes that honest baseball will do the trick. . . .

The Cardinals preserve considerable dignity in their major league promotion stunts, but are receptive to any stunt in their minor league branches. For instance, at the Huntington, West Virginia, camp of the organization, the services of Miss Sally Rand and her fan were enlisted to boost ticket sales. The ballyhooers had Miss Rand photographed from a variety of angles while autographing a baseball, later presented to Huntington's "loudest rooter." The club also reported to St. Louis that considerable publicity had been obtained through a talented young frankfurter salesman called "Salty Dogs." . . .

John McGraw might have considered that irrelevant. In any case, the Cardinal farm at Hutchinson, Kansas, had conspicuous success with "Blue Shirt Night" on which all so attired were admitted for a reduced price. Hutchinson also produced "Family Night," when fathers, no matter how prolific, might bring the whole family for a flat charge of forty cents. There has been a "Beauty Contest Night," "Free Automobile Night," "Mayor's Day," "Hotel Day," "Ladies' Day," and every other manner of day and night at various points on the Cardinal map.

All these new ideas were reported to St. Louis and published in the *St. Louis Cardinals' Publicity and Promotion Bulletin*, a house organ. Readers of the *Bulletin* were reminded, however, that the mere fact that a stunt was given space did not necessarily indicate approval by the home office. . . .

In St. Louis, the Cardinals' most successful promotion scheme consists in designating "Town Days". For instance, there might be a Nokomis, Illinois, Day on which, if Nokomis fans saw fit to buy at least 100 tickets in a bunch, their mayor would be suffered to throw out the first ball, shake various illustrious hands, and see his hometown band shuffle around the infield where shortly the heroes of the Cardinals would perform.

The Cards' routine publicity efforts call for regular dispatches to the country editors (who are supplied with passes on demand), railroad and bus line handbills, hotel lobby cards, radio programs (time free to the club), and distribution of the *Cardinal News*, a four-page collection of chit-chat and Did-You-Know-That-Rip-Collins-Is-Building-A-Fence-Around-His-House-With-Broken-Bats items.

In the field of good will, there are countless luncheons and church suppers always clamoring for personal appearances by the Cardinal stars and it is the duty of the publicity department to see that each player does his share of these chores. Mr. Rickey and the club president, Sam Breadon, are insistent about this detail and it is not unusual for a ball player to be routed out at dawn of a Sunday morning for breakfast with the Holy Name Society. But Mr. Rickey asks no more of his players than he is willing to do himself. A tireless worker, he is never too weary to make a speech and is particularly adept at delivering pep talks liberally sprinkled with spotless anecdotes and adroit references to "the Great Scorer." He can reduce Rotarians, Optimists, and Lions Clubs to tears in four minutes by the clock, attaining himself an advanced state of nervous prostration at the same time. . . .

No team in either league enjoys better press relations than the St. Louis Browns, even if the attendance figures do prove that the most enthusiastic publicity will not make a tail-end club pull money at the gate. The reason for the Browns' fine press is Rogers Hornsby, a veritable Edward L. Bernays at the business. Mr. Hornsby is universally liked by reporters because he does not evade their questions. If a query calls for a direct answer, the articulate Rogers will deliver the order. It may strike the layman as strange that this straightforwardness should be so rare in a baseball man who usually has nothing more important to conceal than the progress of a carbuncle on his star pitcher's posterior. Yet it is a fact that among countless managers and club officials, a great secrecy is made to shroud the slightest news. . . .

As a sample contrast to the Hornsby type, there is Bill Terry, hard-working and consciencious manager of the New York Giants, who apparently cannot open his mouth without thrusting a No. 11 into it. Terry's managerial career has been one long succession of unfortunate utterances, but it was an early out-of-hand remark about "$35-a-week sports writers" that got him the gong for keeps. Since then, he has been quoted with scrupulous accuracy and that, considering Mr. Terry's failing, is an awful revenge. His classic inquiry, "Is Brooklyn still in the league?" made him the foremost candidate for lynching in Flatbush and more than satisfied the outraged honor of the press. Later on, Bill made reluctant advances to the newspaper boys, but the atmosphere at his cocktail parties was as cool as the shakers.

All this aside, it will remain true that the money-making teams will always be those which win more often than they lose. But the new concern of baseball for press and public is acknowledged generally as a wholesome symptom. Baseball writers themselves have received most of the innovations cordially, although they regard some forms of the new promotion with wry faces. For one thing, they resent any corruption of the game itself; for another, they are dead set against handouts, preferring to get their facts direct from the heroes.

Thus, the press agents in baseball are appreciated mainly by the country editors who formerly were treated like poor relations, but now are frequently amazed to find themselves violently shaken by the hand, alloted a bottle of three per cent beer, and, in isolated cases, ushered into the presence of a third-string utility outfielder or some comparable celebrity.

Whatever the worth of it all, baseball is currently enjoying excellent business in major and minor leagues. In fact, it appears that the problem may some day be not the lack of patronage but the lack of enough young men with a talent for actually playing the game.

82

Dizzy Dean Breaks Toe in All-Star Game (1937)

SOURCE: *Washington Post*, July 8, 1937

Between 1932 and 1936 Dizzy Dean dominated batters like few other pitchers have, winning 120 games and leading the St. Louis Cardinals to the world championship in 1934. However, during spring training in 1937 rumors spread that Dean's fast ball was gone. Still, Dean won his first five decisions and was chosen to start the 1937 All-Star Game in Washington DC. During the third inning Dean, behind 2–0 on a titanic Lou Gehrig home run, was further victimized when Cleveland Indians outfielder Earl Averill slammed a line drive into Dizzy's left big toe. Insisting on pitching before the toe had fully healed, Dean was forced to adjust his natural motion, which either caused arm damage or accelerated the decline of his speed caused by years of overwork. Shirley Povich, one of the most celebrated sportswriters of the century, did not mention Dean's injury in his article.

AMERICANS WIN BATTLE OF STARS, 8–3

Gehrig's Homer Starts Carnage as Yankees Dominate Game
Gomez, Harder in Form; Medwick Gets 4 for 5; 32,000 Attend
By Shirley Povich

A neat packing job by Manager Joe McCarthy with President Franklin D. Roosevelt looking on—perhaps wistfully—upheld the validity of the American League's claims to big league supremacy yesterday in fan-filled Griffith Stadium.

Downtown, at the Capitol, the United States Senate was still wrangling over his Supreme Court bill, but from his banner-bedecked box at the ball park, Mr. Roosevelt watched a wily baseball manager steal his own thunder.

McCarthy packed the American League All-Star lineup with five of his own New York Yankees, thus gaining a 5-to-4 majority, and with their bats they pounded out a thoroughly constitutional decision against the National League All-Stars.

By the score of 8 to 3, the American League won the fifth annual All-Star game—its fourth success in the classic—but it was a New York Yankee team, disguised as the American League All-Stars, which beat the National Leaguers.

It was the five Yankees in the American League lineup who commanded the cheers of the 32,000 cash customers who blotted out every seat in Griffith Stadium and crammed the aisles as Washington staged its greatest baseball show in history—All Stars on parade.

The pomp and ceremony of the pre-game program had hardly ceased when the five Yankees, whose slugging has been wrecking the American League, began to pump the ball for extra base hits. Dizzy Dean, Carl Hubbell, Van Mungo—the National League's pitching pride—were as chaff before that Yankee onslaught.

Seven of those eight runs the American Leaguers scored were produced by the Yankee bats of Lou Gehrig, Joe DiMaggio, Red Rolfe and Bill Dickey. Seven of the American League hits were registered by those same Yankees. And of that fifth Yankee—Lefty Gomez—that deserves another paragraph.

Lean, lanky Gomez, whose frail physique belies the power in his pitching arm, did not partake of the Yankees' slugging, but he was out there for the first three innings pitching the great Dizzy Dean into the ground and turning in a scoreless effort while his Yankee mates were amassing a 2–0 lead against the self-styled great one. . . .

It was Gomez vs. Dean, as advertised, when squatty Umpire-In-Chief Bill McGowan shooed the clubs onto the field. The 32,000 sat back for their first taste of what was looming as a superb pitching duel. But it was a one-sided duel they were to see.

VAUGHAN SMACKS SINGLE

Third Baseman Arky Vaughan, of the Pirates, justified his National League batting championship of 1936 when he bashed a hot single into right centerfield with two out in the first inning. But that was the first and last hit off Gomez. Not another National Leaguer reached base in those first three innings as the fastballing Gomez burned his delivery into the big mitt of Bill Dickey.

Greeted with scattered boos as he walked to the mound, Dizzy Dean began to win favor in that first inning when he held the American Leaguers hitless. He walked Joe DiMaggio with two out, but he struck out the dangerous Gehrig with a sharp-breaking slow curve that produced a futile Gehrig swing and a broad Dean smile.

But in that second inning, Dean began to fade. Cleveland's Earl Averill greeted him with a sharp single into rightfield and after Joe Cronin had flied to Demaree, Bill Dickey whacked a single through the box that put Averill on second. But in this crisis, Dean performed nicely, retiring Sammy West on a fly to Demaree and striking out Gomez.

GEHRIG COMES THROUGH

They caught up with him in that third, though. He had two out when DiMaggio, the goat of the 1936 All-Star game, rammed a single into centerfield. Then

Dean faced Gehrig once more. He had the count three and two, and he tried to slip that same curve ball on which Gehrig had fanned in the first inning. He didn't do it. Gehrig caught it on the business end of his bat and it was two runs for the American League as the ball sailed handsomely into the haze beyond the rightfield fence for a home run.

83

Gabby Hartnett's "Homer in the Gloaming" (1938)

SOURCE: *Chicago Daily News*, September 29, 1938

After chasing the Pittsburgh Pirates for much of the 1938 season, the Cubs finally passed their rivals with one of the most dramatic home runs in baseball history. Tied 5–5 with the Pirates in the ninth inning, the game, by agreement of the umpires, was to be stopped after the Cubs' Gabby Hartnett's at-bat due to darkness. The veteran catcher-manager propelled his club to victory, and into first place, by slamming his "homer in the gloaming," inciting such an enthusiastic response that Hartnett was barely able to touch all four bases before being engulfed by Cubs fans who had rushed the field.

The editor of this column, John P. Carmichael, was at the beginning of one of the most illustrious careers in American sportswriting. His column, "The Barber Shop," ran in the Daily News *from 1934 to 1972. In 1945 he assembled perhaps the first great collection of oral baseball history,* My Greatest Day in Baseball *(1945; rpt., Lincoln: University of Nebraska Press, 1996).*

THE BARBER SHOP
by John P. Carmichael

We surrender to inadequacy. This Cub-Pirate pennant fight has gone far beyond our poor power to picture in words. When you squirm to fashion the proper pinnacle for a "Dizzy" Dean only to find that you need at least its twin, that a Gabby Hartnett may also brush the stars, word-painting becomes a magic art not given to the mine run of mortals to diffuse.

So let this be, today, a confession of helplessness to treat an afternoon which beggars description; an afternoon in the life of a stout-hearted Irishman who, as darkness almost wrapped him from the sight of 35,000 quaking fans, changed the map of a baseball world with one devastating blow. And that he is alive and in one piece at the moment, ready to carry on from that smash, is no fault of a Cub team and a Cub populace gone mad.

For a second successive night we stood in a clubhouse of crazy men in play suits. Only this time they weren't even articulate. We can still see 'em fighting for words, staring at one another with glazed eyes. We can still see 'em pushing Hartnett from wall to wall with the irresistible force of robots gone wild. We can still see Gabby trying vainly to free himself from idolatrous teammates.

We can still see Billy Herman, standing in the middle of the floor, arms akimbo. When he could talk it was first just a whisper of awe: "Lord God Almighty." Dawning consciousness of the moment brought it out again, louder, hoarser: "Lord God Almighty." Then the full realization of the terrific sight he had just watched in the twilight smote him. "Lord God ALMIGHTY," he suddenly screamed and hurled his glove he knew not where.

He wasn't even swearing. It was as though he was asking the heavens above to witness that this thing he'd just seen with his own eyes could really happen to him and those caught up in the maelstrom around him.

Dean's day was great. This one was greater. This was everybody's day until Hart-nett wrested it from them all with that miraculous, breath-taking blow in the ninth with two down, two strikes against him and a tie game about to be put over for a double-header today because it was no longer possible to see in the gloom. Far out in the stands a mailman caught the ball and even while Gabby struggled in the arms of his men, it appeared in the clubhouse with a plea for the Hartnett name.

"Give him a new one and I'll sign it," ordered Gabby. "I want to keep this one forever. I've had the greatest thrill of this old life now."

Over in a corner "Rip" Collins, himself one of the day's heroes at that plate, tried to break the hysteria with his inevitable gag. "I get some credit," he yelled. "Gabby used the Collins stance at the plate." Elbowing his way to Gabby's side strode Trainer Andy Lotshaw, a comic figure with his cap awry and wiping away at streaming eyes with a huge towel.

"You big lug," he wept, "you hit it just like I used to do." He was shoved aside, sniffling, and "Dizzy" Dean leaped upon the managerial desk behind which Gabby had sought refuge. "Diz" teetered there back and forth on the balls of his feet, matted gray hair hanging over his forehead like an old crone's disheveled locks.

"Oh," he moaned. "You . . . you Gabby." He tried to talk with his hands, but lost his balance and fell back into unsympathetic arms. Sheer exhaustion at relief from the tension of what they'd gone through finally drove some to their chairs, where they slumped like marionettes whose guiding strings had let them down. Through the half-open door came the frenzied roar of the crowd from which, only minutes before, Andy Frain's ushers had barely saved Hartnett in his entity.

Now up, now down, now up again, the Cubs and Pirates went all the heart-straining day. The tide of battle surged bitterly through breaks, good and bad. It was almost too much for human flesh and blood to watch. And that hat we do not own is off once more to HIM and THEM.

84

Lou Gehrig Ends His Streak (1939)

SOURCE: *New York Herald-Tribune*, May 3, 1939

The most celebrated streak in baseball history—before the record was broken in 1996 by the Baltimore Orioles' Cal Ripken Jr., that is—ended on May 2, 1939, when Lou Gehrig voluntarily removed himself from the lineup prior to the Yankees' game in Detroit. This article quotes Gehrig and manager Joe McCarthy at length, and also mentions the fascinating irony of the presence of Wally Pipp—who lost his starting first base job to Gehrig in the second game of the streak—in Briggs Stadium for the game, which the Yankees won, 22–2.

GEHRIG'S 2,130-GAME STREAK ENDS AT OWN REQUEST; YANKEES, WITH DAHLGREN AT FIRST, WIN, 22–2

Iron Horse, Saddened by Slump, Benches Himself to Help Team Creator of Many Records Since June 1, 1925, Acclaimed by Detroit Fans as He Yields Post; Pipp, His Predecessor, Sees String Snapped

By Arthur E. Patterson

DETROIT, May 2—Joe McCarthy, manager of the Yankees, flew in from Buffalo today. One of the first of his players he met in the lobby was Lou Gehrig.

"Joe, I'd like to talk to you," said the burly first baseman.

"Sure thing, Lou, c'mon around the corner here and sit down." Joe knew what was coming. He had been waiting for it ever since the 1939 season opened.

"Joe," Gehrig began, "I'm not helping this team any. I know I look terrible out there. This string of mine doesn't mean a thing to me. It isn't fair to the boys for me to stay in there. Joe, I want you to take me out of the line-up today."

GEHRIG STREAK ENDS

And so, Lou Gehrig, the iron horse of 2,130 consecutive American League games since June 1, 1925, slowed to a walk, looking almost as awkward at first base as the day he came off the Columbia campus and carrying a sorry batting average of .143, voluntarily ended a streak which probably never will be equaled in baseball.

Before him the eighty-five year history of the game produced nothing like it. Everett Scott played 1,307 games, terminating that skein the year Gehrig's remarkable mark of endurance began.

"I couldn't deny he looked awful," McCarthy told the newspaper men later. "He sure felt blue and I sure felt sorry for him. I hope I cheered him by telling him he would straighten himself out in the warmer weather and get back in there. He really thinks he can and I hope he's right. Just now I'm going to give Babe Dahlgren a real shot at the job. He goes in this afternoon."

Out at the ball park Gehrig good-naturedly posed for pictures before the game on the dugout steps as though watching his mates play. He seemed relieved now that he had made the long-awaited decision. "I made up my mind Sunday night," he told your correspondent. "I knew it wasn't fair to the boys, to Joe, to the baseball public and to myself to stay in there."

PRAISES PILOT'S INDULGENCE

"It got to be plenty tough walking up to the plate with winning runs on the bases and leaving them there. Joe has been perfectly swell about it all. He would have left me in there until the cows came home, I guess, but it wasn't doing any good."

In his 2,130th consecutive game Sunday, Gehrig went to bat four times against the Washington Senators, each time leaving men on bases. There was one on when he flied to center, one on when he flied to right, two aboard when he grounded to the second baseman and against Pete Appleton, last pitcher in the streak, two aboard when he flied to center.

If the final fly had been pulled to right, it might have gone into the seats for a homer. It was Lou's best clout during the season. That night he decided it was no use going on.

In his long and meritorious career, Gehrig has established many records. He has been one of the outstanding sluggers of the game, keeping pace for a time with the one and only Babe Ruth. He has played in seven World Series, these games being excluded from his official streak. The game has rewarded him handsomely and it is estimated he has saved $250,000.

NO THOUGHT OF RELEASE

At present he is under contract for the 1939 season at a figure said to be $34,000. There is no thought of releasing him and he probably will be around when and if the Yankees step into their fourth straight conflict with the National League pace-setter in October.

While Gehrig was answering questions, the bell for the Yankee batting practice rang. Lou jumped up and stretched. "Well now I'm just going out there and spread out."

He romped past first base. Dahlgren was there already. He ran out into center field and speared flies during the drill. He didn't go to bat at all, nor to first base. When the game was about to start, Gehrig, as team captain, took the Yankee line-up card to the plate. The crowd, having already heard the news, cheered him, then Ty Tyson appealed through the microphone for a big hand, letting all the fans in on Gehrig's decision. They roared and clapped. Gehrig "kidded" with the umpires, doffed his cap to the crowd a few times, dropped the score card on Joe McCarthy's lap and then retired to a corner of the dugout. He whipped out a handkerchief and wiped away a few stray tears. Could you blame him?

YANKEES CRUSH TIGERS

The Yankees, grim through it all, then went out and smashed the Detroit Tigers, 22 to 2.

Oddly enough, the man whom Gehrig displaced at first base for the Yankees that second day of June, after his pinch hit for Peewee Wanninger, June 1, was in the stands today. Reporters bumped into Wally Pipp in the lobby as they rushed to the wires with Joe McCarthy's announcement.

"I'm afraid I can't get back into shape to take over again," said the Grand Rapids businessman with a grin. "I'm happy that Lou did it himself, and say, it's a great story for you fellows, isn't it?"

Out at the park, Dixie Walker, former Gehrig teammate, agreed with Pipp. "So Lou's going to rest today. Well, it's nice he did it this way. It would not seem right having some guy take him out, would it, now?"

"Yeah," chipped in Hank Greenberg as he emerged from the dressing-room tunnel. "It looks like the great Yankee dynasty is beginning to crumble."

That comment by Greenberg, you understand, came before that 22-to-2 trouncing.

85

Hall of Fame Opens (1939)

SOURCE: *The Sporting News*, June 22, 1939

The Baseball Hall of Fame opened its doors to tourists on June 12, 1939. For the occasion many of the previous inductees, including Babe Ruth, Ty Cobb, Honus Wagner, and Cy Young, were brought together in Cooperstown to celebrate what was believed to be baseball's centennial. Evidence that disproved the role of Cooperstown and native son Abner Doubleday in the "invention" of baseball, as revealed by a special commission in 1907, however, was available. Within two years of the decision two journalists, Collier's *Will Irwin and* Sporting News *editor Alfred Spink, questioned the commission's conclusions. On February 10, 1936, New York Sun reporter Will Wedge—later a Hall of Fame historian—wrote an article detailing research in the West Point archives by Captain M. P. (Pat) Echols that revealed that Doubleday was on campus during all of 1839 and did not like outdoor sports in any case. The most persuasive dissenter, New York Public Library librarian Robert W. Henderson, published an article in the June 1939 issue of* Current History, *excerpted from a longer article in the April 1939 Bulletin of the New York Public Library, which asked if baseball was celebrating a "fake centennial." Eight years later Henderson wrote a book, featuring an introduction by Irwin, that thoroughly dismantled the Cooperstown/Doubleday myth—but to no avail.*

The Sporting News printed a special section in this edition focusing on the Hall celebration. Included were a lengthy history of the game by Fred Lieb, who wrote the article below, and an interview with the oldest former major league player, ninety-two-year-old Deacon White. Lieb, who was as knowledgeable about the game's history as any sportswriter, tried to balance the inconsistencies between the Doubleday myth and the known existence of similar ball games before 1839.

COOPERSTOWN CAVALCADE MARKED BY GREATEST GALAXY OF PAST AND PRESENT DIAMOND STARS EVER ASSEMBLED

Exhibition, Staged on Historic Doubleday Field, Showed Evolution of Game from "Town Ball" to Modern-Day Sport; Hall of Fame Members Provided Biggest Thrill for 10,000 Onlookers

By Frederick G. Lieb

The splendid progress made by baseball in its first 100 years and the expectancy of even greater things for the future was the theme for the Cavalcade of the Game staged at Cooperstown, N.Y., June 12, by the major leagues and the enterprising citizenry of the 2,800-population New York town which has two great prides—that it is the birthplace of James Fenimore Cooper, early American novelist, also the birthplace of America's National Game.

It was a grand idea of the committee to start the program at Doubleday Field with an early exhibition of town ball, with the boy participants and their girl rooters dressed in the garb which was sported by the lads and lassies of Cooperstown at the time James Cooper looked down on that same nearby Otsego Lake, the Glimmerglass of his Indian friends, for inspiration. Boys appeared in long sailor pants, heavy boots and the odd flat derbies worn by our great-grandpappies. There apparently was little system to town ball. One boy batted and the group of 20-odd boys in the field shifted for the various batters. The base lines were only 60 feet; the batters could take as many strikes as he liked and the baserunner was retired after being "soaked" with the ball. One wonders what would happen today if some of our strong-armed gladiators had that privilege.

One can believe that baseball, such as we understand it, was started by Cadet Doubleday in Cooperstown and still recognize that town ball, rounders and other games in which boys struck a ball with a bat were played long before 1839.

The second section of the show at Doubleday Field, the game between two soldier teams, wearing the whiskers and uniforms of the Knickerbockers and Excelsiors of the 1850s, really showed the order which was brought out of the earlier chaotic game by the first crude rules and playing space drawn up by Doubleday. It still wasn't the baseball of 1939, but it resembled the present game far more than it did the harum-scarum unorganized game which preceded it. . . .

Including the living immortals who took part in the dedication of the Baseball Museum and Hall of Fame, it is doubtful if so many great players, past and present, ever were assembled in one place. It even is doubted if so many outstanding players of the past as the 11 living immortals—Connie Mack, Ty Cobb, Honus Wagner, Napoleon Lajoie, Cy Young, Walter Johnson, Babe Ruth, Tris Speaker, Eddie Collins, George Sisler and Grover Alexander—ever before were assembled in one place. Even an old stager like Hughie Fullerton, who has seen thousands of players come and go since the '90's, admitted a thrill as these brilliant stars of baseball's last 50 years were called upon to say a few words to the crowd.

In looking at these men, one felt that their likes never would be seen again.

Perhaps with the ten-men pitching staffs of today, it would not be possible for a present-day mound ace, even with the build of a Cy Young, to emulate the Ohioan's great record of 511 victories and three no-hitters, including a perfect game. Or, will the game again see a man like Connie Mack, who has managed one club for 38 years, and has been a pilot for nearly 50 years?

Then, Babe Ruth's 714 home runs, not including 15 in World Series, apparently are safe, as is his former top salary of $80,000 a year. It is questionable if we ever will see another player match Ty Cobb's record of 12 batting championships in 13 years and the countless other records, runs, hits, years over .300, and lifetime batting average hung up by the great Georgian.

OLDSTERS LOOK AS GOOD AS THEIR RECORDS

Bob Feller may be a threat to Walter Johnson's strikeout record, but will his arm hold out as long as did the magnificent wing of old Barney? Grover Cleveland Alexander's 16 shutouts in one season also should hold for many years, as should some of the grand performances of old Hans Wagner, Tris Speaker, Eddie Collins and George Sisler.

One was struck by the fine appearance of these famous gladiators of a glorious period of the game's history. Often one wonders what becomes of ball players, the great as well as the lowly, after creaky arms or lack of snap in the step forces them to the side-lines. There they were on the platform. . . .

One of the most pleasing things in the entire Cooperstown show was the fine appearance of old Grover Cleveland Alexander. After his glorious diamond career, Pete, as he was known affectionately to his mates, seemed in danger of slipping from the standard of genteel respectability maintained by his fellow immortals, but Alex took hold of himself in time and no member of the famous 11 received a greater hand than the former Philly, Cub and Cardinal mound ace.

One also sensed the sincerity and love of the game felt by all these men. Connie Mack's voice almost choked with emotion as he expressed his thoughts on baseball of the past and his hopes for the game's future. An honest and justifiable pride was felt by all of the men selected for this top honor in baseball. But, even more so, they hoped they were serving as examples for younger men. As players in the ranks, they perhaps never thought much about such things; they were too busy winning games, knocking out home runs or stealing bases. But, looking at their career in retrospect, they wanted other players to strive as hard for the coveted prizes of baseball as they did. Babe Ruth gave vent to this feeling in his homely language:

"Some of the great players who were in the game when I broke in, got on it (the Hall of Fame All-Star line-up); I got on it; and now it's up to some of the young fellows now in the game to hustle and get on it."

One of the regrettable things about the Cavalcade was the absence of Ty Cobb, greatest player of all time, from the exercises in connection with the dedication of the museum and Hall of Fame. The illustrious Georgian came all the way from Menlo Park, Cal., and was late in arriving on a motor trip from Utica, which he had to make in order to get into Cooperstown.

However, Ty was present in the afternoon part of the program, and then went on to New York to see the Yankees play the Indians. He was particularly interested in seeing Bob Feller.

86

Landis Declares Ninety-one Tigers Free Agents

(1940)

SOURCE: *Detroit News*, January 16, 1940

Commissioner Landis was an avowed opponent of the farm system, conceived by Cardinals general manager Branch Rickey as an inexpensive means of developing future major leaguers. Landis believed that the system unnecessarily slowed the progress of the best minor leaguers and allowed the clubs with the most farm clubs to monopolize the talent pool. On several occasions he invoked rules regulating farm systems to declare numerous minor league players free agents. In 1938 Landis "freed" seventy-four Cardinal players, and two years later he dealt an even harsher blow to the Tigers. By this point, as Benjamin Rader notes in his Baseball: A History of America's Game *(Urbana: University of Illinois Press, 1992), major league clubs had started to curtail their purchase of minor league teams. After World War II new rules were enacted governing the drafting and purchase of minor leaguers, which, coupled with the fading fortunes of the minor leagues, eliminated the broad, Rickey-style farm system that flourished in the 1920s and 1930s.*

THE UMPIRE
By H. G. Salsinger

Judge K. M. Landis' decision, making free agents of 91 players owned by Detroit, and ordering the club to pay a total of $47,250 to 14 players now under contract to other clubs, means a loss of close to half a million dollars. It would require several weeks of examination of books, records and reports by expert accountants, to reach an approximate estimate.

It was not so much the money originally paid the 91 players for signing contracts as the salaries handed them since signing, transportation costs, living expenses while on the road, salaries of scouts, sums paid to minor league clubs for affiliations, numerous deficits squared away to continue "connections," and untold incidental expenses.

This entire investment was swept away when Landis scrawled his signature on the last of seven pages of typewritten sheets, setting forth in elaborate detail the numerous violations of which he found the club guilty.

SPENT FOR WHAT?
Detroit spent money lavishly in creating a network of affiliated clubs, but there is no proof that the club spent wisely. The wisdom of any investment must be

judged by the returns and in the case of the Detroit farm system the returns since 1936 have been so negligible that the club stocked its roster with cast-off veterans.

Detroit owned 165 minor league players last year, but when outfield material was needed the club gave Harry Eisenstat and $15,000 in cash to Cleveland for Earl Averill, a player who was never considered a good competitor, whose major league career was apparently finished two years ago, and who turned in a batting average of .262 for Detroit.

Having claim to 165 minor league players Detroit went to the last-place St. Louis and plucked Beau Bell and Ralph Kress from the Little Brownies' roster.

UNDEVELOPED

There must be something radically wrong with a farm system that enrolls 165 ball players and that cannot deliver one capable of playing with a second division team.

The impression is that Detroit spent its entire efforts shuttling players from one affiliated club to another and none in developing the material on hand.

One hundred and sixty-five ball players are of no use to a club unless they are developed and the Detroit farm plan made no provisions for developing them. At none of the Detroit farms was there a man of major league experience to guide the raw recruits or to coach them. They were in the hands of minor leaguers and left pretty much to shift for themselves. . . .

THEY DID ONCE

There was a time when Detroit farms developed players.

The team that won two pennants and a world championship was developed at Beaumont and Evansville during the late Frank J. Navin regime.

Del Baker, now manager of the Tigers, tutored the players at Beaumont and Bob Coleman was in charge at Evansville.

The policy of "develop-your-own" was shuffled after Mr. Navin's death. The club began acquiring "ready-made" players, nearly all of whom had outworn their usefulness. The club's fortunes have been declining ever since.

GOOD AND BAD

Landis' decision wrecks the Detroit farm system. The loss is heavy, but if the result is a general revision of the club's farm plan, making the development of players the main mission, and, with capable men in command, the decision will have its benefits.

Baseball in Wartime and Peacetime

World War II affected baseball deeply. Many players and fans were drafted into service overseas, and others worked in defense plants. Concern for the postwar economy inspired Spokane, Washington businessmen to plan production of many different aluminum products, including baseball bats.

Racial prejudice was still rampant in factories, on the battlefield, and on the ballfield. Tensions exploded in Detroit in 1943, resulting in thirty-four deaths and hundreds of casualties. It took the threat of two separate marches on Washington by black labor leader A. Philip Randolph to force Presidents Roosevelt and Truman (in 1941 and 1948, respectively) to initiate the integration of the armed forces, but baseball owners still could not be persuaded to break their own color line. The return of veterans generated both enthusiasm, as in the case of Hank Greenberg, and bitterness over contractual inequities which led to the formation of yet another players' union. While the long-overdue integration of baseball by Jackie Robinson was clearly the most significant moment in baseball during the 1940s, marking a new era for the sport, the previous era effectively ended with the death of Babe Ruth, in 1948.

87

FDR Gives Green Light to Wartime Baseball (1942)

SOURCE: *Washington Post*, January 17, 1942

In the aftermath of the Japanese attack on Pearl Harbor and the United States' entry into World War II, baseball owners in the major and minor leagues were concerned about Washington's stance regarding the continuance of professional baseball. They remembered the effect that the 1918 "work or fight" order had on baseball. President Franklin D. Roosevelt responded to a query from Commissioner Landis with a letter, known as the "green light" letter, written on January 15. The unofficial letter made clear that while players eligible for military duty must serve, the survival of the national pastime was essential as recreation for a country at war. Nevertheless, some owners, like Washington's Clark Griffith, who had held out hope for draft exemptions for players, were disappointed with Roosevelt's statement.

Following is the text of Roosevelt's letter, along with Shirley Povich's "This Morning" column. Although Povich may have known of Griffith's views, he noted that Griffith and other owners strongly endorsed the letter. Given the mood in Washington and across the nation, it is not surprising that Povich emphasized baseball's full support of the war effort.

January 15, 1942

My dear Judge:—

Thank you for yours of January fourteenth. As you will, of course, realize the final decision about the baseball season must rest with you and the Baseball Club owners—so what I am going to say is solely a personal and not an official point of view.

I honestly feel that it would be best for the country to keep baseball going. There will be fewer people unemployed and everybody will work longer hours and harder than ever before.

And that means that they ought to have a chance for recreation and for taking their minds off their work even more than before.

Baseball provides a recreation which does not last over two hours or two hours and a half, and which can be got for very little cost. And, incidentally, I hope that night games can be extended because it gives an opportunity to the day shift to see a game occasionally.

As to the players themselves, I know you agree with me that individual players who are of active military or naval age should go, without question, into the services. Even if the actual quality of the teams is lowered by the greater use of older players, this will not dampen the popularity of the sport. Of course, if any individual has some particular aptitude in a trade or profession, he ought to serve the Government. That, however, is a matter which I know you can handle with complete justice.

Here is another way of looking at it—if 300 teams use 3,000 or 6,000 players, these players are a definite recreational asset of at least 20,000,000 of their fellow citizens—and that in my judgment is thoroughly worthwhile.

With every best wish,

Very sincerely yours,

[Signed] Franklin D. Roosevelt

That man in the White House did, indeed, earn the label of the Nation's First Fan yesterday. When President Roosevelt, no less, gave the green light to organized baseball as an acceptable war-time function, the game was receiving the most extraordinary compliment of its 102-year history.

The President in declaring he saw a war-time need for the recreation provided by baseball, set at rest the fears of clubowners for their game but the clubowners and players can still butch the situation for themselves if they lose sight of Mr. Roosevelt's one injunction. It behooves them to take seriously the duty the President pointed out when he declared, "individual ball players subject to service in the armed forces should carry out such obligations without question."

That means no attempts at wire-pulling, no subterfuge by star players to duck military duty with or without the support of their clubs, and no absurd claims for exemption. Such tactics would profane the very special distinction of White House blessings now bestowed on baseball, and would cause official disapproval of the game quicker than any other development. Mr. Roosevelt has put baseball on its honor, in a sense.

Thus far, however, organized baseball has merited all of Mr. Roosevelt's confidence that players will not duck their military duty. Already, it appears, more figures from the major and minor leagues have been drafted or enlisted than throughout World War I, when organized baseball's record was none too shining, with the shipyards a haven for scores of players.

FANS CERTAIN TO APPLAUD ACTION

To the credit of men like Clark Griffith, Tom Yawkey, and Walter O. Briggs, who saw such valuable chattels as Cecil Travis, Buddy Lewis, Ted Williams and Hank Greenberg inducted into the service, theirs was a completely patriotic reaction. "The Washington Club expects every man, star or rookie, to do his duty," said Mr. Griffith, at the first hint that any of his players would be drafted, and that attitude was echoed by other club owners.

That Mr. Roosevelt's action in encouraging continuation of organized baseball during the war crisis will be generally applauded seems certain. As he pointed out baseball has a definite recreational asset in times of stress and 300 teams, using between 5000 and 6000 players provide recreation for themselves just how important will be measured by attendance at games.

Mr. Roosevelt, incidentally, may go down as the best friend organized baseball ever had in the White House. At a time when the industry was wrapped in uncertainty to the point that Commissioner Landis felt it important to ask the White House to determine the game's wartime status with spring training only a few weeks away, doubt and nebulae were swept away by Mr. Roosevelt in one positive stroke.

TREMENDOUS BOON TO OWNERS

It was an added windfall to baseball when Mr. Roosevelt also gratuitously suggested more emphasis of night games, to permit attendance by defense workers who otherwise might not be able to partake of the sport. If the club owners had outlined to him their fondest prayers, and begged his indulgence, they could have received no greater boon. It means the expensive lighting plants, valued now at nearly $2,000,000, would not be costly white elephants; it means increased gate receipts at a time when defense work threatened attendance at day games, and it means, of course that the Nation's fans will have greater opportunity to see ball games.

President Roosevelt may have, in effect, overruled Commissioner Landis in the latter's own domain, on the subject of night baseball, because only a few weeks ago Landis vetoed a proposal by Clark Griffith that the number of night games be increased from 7 to 14. Now, with an approving nod from the White House, Griffith will reintroduce his request, and Landis will scarcely refuse to take the hint from the White House.

The President's action may mean financial salvation to such as the St. Louis Browns, who lost $100,000 last year partly because of the loss in revenue occasioned by the seven-game limit on night games. The Washington Club, for example, played to an average of fewer than 4000 fans in afternoon games at Griffith Stadium last season, but averaged 20,000 for night games.

88

Baseball on Film (1943)

SOURCE: *1943 Baseball Guide*

The establishment of film bureaus in baseball was the idea of Lew Fonseca, former major league player and, starting in 1935, American League promotional director. He believed that the formation of film bureaus would facilitate the distribution of films to civic associations, organizations and other groups interested in seeing major league baseball. During the war the work of the league film bureaus became even more important, as the reels brought baseball to soldiers half a world away. The following article, by former major leaguer Ethan Allen, described the relevance of baseball footage to soldiers.

THE NATIONAL LEAGUE FILM BUREAU
By Ethan Allen

The National League Film Bureau, established in 1938, has produced four motion pictures of three to four reels length. The first, BASEBALL, THE NATIONAL GAME, depicted the game's history, being designed primarily to commemorate its one hundredth anniversary. PLAY BALL, AMERICA, the second production, presented a detailed analysis of individual and team play. The latest pictures, WINNING BASEBALL and SAFE AT HOME, were planned for general audiences and include informative and amusing sequences about plays and players. Pathe News also released two Sportscopes from these productions. They are called PENNANT CHASERS and PUBLIC SPORT NO. 1, and have been distributed in English- and Spanish-speaking countries.

In addition, a one-reel film of the 1940 World Series and a two-reel "BASEBALL, Techniques and Tactics," have been produced. This last one resulted from a request of The Coordinator's Office of Inter-American Affairs for an instructive baseball picture for use in Central and South America. For that purpose Spanish and Portuguese sound tracks have been added to this film, which is now available in the Coordinator's Office in those languages. An English version also is filed with the National League office.

These films have been welcomed most heartily by many and varied audiences. At present, the four basic National League pictures are being exhibited before our armed forces in Australia, New Caledonia, England, Ireland, Mexico, Panama, Puerto Rico, South America, Iceland, Alaska, and elsewhere throughout the world. They also are reaching service camps and stations in the United States via traveling units of the United States Organizations.

An urgent plea for sport films brought a prompt dispatch of three of these pictures to New Caledonia. Two others were presented to Father Hubbard, "The Glacier Priest," after a radio talk in which Father Hubbard told how Army and Navy men in the Aleutians were requesting baseball pictures. The interest in these films in remote places shows that American soldiers and sailors girdling the globe are taking baseball with them to such extent that it may very well become an international game.

Due to existing conditions, with Army and Navy requirements coming first, as is, of course, the desire of every American, and with film priorities limiting the number of prints of these pictures that can be made available to general audiences in the United States, such circulation here will be considerably curtailed. Under the circumstances all applications for any of these films will have to be sent directly to the offices of National League clubs.

89

Race Riots Threaten Baseball in Detroit (1943)

SOURCE: *Detroit Free Press*, June 23, 1943

On June 20 and 21 long-simmering racial tension finally exploded in Detroit with disastrous results: twenty-five blacks and nine whites lost their lives in the ensuing riots, over seven hundred people were injured and thirteen hundred were arrested. As martial law was declared one concern of authorities was the control of crowds at Briggs Stadium and at horse racing at the state fairgrounds. Sporting events at both venues were cancelled on June 22, but were allowed to continue the next day. In this regard Michigan's Governor Kelly and President Roosevelt seemed to agree about the role sports played in easing tensions in wartime America.

BASEBALL, RACES OK; CURFEW STAYS

Troops, Police Disperse Youths; Death Toll Hits 29; 32 Go to Jail

Gov. Kelly at midnight Tuesday eased restrictions of his martial-law regulations in Detroit to permit baseball and horse racing, saying as he completed a tour of riot-torn areas that "a large measure of quiet had been restored."

"I am thankful for the co-operation of the citizens of Detroit, and of the Army whose forces patrolled the city," said the Governor. "I believe that this modification of the regulations will help restore the city to a normal basis."

Several scattered reports of rioting were received by police and Army forces that cruised the streets where blood had been shed 24 hours before.

WOMAN SUCCUMBS

There was only one serious injury, however, although a white woman who had been injured the preceding day died in Receiving Hospital, bringing the riot death toll to 29.

The most serious rioting Tuesday evening occurred around Perrien Park, Chene and Warren, where six cars containing Negroes were stoned by mobs of white youths. Army troops and police finally succeeded in dispersing the mobs there and elsewhere.

A mob gathered earlier in the evening at Warren and Hamilton, and some stones were thrown, but no serious injury was reported there.

The only serious injury reported during the night was the shooting of Julian Witherspoon, twenty-six-year-old Negro, who is in serious condition at Receiving Hospital after being shot in the right side by State Trooper Ted Anders.

According to Patrolman Ed Grace, who was with Trooper Anders, Witherspoon walked out of the St. Antoine YWCA at about 11 p.m. while the officers were questioning three Negroes out after curfew. They said Witherspoon yelled "Heil Hitler" at the officers several times and as Anders started over to question him, he made a motion as if to draw a gun.

Mrs. Sally Grabowski, white, of 5100 St. Aubin, died in Chenik Hospital at 9 p.m. She was shot behind the left ear at 7:45 p.m. Monday by a sniper in a building at 5036 St. Aubin. . . .

OTHER RESTRICTIONS STAY

In modifying the restrictions to let the Tigers play and the horses to run at the State Fairgrounds, Gov. Kelly emphasized that the ban on evening gatherings was still in force. Only day-time sports events will be permitted, he said.

Briggs Stadium and the Fairgrounds will be guarded, solely as a precautionary measure, he added, by companies of State Troops.

90

Landis's Last Act (1943)

SOURCE: *Philadelphia Evening Bulletin*, November 24, 1943

Kenesaw Mountain Landis was hired by baseball owners to convince the public that they were serious about stamping out gambling and its influence on the game. Landis never wavered from that task. In the final major act of his career, Landis expelled Philadelphia

Phillies owner William Cox for, among other things, betting on baseball games. Landis died almost exactly one year later. The Carpenter family, which took over the Phillies from Cox, maintained their control over the club for some forty years.

PLAYING THE GAME
By Ed Pollock

Its reputation smeared by the World Series scandal of 1919, organized baseball the following year took Kenesaw Mountain Landis off a Federal court bench and made him the supreme ruler of the game. His job was to clean up baseball.

Now 77 years old, Landis is still the leading clean-up hitter in baseball and as much of a rootin', tootin', shootin' dictator as he was in 1920.

Yesterday the commissioner announced a clean-up of the Phillies. He fired William Drought Cox, the ill-starred club president who in nine months is said to have made more enemies and influenced fewer people in baseball than any man in the game.

Through all of Cox's controversial actions—his slurs on the all-star game, on Ford Frick and fellow club-owners, his dismissal of Bucky Harris, his rows with minor league clubs—Landis said very little. In effect, all he did was give Cox plenty of rope. The Phils' ex-president eventually made a gambler's noose and put it around his neck.

The charge against Cox which Landis made public was "betting on baseball games." This is against the commissioner's rules. Other charges, if any, don't matter now. Gambling was enough to remove him.

It took many months to straighten out the Phillies when Gerry Nugent could no longer carry the financial burden and had to give up. When baseball wanted to force out a club president for conduct unbecoming an executive, a willing investor was found in a short time.

Perhaps Commissioner Landis was not responsible for producing the new owners—Robert R. M. Carpenter, Sr. and Jr.—but such dispatch is typical of his office.

THEN AND NOW AT PHILS' OFFICE

The scene in the Phillies' office when Cox took over and Nugent went out was what you would expect at a funeral. Club employes looked like red-eyed mourners. They walked on tiptoe and spoke in whispers. Even boisterous newspaper men conversed in undertones.

It wasn't that they disliked Cox. They didn't know him. But Nugent was popular and they hated to see him go.

It was different yesterday when Carpenter took over and Cox went out. The scene was what you would expect in the winning team's dressing room. There was handshaking, backslapping, wisecracking. Employes were red-eyed again—this time from laughing. Newspaper men were loud, boisterous.

It wasn't that they like young Bob Carpenter. They scarcely know him. But Cox was unpopular and they were glad to see him go.

91

Are Black Players Up to Major League Snuff? (1944)

SOURCE: *Negro Baseball Pictorial Year Book*

During the 1940s black journalists put increasing pressure on the major leagues to integrate their clubs. The service of African American soldiers in World War II made baseball's self-imposed segregation seem even more offensive than it had before. The cover of the Negro Baseball Pictorial Year Book *made that point plain by showing a Homestead Grays pitcher and a black, grenade-throwing soldier in identical poses. Given this context, one would expect that an article such as this one, by well-known* Baltimore Afro-American *sportswriter Sam Lacy, would promote Negro League stars as major league–caliber players. While Lacy stated the obvious—that many in the Negro Leagues were certainly talented enough to play in the American or National League—he offered some surprising reservations about certain black stars, most notably Josh Gibson and Roy Campanella. Ten of Lacy's articles on race and baseball are reprinted in* Black Writers/Black Baseball: An Anthology of Articles from Black Sportswriters Who Covered the Negro Leagues, *ed. Jim Reisler.*

WILL OUR BOYS MAKE BIG LEAGUE GRADE?
By Sam Lacey
Sports Editor, Afro-American Newspapers

So much has been said and written in recent months regarding organized baseball's discrimination against colored players, it is inevitable that the question would eventually arise: "Are Negro players actually qualified to play in the major leagues?"

By reason of my close association with the campaign to break down the bars against colored players, I have been approached innumerable times with either that question or with others identically the same in effect. Invariably, my answer has been, "I haven't the slightest doubt that several Negro players are potentially big league material."

There may be some to question the manner in which I framed that reply; it could be that they are not altogether satisfied with my refusal to express myself with an unequivocal "yes" or "no." That is understandable and probably bears explaining.

Measured by present standards, I am reluctant to say that we have a single man in the ranks of colored baseball who could step into a major league uniform and disport himself after the fashion of a big leaguer.

Without doubt, there are some of our players who would meet the test in certain departments. As a matter of fact, there are those among our league players who might possibly excel in the matter of hitting or fielding or base-running or pitching. But, for the most part, the fellows who could hold their own in more than one of these phases of the game, are few and far between—perhaps nil.

It is for that reason that I say we have among us men who are "potential" big leaguers.

I fully believe that the average colored player, taken into organized baseball, given the same opportunities provided for white candidates, and subjected to the same program of handling and training, would develop into the same quality of performer as the average white recruit.

Certainly, with organized baseball suffering from the dearth of talent brought on by the war there can be no question that there are many players on top colored teams who compare favorably with the nondescript lot that makes up several of the American and National leagues' teams today.

However, my interest does not center solely around the major league teams of the present; hence my contention that most of our players are mere "potentials." I am deeply concerned with getting a chance for colored players who will be able to match strides with the game as it is stepped up after the war.

GIBSON A NATURAL HITTER

Taking into consideration first some of the players I have in mind when I speak of those who might possibly excel in certain departments—and when I say excel, I mean doing a better job than a whole lot of the major leaguers—suppose we take stock of our best hitters.

Josh Gibson, to my way of thinking, is one of the greatest natural hitters the game has ever known, and my observations date back through the eras of Ty Cobb, Babe Ruth, Joe DiMaggio, George Sisle [sic], Rogers Hornsby, Harry Heilmann, Tris Speaker, Frank Baker, Lou Gehrig and a host of others.

I don't think that the man ever lived who possessed a keener batting eye or boasted a more finely developed competitive spirit than the home-run champion of colored baseball.

That, perhaps, will be charged to me as a rash statement, especially in view of my naming nine men whom the world will long recognize as batting stylists of the first water. Persons making that accusation will scoff at my opinion, pointing out that Gibson's feats have been accomplished against pitching far inferior to that faced by the aforementioned major league stars.

My answer to them is that Gibson has hit the best pitching thrown against him and that is as much as one can ask. No man can be expected to pass a test before he takes it. In addition, and this is most important, it will be borne in mind that Josh is a righthanded batter.

With the exception of Hornsby, DiMaggio and Heilmann, the longest hitters in the annals of the major leagues have been lefthanded batters, and baseball folk know lefties enjoy a tremendous advantage at the plate.

Gibson, however, in my book, measures up as a major leaguer only in this department. He, like Roy Campanella, is far below the standards set by the average big leaguer as a defensive catcher. He neither receives well, is adept at handling pitchers, nor throws to bases with any passable degree of accuracy and consistency.

Yet, even at 34, Josh is one of my "potentials." Why? Simply because there have been many catchers in the big time who were developed into first-class receivers after they moved up. Given the same careful schooling that is meted out to a prospect from the International League (minor), Gibson has every reason to believe he would master the receiving art and be able to hold his own for a few years in big time company. . . .

To my way of thinking, our best candidates for big league berths are in the armed services, which is as it should be. Howard Easterling, for example, had everything. The former Homestead Grays' luminary has sure hands, was a versatile fielder and a dependable batter. But 22 years old, he was an ideal choice as a candidate for organized baseball.

Another youngster who showed tremendous promise before the call to the flag was sounded for him, is Larry Doby, the Newark Eagles' find of the 1942 season. Doby, like the Homestead Grays' 4-F Dave Hoskins, has a lot of rough edges to be shaped off but, back in pre-war form, would be a "potential" of top-drawer proportions.

Sammy Hughes, though approaching the unforgiveable age as far as baseball is concerned, is another who might be able to serve in good stead in the major ranks. The Baltimore Elite Giants' management would probably wager on his ability to keep step with topline infielders of the other races.

Satchel Paige, judged on his ability as a moundsman, undoubtedly would have covered himself with glory in anybody's league in his heyday. But Satchel soon learned that he could make more money as a showman than he could ever hope to draw as a brilliant flinger. The result was that the redoubtable Kansas City Monarch ace turned his slab assignments into a combination vaudeville act and pitching performance. . . .

I thought highly of the selections made by newspaperman Wendell Smith for the tryouts conducted by the Boston Red Sox. Of the three—Jackie Robinson, Jethro and Marv Williams—I liked Robinson for more reasons than one.

Having played football with an otherwise all-white team at UCLA, the Kansas City shortstop would be well versed in diplomacy. He would have neither the inferiority complex we must avoid nor the cocky bull-dozing attitude we likewise should abandon. All his life has been spent in an interracial setting, a fact that is bound to be a distinct help to the trail-blazer. . . .

I have written at length 'til now on the quality of Negro baseball, based on nothing more than what is my belief. That is as it must be since major league magnates have maintained a studied boycott of talented colored performers.

The answer to the posed question of whether or not they are actually good enough for the majors remains to be investigated.

This writer, frankly, has to make a conscious effort to keep an open mind on the subject. Reason instinctively rebels against the proposition that a man of one race cannot play the game as well as the men of all others.

The important thing, as I see it, is that any colored man who goes up must be given a proper chance to make the grade. If he bobbles an easy chance, or if he fans at a crucial moment, there should be no immediate indictment of him.

All of us will do well to bear in mind that the player might be affected by either one of two things. He could fail at the moment because he is in a slump or because he is a product of Negro baseball. It would would be best remembered that a slump is a temporary thing while the color of the man's skin is here to stay.

Notwithstanding all of this, we still cannot get around the hard cold fact that a fly ball looks the same in Yankee Stadium or in Hickory Switch; that a home-run is good for four bases in any man's language.

92

Aluminum Bats Planned in Spokane (1944)

SOURCE: *Spokane Spokesman-Review*, July 20, 1944; *Newark Star-Ledger*, September 19, 1944

During times of war, government and business work together to invent and improve products that are useful not only during but long after the conflict. In 1944, businessmen in Washington State, anticipating the end of the war, planned postwar uses for their state's abundant resources when they would no longer be needed for the production of aircraft. One product discussed was a metal baseball bat—a full quarter-century before it achieved popularity in amateur baseball.

This article generated a brief Associated Press article that appeared in the New York Times *and a number of other papers. Two months later, after a speech to the Spokane Chamber of Commerce by an engineering professor on the idea, another AP article appeared in various papers across the country. No other references to aluminum bats are found until the late 1960s.*

USE MAGNESIUM BASEBALL BATS

Engineers Hear Talk on New Aluminum Uses

Magnesium baseball bats with a metallic ping will be on the market this fall, the Associated Engineers learned yesterday at a Davenport luncheon called to hear Raymond Miller, industrial analyst of Bonneville power administration, discuss "Aluminum From Washington Clays."

The baseball bats are now being made at the light metals laboratory at Pullman, A. E. Drucker, retiring dean of the Washington State college school of mines, revealed. So are magnesium fruit ladders for orchards, and scores of other small metal articles.

NEED NEW METAL USES

"Spokane business men must take the lead in devising new uses for the light metals if the city expects to retain the aluminum and magnesium plants established here because of the war," Miller said. "The Spokane aluminum reduction plant is the largest in the northwest and third largest in the United States. The sheet mill is the only one west of Chicago and the second largest in the country.

"But if you do not extend yourselves to greater efforts, results will be inadequate to insure the future of the industry. You must concentrate brains, time, experience and money on the effort.

"The Spokane rolling mill will be limited in its distribution area to western markets. If the west does not use the 120,000 tons of aluminum it can produce in a year, the mill will operate at a reduced rate and correspondingly higher cost. A point could be reached that would make it uneconomical."

TRANSPORTATION NEED IS FACTOR

Transportation equipment, both ground and aerial, is one field, Miller said, but possibilities exist in kitchen utensils, cans, pails, barrels, lighting fixtures, range and refrigerator parts, license plates and other stampings, and miscellaneous sheet metal work.

Relatively few plants to make planes and cars will be established in the northwest, he added, but the field is wide open for manufacture of small light metal products.

"Spokane can not afford to neglect the opportunity to make the Inland Empire a center for light production and manufacture," he said. "What is done in the next few years will stamp Spokane as a thriving industrial city, or one that has lost its greatest opportunity. . . ."

Questioned by A. Ben Fosseen, Miller said the Pullman plant now employing 35 men along lines laid out by Dr. Drucker and A. A. Kearney of Inland Empire Industrial Research, Inc., is "fundamental." He then called on Drucker, who told of the suggestion of Jack Friel, W.S.C. athletic coach, about aluminum baseball bats.

"Brown & Holter of Pullman and Cheney are turning out bronze items for the navy and expect to convert to aluminum and magnesium after the war," Drucker said.

ALUMINUM BATS PROVING PRACTICAL

SPOKANE, Wash. (AP)—Professor E. B. Parker of the Washington State College School of Engineering says aluminum baseball bats are meeting with such good reception that they are causing concern down south whence comes the hickory for bats.

The aluminum bat, Joe Di Maggio Model, was developed at the college in experiments to find new uses for light metal of the Pacific Northwest.

It has inspired, Parker told the Chamber of Commerce today, "scores" of letters of approval from players.

93

Junior World Series Game Draws
over Fifty Thousand (1944)

SOURCE: *Baltimore Sun*, October 19, 1944

The Junior World Series between American Association champ Louisville and Interna-
tional League titlist Baltimore was a struggle that attracted as much attention as the
intra–St. Louis World Series being staged at the same time. Nearly fifty-three thousand
Baltimore fans, hoping to see their club take a commanding 3–1 lead in the JWS, mobbed
Municipal Stadium—originally constructed for football—to cheer the Orioles to victory.
However, despite a valiant comeback from a 5–0 deficit, the Orioles left two men on in
the bottom of the ninth to lose, 5–4. Baltimore rebounded to win the following games to
claim the JWS, four games to two.

52,833 SEE LOUISVILLE BEAT ORIOLES TO EVEN SERIES

RALLY IN NINTH INNING THRILLS FANS BUT
FALLS SHORT IN 5-TO-4 GAME
Dwight Simonds, Colonel's Relief Pitcher, Strikes Out Side in Final
Inning—Teams Tied at 2-All

Those fighting Colonels from Louisville, playing before 52,833 paid fans, defeated the Orioles last night in the Stadium, by a 5-to-4 score, to even the Junior World Series at two games each.

Although the Birds were unable to win the contest before this record-breaking assemblage, they gave the huge turnout one of the most thrilling games imaginable.

The Flock fought gamely enough to overcome a 5–0 deficit and come within one run of tying up the ball game. They put on their final bid in the ninth inning, when they scored their last run and had the tying and winning runs on base with two down.

Sherman Lollar found himself elected in this do-or-die spot. The young catcher had already smashed the ball for a double and two singles and the crowd was in a wild uproar of anticipation.

13TH TO STRIKE OUT
But Dwight Simonds, who had relieved Ray Patton in the seventh, bore down on Lollar and struck him out. He was the third man to fan in the inning and the 13th in the game.

The hitting was limited to nine safeties on each side. Hal Kleine started for the Orioles, but he was unable to get past the first inning when the Kentucky batters got to him for three hits and a run. Before the evening was over, Johnny Podgajny, the old fire horse; Sam Lowry and Rolland Van Slate all swung into pitching action.

Patton, the Kentucky barefoot boy, gave a great demonstration of pitching courage and savvy during his stay on the hill. This big raw-boned right hander drew admiration from the throng in the fifth when he walked the first three men, but fought his way through the inning without a score.

CROWD ROARS

This frame was really a high light. The crowd tore the night apart with a continued roar as the session opened. This crowd contained more people than the big rawboned mountain boy had ever seen.

This tremendous roar disconcerted him and he walked Monaco, Latshaw and Benjamin in succession. With Moss up the excitement reached tremendous heights. But the Howitzer, held to a single safety during the night, bounced to Patton who tossed to the plate to force Monaco and Moss was doubled at first.

Patton then threw out Macklewicz. It was an exceptionally fine bit of pitching under extreme pressure and the big lad received a roar of appreciation from those who had been doing their best to unnerve him.

Bob Latshaw once again was the stick stalwart as he had been so often through the long playoffs grind. It was the lanky first baseman who put us in the ball game in the sixth with a three-run triple that caused the stands to explode.

SLUGGERS STRIKE OUT

It was Latshaw again who started the ninth inning with a double. But Simonds was doing a great job on the hill in a relief role and he stopped the last-ditch rally one short of the tie. He fanned Benjamin and caused Moss to beat the air with tremendous swings.

Mackiewicz managed to blast a scratch hit to Shofner to keep hope alive. In this spot the pressure got hold of Polly. He fielded Skaff's drive nicely, but his throw to first was wide and Latshaw scored. This brought Lollar to the plate and bingo—he fanned also.

While the fans were disappointed, they were busy admitting to each other that they had sat through a ball game which had turned out a crowd that topped the previous high mark in the 1923 Junior World Series, set at Kansas City. With the Orioles playing there, 23,105 fans turned out in their brand-new ball park.

COLONELS SCORE FIRST

Kleine opened his mound campaign well enough by fanning Steiner. But the fleet Genovese drilled a safety to left, and Browne followed with one to right, sending him to third, from where he scored after Mackiewicz had taken in Polly's long fly. Barath smacked another single. Manager Thomas lifted Kleine and Podgajny took over.

Johnny stopped everything only until the third. In this the Kentuckians greeted Johnny lovingly, if somewhat roughly. Steiner fashioned a single to center, but Benjamin took care of Genovese's fly. When Browne forced Steiner at second things appeared in hand.

Polly, however, is quite a hitter when there are chips on the table. He exploded a drive into the bleachers right over Benjamin's head. While the fans were still trying to get their Adam's apples back in place, Barath touched off another. The only difference was that this one was longer and farther away. Cotelle rolled out to end it, but the Colonels had a 4–0 lead.

KENTUCKS SCORE AGAIN

This was bad because the barefoot boy was holding the Birds in check with distressing efficiency. It got even worse when in the next inning Ex-Bird George Savino scratched a hit to Monaco. Skaff gathered in Shofner's pop, but Patton turned in a sacrifice bunt, sending Savino to second.

Once again Steiner came through. His safety to right sent Savino over the plate for a 5–0 lead. It began to take on the semblance of a rout. Genovese flied out to Moss who made a great catch against the stands way out beyond the end of the foul line.

From that point the visitors were through. They got only one hit from there on and were never in a position to make even a threatening gesture. This, however, became a slight interest to the fans who were giving their all to help their own ball club.

LOUISVILLE

	Ab.	R.	H.	O.	A.
Steiner, 2b	4	0	2	2	0
Genovese, cf	4	1	1	3	0
Browne, 1b	4	1	1	5	0
Polly, 3b	3	1	2	2	0
Barath, lf	4	1	2	0	0
Howerton, lf	0	0	0	0	0
Cotellez, rf	4	0	0	0	0
Savino, c	4	1	1	14	1
Shofner, ss	3	0	0	0	1
Patton, p	1	0	0	1	2
1Piet	1	0	0	0	0
Simonds, p	1	0	0	0	0
Totals	33	5	9	27	4

1Batted for Patton in sixth.

ORIOLES

	Ab.	R.	H.	O.	A.
Monaco, 2b	3	0	0	3	4
Latshaw, 1b	4	1	3	10	1
Benjamin, lf	3	0	0	1	0
Moss, rf	5	0	1	1	0

ORIOLES

	Ab.	R.	H.	O.	A.
Mackiewicz, cf	5	0	1	3	0
Skaff, 3b	5	1	1	3	1
Lollar, c	5	0	3	2	1
Braun, ss	3	1	0	3	2
Kleine, p	0	0	0	0	0
Podgajny, p	2	0	0	1	3
1Riley	0	1	0	0	0
Lowry, p	0	0	0	0	1
2Kahn	1	0	0	0	0
Van Slate, p	0	0	0	0	0
Totals	36	4	9	27	13

1Batted for Podgajny in sixth.

2Batted for Lowry in eighth.

Score by innings:

Louisville	1	0	3	1	0	0	0	0	0—5
ORIOLES	0	0	0	0	0	3	0	0	1—4

Error—Polly. Runs batted in—Polly (3), Latshaw (3), Steiner, Barath. Two-base hit—Lollar. Three-base hit—Latshaw. Home runs—Polly, Barath. Sacrifice—Patton. Double plays—Patton, Savino, Browne; Skaff, Monaco, Latshaw. Left on bases—Louisville, 4; Orioles, 11. Base on balls—Patton, 7; Lowry, 1; Van Slate, 1. Strikeouts—Kleine, 1; Patton, 7; Simonds, 6; Lowry, 1. Hits—Kleine, 3 in ⅔ inning; Podgajny, 6 in 5⅓; Lowry, none in 2; Van Slate, none in 1; Patton, 6 in 6; Simonds, 3 in 3. Winning pitcher—Patton. Losing pitcher—Kleine. Umpires—Tobin, Peters, Van Grafian, Kelly.

Time—2:40. Attendance—52,833 (paid).

94

"Nats" Net Only One Home Home Run All Year (1945)

SOURCE: *Washington Post*, September 8, 1945

Dominating the Washington Post *sports page on September 8, more than the hiring by the University of Maryland of Lieutenant Commander Paul (Bear) Bryant as its football coach, was a dramatic 3–2 win by the Senators over the Browns. The victory kept the "Nats" within one and one-half games of the league-leading Tigers. Washington managed to keep close to the sluggers from Detroit despite hitting only one home run in spacious Griffith Stadium all season—an inside-the-park drive by Joe Kuhel against the Browns that sealed the win. In spite of the return of war hero Cecil Travis in the following game, however, Washington couldn't pass Detroit.*

NATS EDGE BROWNS, 3–2, ON WOLFF'S 4-HITTER

Kuhel Hits Homer, Case Steals Home

By Shirley Povich
Post Staff Writer

George Case stole home, Roger Wolff pitched a four-hitter and Joe Kuhel clouted a home run, and those assorted feats lifted the Nats to a 3–2 victory over the Browns last night at Griffith Stadium. A noisy gathering of 13,514 fans were quite pleased with it all.

It was a nice ball game for the Nats to win, because earlier in the day the Tigers had licked the Yankees, and Washington stayed within a game and a half of the league lead. The Nats widened the gulf between themselves and the third-place Browns to 4½ games, with the Yankees a half game farther back.

MUNCRIEF TOSSES 4-HITTER, TOO

It wasn't any breeze though. Bob Muncrief was out there pitching a four-hitter for the Browns and shutting the Nats out after the third inning. Wolff saw most of his 3–0 lead vanish in the sixth inning, when the Browns came up with two unearned runs after an error by George Myatt, and they had both the tying and winning runs on base in that inning.

Case was the big shot of the Nats' victory. He stole three bases during the night, and his steal of home in the first inning precipitated an uproar that resulted in the banishment of Manager Luke Sewell and Catcher Frank Mancuso of the Browns from the ball game.

The Nats got that first run off Muncrief without a hit. Case walked and stole second and moved to third on Myatt's infield out. He languished there while Lewis grounded to Muncrief, but on the first pitch to Kuhel, Case broke for the plate . . . He wasn't fooling.

SEWELL, MANCUSO CHASED

Muncrief, caught in the midst of a long and lazy windup, got his pitch away too late. Case slid in safely under the throw on a close play. Catcher Mancuso and Sewell squawked loudly that Case was out. Umpire Joe Rue said he didn't think so, and so far as he was concerned the only men out were Sewell and Mancuso. He thumbed 'em off the field.

Case opened the third with a single to left and stole second quickly. He moved to third on Myatt's fly to center and raced home on Lewis's fly to center. He might just as well have saved his breath, because a bit later Joe Kuhel slammed a line drive into the center-field corner for a home run. It was, incidentally, the first Washington home run of the season in Griffith Stadium.

The Nats got only one more hit for the rest of the night off Muncrief. Lewis' bunt in the sixth, but Wolff and his knuckler were making their 3–0 lead stand up nicely until the sixth.

Wolff had two out in the sixth when he issued his only walk of the game, to Byrnes, and Finney followed with a single to center. Wolff thought he was out of trouble when McQuinn grounded to Myatt, but Myatt fumbled and Byrnes raced home from third. Then Moore singled and Wolff was in deep trouble until he personally disposed of Stephens on a tap back to the box.

Case's three thefts lifted him into a tie with George Myatt at 28 steals each, but George Stirnweiss is leading the league with 29.

95

Greenberg Returns from War, Homer Wins Pennant (1945)

SOURCE: *Detroit Free Press*, October 1, 1945

Hank Greenberg marked his return to major league baseball on July 1, 1945, after four years of military service, with a game-winning home run. That blast helped the Tigers remain in first place. On the season's final day, with several members of the Washington Senators in Detroit for a playoff game in the event of a tie, Greenberg duplicated the feat. By hitting a pennant-clinching ninth-inning grand slam Greenberg sealed the Senators' fate and further solidified his status as a hero in Detroit. He went on to lead Detroit to a victory in the World Series over the Cubs, but this was his moment of glory for the Tigers this season.

HANK'S BAT WINS FLAG

4-Run Clout in 9th Beats Browns, 6–3
Newhouser Racks Up No. 25 in Relief Role
By Lyall Smith
Free Press Sports Editor

ST. LOUIS—Call Hank Greenberg a champion of champions.

Call him the hero of Bengaltown! Call him the man who came through with a ninth-inning home run with the bases loaded to bring the Tigers their seventh American League pennant in 45 years!

Call him the man who made Manager Steve O'Neill a flag winner for the first time in a managerial career that stretches back to 1929!

Call him all the flowery things you want, for the big left fielder stepped up to the plate and beat the defending league champions, the St. Louis Browns, 6 to 3, with a home run for history.

Drama . . . thrills . . . nerve-wracking realization of a frustrated dream of 1944. They all were there.

GREENBERG'S four-run circuit smash into the left-field stands came off Nelson Potter, ace of the Brownie mound staff.

The ninth inning was the time. The Tigers were trailing, 3 to 2, with one out and the bases clogged with anxious runners who carried a trip into the 1945 World Series on their mud-laden spikes.

Hubby Walker, who batted for Hal Newhouser, started the big ninth-inning uprising with a single. Skeeter Webb bunted and Hubby slid through the mud and water to beat the throw to second. Red Borom went in to run for Walker.

EDDIE MAYO laid down a bunt and both runners advanced. Potter issued an intentional pass to Doc Cramer, filling the bases. That placed the responsibility on the shoulders of Big Hank.

The count was one ball and one strike on Hank, the man who came back from four years in the service of his country to play baseball.

Potter wound up and threw a high fast one toward the plate. Hank hit the ball on a line out of the field into the left stands at the 351-foot mark to drive home Red Borom, Skeeter Webb and Doc Cramer.

BY THE TIME Hank reached home plate, he was caught up in a maelstrom of humanity that was every Tiger on the team. He was hugged and roughed and kissed and pummeled.

It was 1940 all over again. That was the last time the Tigers won the A.L. pennant. They did it that year when Rudy York hit a two-run homer off Bobby Feller to clinch the flag.

But they didn't have to do it under such adverse playing conditions as Sunday. Storms had drenched the field for 10 straight days; the temperature was 57; only 5,582 fans were huddled in the dank park to see baseball history made by a man who hit his thirteenth home run since he came back from the wars last July 1.

96

Jackie Robinson Signs with Dodgers (1945)

SOURCE: *Brooklyn Eagle*, October 24, 1945

On October 23, in perhaps the most significant act in major league history, the Brooklyn Dodgers signed Jackie Robinson to a minor league contract. The significance of Robinson's signing is not merely that it was yet another first for an African American, but that it was achieved in the national pastime. Even people who disliked baseball, or hated sports, instantly understood the importance of the integration of an institution recognized worldwide as a symbol of the United States. Those who would dismiss the relevance of sports in our society should recognize that its popularity with a significant percentage of the population is not trivial and cannot be ignored. Had Robinson been the first black attorney general, or the first African American general, his ascendance, while undoubtedly important, would not have had nearly the cultural resonance as did his acceptance (however reluctant and overdue) by major league baseball teams and fans. Sports heroes are remembered because they act out our dreams and fantasies, and in fulfilling the dream of racial integration on what to many is the field of dreams, Jackie Robinson became one of the most powerful symbols of success in modern American history.

Dodgers Scouted Robinson for Big-League Role
Deal Made in August—Jackie to Train in Fla. With Flock, Royals
By Harold C. Burr

President Branch Rickey of the Brooklyn Dodgers has broken through the color line in signing the first Negro ball player to appear in Organized Baseball in the 70 years of its life. The player who enters through the opened door is Jackie Robinson, shortstop and UCLA football star.

During the 1945 season, Robinson was a member of the Kansas City Monarchs, hitting .340. He came to the Monarchs after serving as a second lieutenant in the army. He was quietly brought to Brooklyn in August. Rickey explained what he had in mind and Jackie agreed to sign Nov. 1.

Robinson was carefully scouted by Tom Greenwade, George Sisler and Clyde Sukeforth, the Rickey bird dogs. The boy was signed yesterday to a Montreal bonus contract, the Brooklyn club's Double A International League farm. But in reality he was scouted as a major league prospect. Robinson will go to the Dodger and Montreal combined training camp at Daytona Beach, Fla., in the Spring.

Jackie previously had received a tryout at Fenway Park, Boston, by the Red Sox. Of the three Negroes tried out on that occasion, Robinson received the most favorable attention from Manager Joe Cronin. But the Red Sox made no attempt to sign him and the Dodger scouts took over and reported to Rickey that he was the best of the Negro prospects.

MAY COST CLUB PLAYERS

"Mr. Racine and my father," Branch Jr. said, "will undoubtedly be severely criticized in some sections of the country where racial prejudice is rampant. They are not inviting trouble, but they won't avoid it if it comes. Robinson is a fine type of young man, intelligent and college-bred."

Young Rickey admitted that the move might cost the Dodgers a number of ball players.

"Some of them, particularly those who come from certain sections of the South, will steer away from a club with a Negro player on its roster. Some players now with us may even quit, but they'll be back in baseball after they work a year or two in a cotton mill."

Racine, whose Montreal team won the International League's regular-season championship, said he expected no opposition either from the league or from fans. "Negroes fought alongside whites and shared the foxhole dangers," he said, "and they should get a fair trial in baseball."

Jack Roosevelt Robinson is 26 years old. He weighs 190 pounds, stands 5 feet, 11½ inches tall.

At UCLA, Robinson received numerous nominations for All-American honors in 1940 and 1941. He played in the 1942 All-Star game at Soldier Field, Chicago, and went to Honolulu for another All-Star game, and took part in about a dozen pro football games in the Coast League. He went into the army as a private in April, 1942, attended Officers' Training School and was commissioned as a second lieutenant in November, 1942. Early this year he was given an inactive status.

The signing of Robinson produced a wave of wild reports. Among them was a yarn that the Dodgers had 25 other Negro prospects in mind. The Mahatma made haste to enter his denial.

WILL CONTINUE TO SCOUT

"I haven't 25 prospects," declared Mr. Rickey. "The number I have in mind is nowhere comparable to that figure. I will continue to scout Negro talent. I know of no reason why I shouldn't go after any ball players regardless of color. If I thought it would hurt the Negro, or our players, I wouldn't have done it."

Mr. Rickey was asked about the problem of living and traveling while the Royals are on the road.

"The boy himself answered that question. 'I wouldn't want to go where I'm not welcome,' was the way he put it."

The president of the Dodgers explained why he hadn't broken ground before.

BLASTS GRIFFITH

"When I was in St. Louis Negroes were not allowed in the grandstand. Hence I could not arrange for tryouts. If I was in authority, I would have changed that. I got the idea when I came to Brooklyn after watching Negro teams play at Ebbets Field. Baseball is a game played by human beings, regardless of color, and I want to have winning baseball."

President Clark Griffith gave out a statement in Washington condemning Rickey for raiding an organized professional league. Rickey came back with a hot retort.

"The Negro leagues, as they are today constituted, are in the nature of a racket and Griffith knows that. History will record that Mr. Griffith introduced Negro ball in the major leagues. I want to help the Negro leagues organize. I'm doing this in spite of outside interests and pressure groups who are exploiting the Negro rather than helping him."

Rickey said he had a heavy telegram reaction, mostly favorable.

97

Pacific Coast League Requests
Major League Status (1945)

SOURCE: *The Sporting News*, December 13, 1945

The Pacific Coast League (PCL) was the most successful minor league in the first half of the twentieth century. From its first year, 1903, PCL teams drew more fans and produced more major leaguers than any other minor league, and since the PCL *operated without competition from nearby major league teams, it developed an especially strong identity with its fans. After the 1945 season the* PCL *asked its fellow minor leagues to support its petition to be upgraded to major league status. Critics acknowledged that San Francisco and Los Angeles could support major league teams, but they believed the other* PCL *cities were too small and that their parks were inadequate.* The Sporting News *polled nineteen reporters and sports editors from* PCL *cities on the viability of the league's petition, and found that they had different opinions. Reprinted below are a selection of the comments on the subject.*

COAST WRITERS SPLIT ON BIG LEAGUE RATING

Most View Step-Up as Premature
Half of Parks Inadequate, Maintain Scribes Who Criticize Proposal
By Carl T. Felker

The Pacific Coast League's expressed desire to attain major league status brought a sharp division of opinion among the league's sports writers.

A symposium on the subject, conducted by THE SPORTING NEWS, showed a slight majority opposed to such a step at this time. Even those who favor the advancement qualify their approval, in most cases, by admitting the league is not quite ready in all respects to measure up to major league standards.

Many of the writers point out that at least four of the league's parks—at Sacramento, San Diego, Oakland and Portland—are inadequate in seating capacity and other facilities for major league ball. Approximate capacities at these parks are: Oakland, 11,000; Sacramento, 11,000; Portland, 12,500; San Diego, 12,000.

The Oakland owners are spending $125,000 to improve their park for 1946. It is said the Hollywood club, which leases Gilmore Field, with a capacity of 12,000, recently figured on adding 5,000 seats and found the estimated cost was $200,000—providing labor and materials could be obtained.

Other obstacles to an advancement to major league rating, as emphasized by writers criticizing the idea, are the increased overhead, including player salaries, and the necessity of a substantial boost in admission prices. Doubt was expressed as to whether the league was in a position to meet the steep increase in expenses.

Such terms as "pipe dreams," "inviting financial disaster," and "it's no use kidding ourselves" were used by scribes who viewed the proposal as impractical at this time.

On the other hand, many of the writers declared that advancement to major league standing was inevitable for the Coast, and that the only question was the proper timing.

Following are the opinions:

Gate Figure Encouraging
By Ned Cronin
Sports Editor, Los Angeles Daily News

The Coast League may not have the physical equipment for eight major league clubs at present, but it is the opinion out here that it is better to start the ball rolling too soon than too late.

Clubs with smaller parks already have made plans to enlarge the seating capacities to the point where they could compare with major league standards. There may be a couple of weak spots in the circuit, just as there are in both major leagues, but it is expected that the teams in the larger cities will make up the difference and be able to carry the load.

If the Coast league isn't ready right now for big league baseball, at least it is rounding third base and only one jump away from scoring.

Attendance figures prove the interest is here. Given the talent and all-round playing facilities, there is little doubt that a third major league could survive and flourish on the West Coast.

Delay in Step-Up Urged
By George Bertz
Sports Editor, Portland Journal

In its entirety, the Pacific Coast League is not ready to step up to the top.

Although big enough in population and with fans' interest at the highest pitch in the history of the diamond sport on the Pacific seaboard, I do not believe the move would be justifiable at this time.

In the first place, all of the cities do not have parks capable of handling the crowds that are necessary to meet the added payroll that would be bound to come with the major rating. Secondly, the clubs would have to rid themselves of many of the veterans now gracing their lineups in favor of younger and faster players.

I believe the Coast League would be far better off to delay the step until such a time as all clubs have had an opportunity to develop and retain talent. That, in my opinion, will take from two to three years.

Warns Against Hurry
By Stan Speer
Of the Oakland Post-Enquirer

My contention is that the Coast league is far from being ready to graduate into a third major league. Many of the parks are not suitable and it is unlikely that the population will remain the same, due to the overcrowded conditions.

It is doubtful that the club owners could afford to pay topnotch salaries, even if there would be enough good players to comprise the rosters of the eight-club circuit. Another question is what leagues would compete in the World Series?

It might be considered a wise move for league officials to lay plans for such a move, but wait until a few years before putting the idea into practice after watching postwar developments in all eight Coast loop cities.

1946 Time to Start
By Bill Leiser
Sports Editor, San Francisco Chronicle

If all the owners are as serious as Paul Fagan of San Francisco and are ready and anxious as he is to do all that has to be done, the Coast league could make itself a worthy major league in three or four years and 1946 is as good a time to start as any.

98

Review of AAGPBL Season (1946)

SOURCE: *Kenosha Comets 1946 Year Book*

In 1943 Chicago Cubs owner Philip Wrigley, seeking to capitalize on the popularity of women's softball and to reinvigorate interest in baseball while the best players were at war, founded the All-American Girls' Professional Baseball League (AAGPBL). The highlight of the first season was a night doubleheader played for the benefit of the Women's Army Corps at Wrigley Field—the only night games played there prior to 1988. The league quickly expanded from the original four teams to eight, and throughout its twelve-year existence the rules and measurements became closer to those used in major league baseball. As the following article states, however, the "femininity and behavior" of the athletes was just as important to league officials as the level of play, which was consistently high.

ALWAYS SOMETHING EXCITING

Never a dull moment at an All-American Girls' Baseball Game

That's the prophetic theme again in vogue for 1946, calculated to induce constant action at the turnstiles at all home attractions for the eight clubs.

The attendance forecast this summer is "a million," according to league headquarters. Six clubs in the 1944 circuit attracted 259,000 fans for 110 games. In 1945, the same setup drew 450,000 for the same span of contests, reflecting the terrific spread of enthusiasm all over the circuit. The game really "caught on."

Now, with eight teams in the pennant pursuit, due to the awarding of franchises to Muskegon, Mich., and Peoria, Ill., both noted as spirited cities for sports attendance, the box office business should boom for the 112 assignments on the 1946 books.

President Max Carey says: "this girls' game is loaded with dynamite!" Action, suspense, thrills regale the fans at every game. The lineups are colorful and contain outstanding players from all sections of the United States and Canada.

Chaperones are provided for each club, and the highest standards of conduct are maintained, Carey explained. He pointed out that players are selected for ability, femininity, and behavior. With major and minor league managers in charge, the girls are assured of topnotch training in every phase of the national game. The double umpire system adds further baseball authority to the league.

IMPRESSIVE FEATS IN RECORDS

Three impressive feats grace the record books in batting, pitching and stolen bases for the All-American Girls' Baseball League. The figure Filberts take keen concern in gleaning the statistics which invariably put the stamp of "outstanding" and those who create the marks.

In the offensive department, Terrie Davis, fleet Rockford Peaches star from Canada, bashed the ball for an average of .332 during the 1943 stretch of 102 games. Besides her consistent clouting, she alternated as a topflight outfielder and infielder.

The 1945 campaign produced sturdy Connie Wisniewski of Detroit as the pitching phenom. Ace of the Grand Rapids Chicks' pitching platoon, Connie posted 32 victories balanced against only 11 reversals. The previous season she was practically as sensational with the Milwaukee Chicks, who defeated the Comets in the seventh and final game of the play-off series for the title.

Sophie Kurys, spark-plug of the Racine Belles infield at second base, committed the greatest thievery on the path-lines. In 116 games, she grabbed off 166 stolen bases. Fairly fast, with a good sense of timing, she is crafty heading for a base and has mastered the sliding technique with the finesse of a major league player. She can feint from would-be taggers with a deceptive hook, and she isn't afraid to take a chance with a long, hard roll along the ground with a headlong dive.

EX-MAJOR STARS ARE MANAGERS

A competent personnel conducts the affairs of the All-American Girls' Baseball League. Max Carey is president. With a background as player, coach and manager in major league baseball for 24 years with the Pittsburgh Pirates and Brooklyn Dodgers, he is the logical choice for the top position.

Carey served as manager of the Milwaukee Chicks in 1944 when they defeated Kenosha for the play-off title after going the full seven contests at Lake Front Stadium here. Noted as one of the greatest base-stealers in major league history, Carey taught his Chicks how to prowl the path-lines, and their speed and adeptness in that department eventually paid-off with the championship.

Frank B. Avery has the role of vice-president and promotional director. His handling of the spring training camp and exhibition tour of the south this spring is a real tribute to his efficiency.

Secretary and assistant to President Carey is Miss Marie E. Keenan, director of publicity. Co-operative at all times, she has gained the good will of sports writers, syndicates, magazines, and radio stations all over the country. National publicity has come to the league through her efforts. This season she is being aided by Paul

Lamar, widely known radio script writer, who is handling league publicity in effective style.

NEW CONVERTS EVERY YEAR

The All-American Girls' Baseball League converts new fans every season. This year there will be hundreds of servicemen seeing the "sweethearts of swat" in action for the first time. These newcomer spectators will be wondering what it is all about.

At the very outset, the uninitiated are emphatically informed that the girls play baseball and NOT SOFTBALL!

The bases are 70 feet. The pitching distance is 43 feet. The ball used is 11¼ inches. Baseball rules are employed except for underhand pitching.

Under this setup, a new open game results with bunts, home runs, stolen bases, and double plays. Players lead off and base thievery is one of the highlights of the action. Numerous girls in the league are highly adept at larceny on the baselines. Shirley Jameson, Kenosha's speedy outfielder, is a veritable flash in sack stealing while Sophie Kurys of Racine is another source of constant worry to opposing pitchers because of her cunning in pilfering the padded cushions. She set a league record of 166 for 116 games. These are only two of the standout stars, and they are legion.

EIGHT CLUBS IN LEAGUE

An association of eight member clubs, the All-American Girls' Baseball League is owned and operated by local civic and industrial leaders on a non-profit basis. Nearly 100 club directors participate in the direction of the circuit.

Exclusive innovations used include allocation system of players which assures even competition. All players are signed by the League office at Chicago after being recommended by commissioners throughout the United States and Canada.

Players are rated and assigned through a stout point system guaranteed to be fool proof. The new total advanced bases scoring column records actual performance of the girls and serves as an accurate key to their true ability in all departments of the game.

99

First Major Leaguer Lost to Mexican League (1946)

SOURCE: *New York Times*, February 19, 1946

Just as major league baseball was about to complete its first season since the before war with a full complement of players, the formation of the Mexican League by the wealthy Pasquel brothers threatened to disrupt baseball's monopoly. The Pasquels offered generous contracts to many major leaguers, but only a handful accepted. The first of these was New York Giant outfielder Danny Gardella, whose signing is detailed below.

After the Mexican League collapsed, former major leaguers who tried to return to their former teams found that they had been blacklisted for as long as five years. Gardella and several others sued baseball, claiming that the suspensions constituted violations of antitrust law to which, they argued, baseball should be subject. Although Gardella settled his case out of court in 1950, eventually a similar case reached the U.S. District Court, which ruled in 1953 that baseball was a sport and therefore not subject to antitrust law. However, the lengthy legal process inspired two congressional investigations into the antitrust exemption in the 1950s.

GARDELLA REVEALS JUMP FROM GIANTS

Tells at Miami Camp of Signing a Five-Year Contract to Play in Mexico
RESENTS PUSHING AROUND
Ott Names Adams, Lombardi as Only Men of 17 Absent He Is Depending On
By John Drebinger

Special to *The New York Times*

MIAMI, Fla., Feb. 18—The Giants, who had fervently hoped they had seen and heard the last of Danny Gardella until they had made proper disposition of him, were rudely jolted out of their complacency today when their eccentric outfielder reappeared on the scene with a startling announcement of his own.

For, at the very moment Manager Melvin Ott was telling a group of baseball writers that he expected to have something to announce on Gardella within the next twenty-four to thirty-six hours, presumably involving a deal with a minor league club, Dauntless Daniel was hovering just outside the ball park to inform the scribes a few minutes later that he had other plans.

Accompanied by one Robert Jamis, whom he described as his personal manager as well as agent for George Pasqual [sic], reputedly the backer of the newly formed Mexican League, Gardella announced that he has just signed a five-year contract to play in Mexico.

What is more, he revealed that Jamis has also rounded up several other major league players, including two Giants, Nap Reyes, infielder, and Adrian Zabala, pitcher, as well as Luis Olmo, Dodger outfielder.

NOT TO "ENRICH" GIANTS

"You may say for me," asserted Gardella, who seemed to experience no difficulty talking both for himself and his newly acquired manager, "that I do not intend to let the New York Giants enrich themselves any further, at my expense, by selling me to a minor league club, after the shabby treatment they have accorded me here. So, I have now decided to take my gifted talents to Mexico."

He said that at the close of last season the Giants were paying him $4,500 and that they offered to increase this only to $5,000 despite the eighteen home runs he hit. "At that," he added, "I would have accepted this figure had they not started pushing me around."

Regarding the possibility of Reyes and Zabala also jumping to Mexico, Ott partially confirmed this when he disclosed that both were holdouts, along with Sal Maglie, another pitcher, and that Reyes, in particular, has threatened to bolt to the Mexican circuit. Mel, however, did not appear greatly concerned over these fresh problems his Latin players are posing for him.

REYES DEMAND REFUSED

"Reyes is demanding a $4,000 increase, and when I told him we considered this too much, he said he could do better in Mexico. I then told him that that would be quite all right by me."

"You know," concluded Ott, "the time has passed when we have to worry about players like that. It was different in the days when we often didn't know when we would be able to put nine men on the field, but we now have a camp full of fine players, and I don't think any of the others will be missed."

100

American Baseball Guild Formed (1946)

SOURCE: *Boston Globe*, April 18, 1946

In April 1946, for the fourth time in major league history, the proposed formation of a new major league coincided with attempts by baseball players to unionize. In the late 1880s the establishment of the Brotherhood of Professional Base Ball Players led directly to the formation of the Players' League in 1890. A decade later Ban Johnson took advantage of the dissatisfaction which led to the creation of the Players' Protective Association to attract players to the American League. Organizers of the Federal League wooed members of the new Professional Baseball Players' Fraternity, knowing they would be receptive to liberal contract terms. Likewise, in 1946 both the Pasquel brothers and American Baseball Guild founder Robert Murphy recognized that an opening existed for the recruitment of players angry with their current status. Murphy attracted many major leaguers to his organization, and managed to win a number of concessions from the owners, including a raise in minimum salary and the payment of spring training expenses, which is still known to some as "Murphy money." The Guild survived barely one year, but it was replaced by the Major League Baseball Players' Association in 1953.

PLAYERS' GUILD FORMED HERE TO BARGAIN WITH BALL CLUBS
By Hy Hurwitz

The atomic bomb of baseball—a players' union—fell in the laps of the major league magnates last night when Robert Murphy, a labor relations counsel and a former Harvard trackman, announced the formation of the American Baseball Guild.

Declaring that a "considerable number of major league players" have already joined his guild, Murphy, who has an office at 6 Beacon st., Boston, yesterday registered the guild as a labor organization in Suffolk County at the Boston City Clerk's office.

A former examiner for the National Labor Relations Board, Murphy said he hopes to represent major and minor league players in collective bargaining with baseball's bosses. He says he will start with the major leagues and work down. "My first move," Murphy told the Globe last night, "is to organize a majority on one big league club. Then I will go to the owner of that club, stating that I represent a majority of the players of his team and request to bargain collectively for them."

Murphy claims that he decided to form the American Baseball Guild after discussing player contracts with members of major league clubs. He stated that his organization was formed "to right the injustices of professional baseball and to give a square deal to the players."

COLLINS REMAINS SILENT

Asked to comment on the baseball union, General Manager Eddie Collins of the Red Sox refused to make a statement. When informed that Murphy hopes to approach major league magnates sometime this season as the legal representative of a majority group, Collins said, "Let him get a majority; he'll have a heck of a time doing it."

Nevertheless, there has been more talk of forming a union among players this season than ever before. There was a heated discussion on the subject as the Boston Braves returned home from Spring training. One of the regular members of the team announced he was in favor of a union and would join as soon as one was organized.

Another first string member of the club, while admitting that baseball contracts, as now written, are all in favor of the club management, suggested that a baseball arbitration board be formed to settle salary disputes. When he recommended Commissioner Chandler, Pres. Harridge and Frick of the American and National Leagues, respectively, two other players remarked, "What good would that do, they work for the club owners."

A conference among Braves players is that a minimum salary should be paid to every one capable of making a major league team, with graduated pay raises if they continue to play in the big leagues.

CHANDLER HAS NO COMMENT

Globe baseball writer Gerry Moore contacted seven players of the Red Sox in Washington last night and each one claimed that he had not been approached by Murphy to join the Guild. The only member of the Sox admitting to be a union member was Trainer Win Green. "And it's the Musicians Union," Green stated proudly.

Moore also spoke with Commissioner Chandler on the Guild formation, but the Commissioner refused to comment.

In legal and labor-minded Washington, The Times-Herald this morning led its paper with the Guild story under an eight column banner.

While this Globe baseball writer heard player unions and minimum salaries discussed only by members of the Braves this Spring, and reported such last week, it is felt certain that the subject has been talked about by athletes on other teams.

At present, the situation may be a laughing matter among certain owners but the American Baseball Guild may spread throughout the country, and owners may be forced into bargaining collectively with the players on the same standards as laborers or office workers under the National Labor Relations act.

Murphy, who formed the Guild here, has had a wide experience in labor-management dealings. He was graduated from Harvard in 1932 and from the Harvard Law School in 1934. From January, 1939, through September, 1942, he was an examiner for the National Labor Relations Board. Since then, he claims, he has represented 40 to 50 firms in labor dealings.

101

Bus Crash Kills Nine Spokane Minor Leaguers (1946)

SOURCE: *Spokane Spokesman-Review*, June 26, 1946

One of the greatest tragedies in professional baseball history occurred on June 24, 1946, when a bus carrying the Spokane Indians of the Pacific Coast League tumbled off a road hugging a mountainside, killing nine players. As the article below stated, the irony is that many of the players had survived World War II.

GEORGE LYNDEN EIGHTH BUS CRASH FATALITY

Sam Collins Carries Big Load as Aid Offers Arrive

George Lyden, 22-year-old righthanded pitcher from Tensed, Idaho, was the eighth victim in the crash and fire of a chartered bus carrying the Spokane Indian team to Bremerton Monday night. Sixteen hours after the tragedy, Lyden succumbed to severe head injuries and burns while in a Seattle hospital. Seven other Spokane players were listed as dead and seven in the hospital with injuries.

"TERRIBLY TIRED"

Admittedly "up in the air and terribly tired," Sam W. Collins, owner of the ill-fated Spokane Indians baseball team, continued to carry on under the ever increasing burden of grief and worry as news continued to come in concerning the tragic bus accident.

With less than three hours' sleep in 48 hours, Collins was back in the team's offices in the Empire State building taking care of the details at this end while Dwight Aden, business manager, and Ken Hunter, publicity director of the team, are in Seattle taking care of the injured players' wants, arranging for rooms for the relatives of the players and many other important details.

The accident occurred at 8 p.m. Monday evening four miles west of the summit in Snoqualmie pass. The Washington Motor Coach company bus transporting the 15 members to Bremerton, plunged down a 500-foot embankment when forced to the side to avoid an oncoming vehicle.

Others dead were: Manager Mel Cole, 25, Wenatchee, Wash., catcher; Victor Picetti, 18, San Francisco, first base; George Risk, 25, Hillsboro, Ore., shortstop; Frederick T. (Marty) Martinez, 24, San Diego, Calif., utility; Pitcher Robert E. Kinnsman, 27, Brooklyn, Wash.; Right Fielder Robert James, 24, Tempe, Ariz.; Robert Paterson, 22, San Francisco, Calif.; center fielder.

Chris Hartje, Spokane catcher who reported to the team a week ago, was pronounced still in danger by attendants at the Harborview hospital, with first and second degree burns over his entire body.

The best doctors and brain specialists of Seattle have been obtained to treat the others injured. Dick Powers, pitcher, and Irv Konopka, former University of Idaho athlete, have fractured cervical vertebrae, but, according to the Seattle doctor, "neither have paralysis."

Ben Gehaghty, scrappy second baseman, had 25 stitches in closing a gash in his head but was doing fine. Pete Barlsoff, pitcher on option from Oakland of the Pacific Coast league was released from the hospital but is on crutches.

Konopka readily admits Barlsoff is the one who saved his life. Barlsoff pulled his husky battery mate out of the fire and took care of him until first aid arrived.

Levi (Chief) McCormack was reported to be doing nicely and is expected to be released from the hospital possibly today. . . .

Gus Hallbourg, right-handed pitcher, is in an Ellensburg hospital with a burned right hand but otherwise is in good condition and will be released soon.

Milt Cadinha, Spokane's ace chucker, and Joe Faria, another right-hander, were not aboard the bus, the pair driving to Bremerton with their wives in Faria's car.

Jack Lohrke, outstanding young third baseman, was recalled by San Diego of the Pacific Coast league and fortunately was taken from the bus at Ellensburg and headed back to Spokane.

Messages of condolence, telegrams offering assistance and the desire of the entire baseball world to aid Spokane in overcoming the horrible disaster were pouring into the baseball office throughout the day. . . .

Of the eight dead, all but Vic Picetti had served in World War II, in either army, navy, coast guard or the marines. Picetti, a youngster with a wonderful baseball future, would have been eligible for the draft in the near future. The young first baseman was regarded as the outstanding major league prospect in the Pacific Coast league last season.

According to an Associated Press report last night Risk's body was taken to Kelso, Wash. He was listed from Hillsboro, Ore., on the team roster but his family home is Cathlamet, Wash.

Although the times are indefinite, the funeral of the others will be: Lyden at Tekoa, Wash.; Cole at Sacramento; Martinez at San Diego; Picetti and Paterson at San Francisco.

Bob James' father arrived from Phoenix, Ariz., and will make the necessary arrangements and Kinnaman's family also is completing arrangements.

102 _____

Proof That Baseball Predates
Doubleday "Invention" (1946)

SOURCE: *New York Times*, July 16 and 17, 1946

Seven years after he first published an article questioning the Cooperstown/Doubleday myth, Robert W. Henderson, the chief librarian of the main reading room at the New York Public Library, received a collection that provided him with more evidence. The L. M. Goulston collection included over one thousand items related to early American baseball. Henderson used this new material in a classic book published the following year, Ball, Bat and Bishop: Five Thousand Years of Sport *(New York: Rockport Press, 1947), which explored the origins of many ballgames but is best remembered for its dismantlement of the Doubleday story.*

The article is followed by an editorial published the next day that applauded the acquisition as "appropriate, scholarly and valuable," and declared that the collection of historic sports material was "a trend."

BASEBALL HISTORY IN GIFT TO LIBRARY

L. M. Goulston Collection Shows Game Played 4 Years Before Doubleday "Invention"

A comprehensive collection of early American baseball books and pictures showing that the game was played in the United States as early as 1835, four years before Abner Doubleday was said to have invented baseball at Cooperstown, N.Y., has been presented to the New York Public Library, it was announced yesterday.

The collection, consisting of more than 1,000 photographs, fifty prints and rare cartoons, books and souvenirs, was a gift from Leopold Moss Goulston, a former vice president of the Boston Braves, in memory of his friend, Leo J. Bondy, vice president and treasurer of the New York Giants, who died in 1944.

One of the books, a juvenile published in 1835 under the title "The First Lie or Falsehood Its Own Punishment," contains an illustration showing boys playing baseball on a diamond on Boston Common.

Placing the illustration of baseball on the American scene still further back, Robert W. Henderson, chief of the library's main reading room, asserted that Washington's men had played the game at Valley Forge. In England, instances of the game were recorded still earlier, he said, and in the early 1700s a clergyman at Maidstone complained that his parishioners were playing baseball and other games on the Sabbath.

However, the first record of baseball in the new collection came in 1820, with the publication in Paris of "Les Jeux des Jeunes Garcons." The book presents a picture and a description of a game called "La Belle Empoisonee," identical with rounders, another name for an early form of baseball.

Other books in the gift, which will supplement the library's famous A. G. Spalding baseball collection, include many treatises on technical aspects of the game. Some of them are "The Art of Batting" and "The Art of Fielding," written in 1885 by Henry Chadwick, called even then the "father of baseball."

Another book contains the by-laws, rules of order and playing rules of the Takewambait Baseball Club of Natick, Mass., for 1858.

The collection also includes three complete sets of photographs of old-time ball players. They are the 250-picture series issued by Old Judge cigarettes in the 1880s one to a package; the 550 colored pictures put out by Sweet Caporal cigarettes in the 1890s, and a set of the Sporting News photographs of 100 players issued in 1910–11.

The entire collection, now being catalogued by library officials, will not be opened to the public for six months.

BASEBALL DOWN THE YEARS

One of the American phenomena we watch with awe and unflagging interest is the steady, honorable growth in dignity of sports. After professional baseball is able to attract to its ruling seat, in turn, a former Federal judge and then a United States Senator, it should not surprise anybody that the gift of a sizeable collection of early baseball books and pictures to the New York Public Library is prized as an appropriate, scholarly and valuable addition. As a matter of fact, the chief officer of the library's main reading room, Robert W. Henderson, is identified in The Encyclopedia Americana as a "sports specialist," which in itself adds dignity to sports while at the same time humanizing the library.

That remarkable institution at Fifth Avenue and Forty-second Street already holds the famous A. G. Spalding baseball collection, so what we are observing is one incident in a trend, rather than a startling innovation.

103

Connie Mack Defends "Nice Guys" (1946)

SOURCE: *The Sporting News,* July 31, 1946

One of the most famous baseball quotations, Leo Durocher's statement that "nice guys finish last," is incorrect—Durocher actually listed a number of New York Giants and commented that "they're nice guys and they're in last place." Connie Mack, widely perceived as one of the nicest men in the majors, objected to Durocher's comments. Mack noted that while he believed in aggressive baseball, he detested dirty, bullying baseball as personified by players like Ty Cobb.

CONNIE MACK SAYS: "GENTLEMEN ALSO WIN!"

Disapproves Lippy's Theory on 'Nice Guys'
By Stan Baumgartner
Philadelphia, Pa.

Connie Mack had stepped off his private elevator and was on his way to the A's clubhouse when we handed him a copy of THE SPORTING NEWS—opened to Leo Durocher's article.

"Nice guys don't win pennants, they wind up in the cellar."

We read a few of Durocher's choicest paragraphs. . . . "Nice guys? I'm not a nice guy and I'm in first place. Look at Mel Ott and the Giants. They're nice guys and they're in last place. Look at that little guy (Ed Stanky). Think he's a nice guy? The hell he is. He'll knock you down to make a play if he has to."

Connie smiled at first, then the friendly twinkle went out of his blue eyes, and he said in a voice husky with emotion:

"You don't have to be a rowdy to win pennants and you don't have to argue with umpires to win ball games.

"We won pennants (more pennants than Brooklyn has ever won and in a tougher league, too) and every one of my players was a gentleman. The 1910 to 1914 clubs were 'nice guys,' if you want to call them that, and they did pretty well and they were a fine, splendid influence for baseball. My 1925 team, which was the foundation of my pennant-winning teams in 1929, '30 and '31, were fine boys, too. They didn't argue with umpires, row with spectators and didn't abuse opposing players."

ROWDIES NOT ALLOWED

"I remember when I was first starting out as a manager," continued Mack. "Monte Cross, one of my stars, got into an argument with an umpire and was put out of the game. When he came to the bench, I gave him a calling down for getting put out. He got pretty hot for the calling down and said: 'If you don't want us to show a little spunk and fight for games, I won't say another thing.'

"When he had calmed down I said quietly, 'Where can you do us the most good, on the bench here or in the game?' He smiled, 'You're right, Connie,' he said. And that has been the principle I have always worked on. There were times when I had to pull such fiery fellows as Mickey Cochrane back to the bench, but it paid off in championships.

"Of course, as I told Pat Tebeau (once manager of Cleveland), it all depends on the type of players you have. Tebeau came up to me one day in New York when I was managing Pittsburgh and he said, 'I understand you have given orders to your men not to argue with the umpires. What kind of baseball is that?'

"I told him: 'That's the only kind of baseball my men can play well. If my boys argue with the umpires, they forget to play baseball. Maybe your men are the kind who can fight and still think clearly.'

"I believe in aggressive baseball—but not roughhouse baseball, and an aggressive player does not have to be a rowdy to earn the respect of his fellowmen. I recall the case of one of my own men. He was a quiet lad, played the game aggressively but well. Ty Cobb came to town—and you know Cobb . . . how he always slid into base spikes high. Detroit was away out in front that afternoon when Cobb slid into base and stuck his spikes dangerously near the infielder's face. He made no outward show of animosity, but quietly put the ball on Ty and said, 'The next time you come into me that way I'm going to jump on your face with both feet and grind my spikes into your throat until you are dead!' Cobb knew that the fellow meant what he said—and never slid with his spikes high again into that fellow's bag.

"And I have another thing to say on that score. Nice guys or tough ones don't win pennants unless they have the material."

104

Jackie Robinson's Major League Debut (1947)

SOURCE: *Brooklyn Eagle*, April 16, 1947

On April 15, 1947, for the first time since 1884—when Moses and Welday Walker played for the Toledo club of the American Association—a black man played in a major league game. Jackie Robinson's debut was not notable for how he played on the field that day, but the importance of his presence on the ballfield far exceeded even his greatest accomplishments in his illustrious ten-year career. This historic debut was missed by Dodger manager Leo Durocher, who on April 9 was suspended for the entire season by Commissioner Happy Chandler for conduct unbecoming to baseball.

"OLD" REISER, "NEW" HERMANSKI STARS, OF DODGERS' OPENING DAY TRIUMPH

Pistol's Double Knocks Out Sain, Defeats Braves
By Harold C. Burr

For years, under the goading of his late manager, Leo Durocher, President Branch Rickey has been conducting a nationwide search for a man who could hit 'em up against the fence at Ebbets Field. And here the guy was under the Deacon's palpitating nose. Pistol Pete Reiser doubled off the wall yesterday—the ball hugged the foul line all through its flight—to bat in the deciding runs in the Dodger's [sic] 5 to 3 win over the Braves.

Of course, one two-bagger doesn't constitute an 154-game schedule and this was

Brooklyn's 1947 inaugural. But it was an auspicious start for the Pistol, who has been regarded nervously as one of the big IF players of the lineup.

Reiser had a perfect afternoon at bat with a single and a pair of bases on balls in addition. His lethal blow knocked Johnny Sain, Boston's 20-game winner right out of the ball game, which gives the feat added lustre. Pete's away to a good start, the same as the rest of the Dodgers.

A secondary hero was Gene Hermanski, one of the younger set of Flatbush grass patrolmen. The Pride of Newark batted in two runs himself with a ground ball and a long fly. On the force play he hit into in the fourth inning, he neatly took out Connie Ryan, preventing the Brave second baseman from doubling up Bruce Edwards to end the round and the flying tackle permitted the run to cross.

There's an old 50-yard line marker out on the grass behind the bag, left behind by the football Dodgers and Hermanski really sent Ryan spinning at midfield. In the field Hermanski did all that was expected of him. In the fourth, with two runners on base, Phil Masi got hold of one and sent it screaming to left center on a low trajectory. Gene judged it perfectly and gathered it on the dead gallop.

REISER OF OLD

It was the old Reiser and the new Hermanski—an unbeatable combination.

Otherwise it looked like any other of those long 1946 afternoons on the Flatbush lawn. The game consumed two hours and 26 minutes. The Dodgers sent three pitchers to the peak, just as of yore—Joe Hatten, Hal Gregg and Hugh Casey, with Gregg receiving credit for the win. But all enemy runs were scored off California Joe, only one of 'em earned.

Little Johnny Jorgensen made his big league debut at third base. The rookie walked his first time up and bounced to Ryan on his other three efforts. But he held his poise before 25,623 critical paid admissions and was a smooth and sure workman when Manager Billy Southworth thought to bunt him into the litters.

Jackie Robinson again went hitless against big league pitching but he sacrificed prettily to advance the walking Ed Stanky along in the winning Dodger rally in the seventh and his speed caused Earl Torgeson to make a hurried throw into short right field and Stanky reached third and Robinson second and set the stage for Reiser's cleanup wallop. Dick Culler took a hit away from Jackie in the fifth with a sprawling stop and flip to Ryan that started a double play just when the Flock threatened to gang up on Sain.

The crowd was disappointing. But Flatbush misses its pepperpot manager and the team didn't look right out there on the field without Durocher to drive 'em on to victory. Another reason why the attendance wasn't up to expectations was fear perhaps of the smallpox scare. Nobody knew if his neighbor in the next seat had been vaccinated or not. Then, too, baseball can't expect a second monster year.

BOSTON	AB	R	H	O	A		BROOKLYN	AB	R	H	O	A
Culler, ss	3	0	0	0	2		Stanky, 2b	3	1	0	0	3
b-Holmes	1	0	0	0	0		Rob'son, 1b	3	1	0	11	0
Sisti, ss	0	0	0	0	0		Schultz, 1b	0	0	0	1	0
Hopp, cf	5	0	1	2	0		Reiser, cf	2	3	2	2	0
McCormick, rf	4	0	3	2	0		Walker, rf	3	0	1	0	0
Elliott, 3b	2	0	1	0	2		Tatum, rf	0	0	0	0	0
Littler, lf	3	1	0	1	0		e-Vaughan	1	0	0	0	0
Rowell, lf	1	0	0	0	0		Furillo, rf	0	0	0	0	0
T'geson, 1b	4	1	0	10	1		Her'ski, lf	4	0	1	3	0
Masi, c	3	0	0	4	0		Edwards, c	2	0	0	2	0
Ryan, 2b	4	1	3	4	7		d-Rackley	0	0	0	0	0
Sain, p	1	0	0	0	1		Bragan, c	1	0	0	3	0
Cooper	0	0	0	1	0		Jor'sen, 3b	3	0	0	4	0
a-Neill	0	0	0	0	0		Reese, ss	3	0	1	3	2
Lan'coni, p	0	0	0	0	0		Hatten, p	2	0	1	1	1
							c-Stevens	1	0	0	0	0
							Gregg, p	1	0	0	1	0
							Casey, p	0	0	0	0	0
Totals	31	3	8	24	13		Totals	29	5	6	27	10

a-Batted for Cooper in 8th.
b-Batted for Culler in 8th.
c-Batted for Hatten in 6th.
d-Ran for Edwards in 6th.
e-Batted for Tatum in 7th.

Boston . . . . .0 0 0 0 1 2 0 0 0—2
Brooklyn . . . . .0 0 0 1 0 1 3 0 x—5

Errors—Torgeson, Edwards. Runs batted in—Edwards, Hopp, Ryan 2, Jorgensen, Reiser 2, Hermanski. Two base hits—Reese, Reiser. Sacrifices—Sain 2, Culler, Masi, Robinson. Double plays—Stanky, Reese and Robinson; Culler, Ryan and Torgeson. Left on bases—Boston 12, Brooklyn 7. Base on balls—Off Hatten 3, off Sain 5, off Gregg 2. Strike outs—By Hatten 2, Sain 1, Gregg 2, Lanfranconi 2, Casey 1. Hits—Off Sain 6 in 6 innings; off Cooper 0 in 1 inning; off Lanfranconi 0 in 1 inning; off Hatten 6 in 6 innings; off Gregg 2 in 2⅓ innings; off Casey 0 in ⅔ inning. Hit by pitcher—By Hatten (Litwhiler), by Sain (Edwards), by Gregg (Neill). Wild pitch—Hatten. Winning pitcher—Gregg. Losing pitcher—Sain. Umpires—Pinelli, Barlick and Gore. Time—2:26. Attendance—25,623.

105

Babe Ruth Dies (1948)

SOURCE: *New York Sun*, August 17, 1948

The two events that marked the end of one era and the beginning of the next were, respectively, the death of Babe Ruth and Jackie Robinson's break into the majors. Grantland Rice, whose career spanned the previous half-century, was uniquely able to comment on the magnitude of Ruth's legend.

SETTING THE PACE
By Grantland Rice

GAME CALLED

Game called by darkness—let the curtain fall.
No more remembered thunder sweeps the field.
No more the ancient echoes hear the call
To one who wore so well both sword and shield;
The Big Guy's left us with the night to face,
And there is no one who can take his place.

Game called—and silence settles on the plain.
Where is the crash of ash against the sphere?
Where is the mighty music, the refrain
That once brought joy to every waiting ear?
The Big Guy's left us, lonely in the dark,
Forever waiting for the flaming spark.

Game called—what more is there for one to say?
How dull and drab the field looks to the eye,
For one who ruled it in a golden day
Has waved his cap to bid us all good-by.
The Big Guy's gone—by land or sky or foam
May the Great Umpire call him "safe at home."

THE GREATEST OF THEM ALL

The greatest figure the world of sport has ever known has passed from the field. Game called on account of darkness. Babe Ruth is dead.

There have been mighty champions in their day and time, from John L. Sullivan to Jack Dempsey—such stars as Bobby Jones, Ty Cobb, Walter Johnson, on and on, who walked along the pathway of fame.

But there has been only one Babe Ruth—one Bambino, who caught and held the love and admiration of countless millions around the world.

From the time he appeared on the big league scene with the Boston Red Sox in

1914 to the day his playing career ended over twenty years later, Ruth was the greatest all-around ball player in the history of the game. He was a brilliant left-handed pitcher—the top power hitter of all time—a star defensive outfielder who could be rated with the best. He was the one ball player who was a master of offense and defense—the nonpareil in both.

But Ruth was something more than a great ball player. He was an emblem, a symbol. No other athlete ever approached his color, not even the flaming Jack Dempsey, who had more than his share.

Ruth's appeal to the kids of this nation was something beyond belief. He loved them and the kids knew it, and there was nothing phony about his act. The kids knew that the Babe was the greatest home-run hitter of all time—that he was one of the greatest pitchers of all time—that he was an able place hitter—that he could do more with a bat and a baseball than any other player who ever lived. And the Babe could. But they also knew he was their pal. I was present when he drove sixty miles one night before a world series game in Chicago to see a sick boy. "And if you write anything about it," he said, "I'll knock your brains out."

He meant it that way.

THE TRUE BABE

I was a close friend of Babe Ruth since 1919, nearly thirty years ago, when the Red Sox and the Giants traveled north together.

The true story of the Babe's life never will be written—the story of wrecked cars he left along the highway—the story of the night he came near dropping Miller Huggins off a train—the story of the $100,000 or more he lost in Cuba one racing winter. (The Babe told me it was $200,000)—the story of the ribald, carefree Babe who ignored all traffic signals.

I was riding home with Ruth one night after a golf game. The Babe was late. He ignored red lights and everything else in a big car. I begged Babe to let me get out and take a taxi. The Babe only laughed.

"These cops are my pals," he said. "A funny thing happened yesterday. Maybe I'd had a shot or so too much. Anyway, my car stalled. A big cop came up and asked what the matter was. 'It won't run,' I said. 'You're drunk,' the cop said. I hit him in the nose. 'Now I know you're drunk, you so and so,' the cop said. He shoved me out of the way and drove me home."

One day the Babe took the wrong way on the road to some golf club.

"Hey, this is a one-way street," the traffic cop hollered.

"I'm only driving one way, you dumb —————," the Babe said. The cop, enraged, came rushing up. "Oh, hello Babe," he said. "I didn't know it was you. Drive any way you want to."

I sat one day with Babe at St. Albans, his golf club. The Babe took out a .22 rifle and he and a pal began shooting away the door knob at $1 a shot. The Babe missed some guy who had just opened the door by 2 inches.

"He should have knocked," the Babe said.

Just one day with the Babe was a big adventure. There was the time he planted a small explosive bomb in some pal's car and almost blew up the place, including the Babe and myself.

"I didn't know it was that strong," was all he said.

He was a rough, rowdy, swaggering figure, more profane than any one I ever hope to meet again, with a strong sense of decency and justice and fair play. He was a sportsman, if I ever saw one. He wanted no advantage at any start.

There was the day Miller Huggins was going to fine Ruth $5,000. He had been absent two days. The fine was to be plastered after the game. All baseball writers were notified. The Babe appeared before the game, red-eyed and dazed looking. He was in terrible shape. He hit two home runs and a triple. Huggins forgot the fine.

These are among the true stories of Babe Ruth, who had no regard for the conventions of the common or normal man, whether this included action or words.

But beyond all this he was open-hearted, friendly, always cheerful, a great guy to be with. I can still hear the roar of his voice, wherever he was. There was nothing quiet and sedate about the Babe. He could recall few names.

"I caught back of him for ten years," Mickey Cochrane once told me. "But he never knew my name. It was 'Hello, kid.'"

Driving around, Babe always responded to those who called out "Hey, Babe." His reply was "Hello, Mom" or "Hello, Pop."

"They can't forget my funny-looking pan," he said once.

They won't forget his funny-looking pan soon. His records were terrific. But they meant little when compared to the man who was so far above all the records he ever set. I never saw him turn a mean trick. No game will ever see his like, his equal, again. He was one in many, many lifetimes. One all alone.

Bibliography

The best histories of baseball in the first half of the twentieth century remain Harold Seymour, *Baseball: The Golden Age* (New York: Oxford University Press, 1971), and the first two volumes of David Quentin Voigt's trilogy, *American Baseball: From Gentleman's Sport to the Commissioner System* (Norman: University of Oklahoma Press, 1966), and *American Baseball: From the Commissioners to Continental Expansion* (1970; rpt., University Park: Pennsylvania State University Press, 1990). Two recent single-volume histories are Benjamin G. Rader, *Baseball: A History of America's Game* (Urbana: University of Illinois Press, 1992), and Charles C. Alexander, *Our Game: An American Baseball History* (New York: Henry Holt, 1991). G. Edward White, *Creating the National Pastime: Baseball Transforms Itself, 1903–1953* (Princeton NJ: Princeton University Press, 1996), William Curran, *Big Sticks: The Phenomenal Decade of Ruth, Gehrig, Cobb, and Hornsby* (New York: William Morrow, 1990), and Richard C. Crepeau, *Baseball: America's Diamond Mind, 1919–1941* (Orlando: University Presses of Florida, 1980), are excellent surveys that focus on this era.

Some of the finest baseball books concentrate on a single season. Among these are the trio by G. H. Fleming, *The Unforgettable Season* (New York: Fireside, 1981), *Murderer's Row: The 1927 New York Yankees* (New York: William Morrow, 1985), and *The Dizziest Season: The Gashouse Gang Chases the Pennant* (New York: William Morrow, 1984). Others include Mike Sowell, *The Pitch That Killed: Carl Mays, Ray Chapman, and the Pennant Race of 1920* (New York: Macmillan, 1989); Talmadge Boston, *1939, Baseball's Pivotal Year: From the Golden Age to the Modern Era* (Fort Worth TX: The Summit Group, 1994); Robert W. Creamer, *Baseball in '41* (New York: Viking, 1991); and Frederick Turner, *When the Boys Came Back: Baseball and 1946* (New York: Henry Holt, 1996).

Although many fascinating and important individuals, such as Connie Mack, umpire Bill Klem, Negro League owner J. L. Wilkinson, journalists Francis Richter and Henry Chadwick, and players like Hal Chase and Tris Speaker, have not yet attracted biographers, many others have. Two of the most colorful baseball men of the era were captured by Robert W. Creamer in *Babe: The Legend Comes to Life* (1974; New York: Fireside, 1992), and *Stengel: His Life and Times* (New York: Simon and Schuster, 1984; rpt., Lincoln: University of Nebraska Press, 1996). Others examined for this book include Eugene C. Murdock, *Ban Johnson: Czar of Baseball* (Westport CT: Greenwood Press, 1982); Henry W. Thomas, *Walter Johnson: Base-*

ball's Big Train (Washington DC: Phenom Press, 1995; rpt., Lincoln: University of Nebraska Press, 1998); Charles C. Alexander, *Ty Cobb* (New York: Oxford University Press, 1984); Paul J. Zingg, *Harry Hooper: An American Baseball Life* (Urbana: University of Illinois Press, 1993); and Harry "Steamboat" Johnson, *Standing the Gaff: The Life and Hard Times of a Minor League Umpire* (1935; rpt., Lincoln: University of Nebraska Press, 1994).

African Americans in baseball, long ignored, have been the subject of many recent books. The best overall history remains Robert Peterson, *Only the Ball Was White* (1970; rpt., New York: Oxford University Press, 1992). Rob Ruck, in *Sandlot Seasons: Sport in Black Pittsburgh* (Urbana: University of Illinois Press, 1987), covers the formation of the Homestead Grays and the Pittsburgh Crawfords. Jules Tygiel's *Baseball's Great Experiment: Jackie Robinson and His Legacy* (New York: Oxford University Press, 1983) is essential reading. Also of interest are Janet Bruce, *The Kansas City Monarchs: Champions of Black Baseball* (Lawrence: University Press of Kansas, 1987); James Bankes, *The Pittsburgh Crawfords: The Lives and Times of Black Baseball's Most Exciting Team* (Dubuque IA: William C. Brown, 1991); and Neil Lanctot, *Fair Dealing and Clean Playing: The Hilldale Club and the Development of Black Professional Baseball, 1910–1932* (Jefferson NC: McFarland, 1994).

The work of baseball's finest photographer is sampled in Neal McCabe and Constance McCabe, *Baseball's Golden Age: The Photographs of Charles M. Conlon* (New York: Harry N. Abrams, 1993). Two volumes of *The National Pastime: A Review of Baseball History*, published annually by the Society for American Baseball Research (SABR), featured photographs from this era. The volumes were *The Dead Ball Era*, vol. 5, no. 1 (1986), and *The Big Bang Era*, vol. 7, no. 1 (1989). Phil Dixon with Patrick J. Hannigan, *The Negro Baseball Leagues: A Photographic History* (Mattituck NY: Amereon House, 1992), is unsurpassed in its coverage. Finally, Geoffrey C. Ward and Ken Burns, *Baseball: An Illustrated History* (New York: Alfred A. Knopf, 1994), the companion to Burns's documentary *Baseball*, is a gorgeous assemblage of images.

Although no history of sportswriting exists, several books on or by sportswriters and sports broadcasters are available. Two of the best biographies or autobiographies are Fred Lieb, *Baseball As I Have Known It* (New York: Tempo Star, 1977; rpt., Lincoln: University of Nebraska Press, 1996), and Charles Fountain, *Sportswriter: The Life and Times of Grantland Rice* (New York: Oxford University Press, 1993). Other reminiscences of sportswriters of this era include Grantland Rice, *The Tumult and the Shouting* (New York: A. S. Barnes, 1954); Paul Gallico, *Farewell to Sport* (New York: Knopf, 1940); Graham McNamee, *You're on the Air* (New York: Harper and Bros., 1926); Ted Husing, *Ten Years before the Mike* (New York: Farrar and Rinehart, 1935); Tim Cohane, *Bypaths of Glory: A Sportswriter Looks Back* (New York: Harper and Row, 1963); and Warren Brown, *Win, Lose or Draw* (New York: G. P. Putnam's Sons, 1947). Curt Smith, *Voices of the Game*, rev. ed. (New York: Fireside, 1992), and Jerome Holtzman, *No Cheering in the Press Box*, rev. ed. (New York: Henry Holt, 1995), collect the reminiscences of veteran scribes and announcers, while Red Barber, in *The Broadcasters* (New York: Da Capo, 1985), offers a personal history of broadcasting. For a contemporary's view of sportswriting, see Stanley Woodward, *Sports Page: The Story behind Newspaper Sports Writing* (New York: Simon and Schuster, 1949).

Many of the best baseball articles have been collected in anthologies. A fine series is The Fireside Books of Baseball, edited by Charles Einstein. Also valuable are the two *Armchair Books of Baseball* edited by John Thorn. Three fine older examples are *The Omnibus of Sport*, ed. Grantland Rice and Harford Powel (New York: Harper and Bros., 1932); *The Greatest Sport Stories from the Chicago Tribune*, ed. Arch Ward (New York: A. S. Barnes, 1953); and *The Greatest Sport Stories from the New York Times*, ed. Allison Danzig and Peter Brandwein (New York: A. S. Barnes, 1951). A more recent example, which also includes many photographs, *The Baseball Anthology*, ed. Joseph Wallace (New York: Harry N. Abrams, 1994).

The foremost baseball reference book is *Total Baseball IV: The Official Encyclopedia of Major League Baseball*, ed. John Thorn and Pete Palmer with Michael Gershman (New York: Viking, 1995). David L. Porter has edited an invaluable series of biographical dictionaries on sports personalities. The three volumes relevant to this book are *The Biographical Dictionary of American Sports: Baseball* (Westport CT: Greenwood, 1987), and the supplements for 1989–92 (published in 1992) and for 1992–95 (1995). *The Negro League Book*, ed. Dick Clark and Larry Lester (Cleveland: Society for American Baseball Research, 1994), is the most complete statistical source for the Negro Leagues. Of importance in its field is *The Encyclopedia of Minor League Baseball*, ed. Lloyd Johnson and Miles Wolff (Durham NC: Baseball America, 1993). Also important are Paul Dickson, *The Dickson Baseball Dictionary* (New York: Avon, 1989); *The Baseball Chronology*, ed. James Charlton (New York: Macmillan, 1991); *John Spalding's Guide to Baseball Guides, Record Books and Registers, 1869–1995*, ed. John Spalding (self-published, 1995); and Bill James, *The Bill James Historical Abstract* (New York: Villard, 1986). The best bibliographic essay on recent baseball books is Larry R. Gerlach, "Not Quite Ready for Prime Time: Baseball History, 1983–1993," *Journal of Sport History* 21, no. 2 (summer 1994).

Acknowledgments

"A New Division in Baseball" (doc. 58), "Landis Took Wise Course, Says Rice" (doc. 61), "Fired as 'Washed-Up' Player in Minors, Ziggy Sears Becomes All-Star Umpire His First Year in Majors" (doc. 78), "Vote for Your Favorite Broadcaster in Majors or Minors" (doc. 80), "Cooperstown Cavalcade Marked by Greatest Galaxy of Past and Present Diamond Stars Ever Assembled" (doc. 85), "Coast Writers Split on Big League Rating" (doc. 97), and "Connie Mack Says: 'Gentlemen Also Win!'" (doc. 103) courtesy of The Sporting News.

"President Heydler's Suggestion" (doc. 66) courtesy of Spalding Sports Worldwide.

Reprinted with permission excerpts from "Officials All Pleased With Night Contest" (doc. 68) by The Des Moines Register, copyright 1930.

"Reporters Split on Whether Fans Booed Hoover at Series Game" (doc. 71) courtesy of Editor & Publisher.

"Satchel Hits and Pitches Team to National Honors" (doc. 77) reprinted with permission. © The Wichita Eagle-Beacon Publishing Co., Inc.

"Baseball and Ballyhoo" (doc. 81) reprinted by permission of the Enoch Pratt Free Library of Baltimore in accordance with the terms of the will of H. L. Mencken.

"Americans Win Battle of Stars, 8–3" (doc. 82) © 1937, document 87 © 1942, "Nats Edge Browns, 3–2, on Wolff's 4-Hitter" (doc. 94) © 1945, The Washington Post. Reprinted with permission.

"The Barber Shop" by John Carmichael (doc. 83) reprinted with permission of The Chicago Sun Times.

"The Umpire" (doc. 86) reprinted with permission of The Detroit News.

"Baseball, Races OK; Curfew Stays" (doc. 89) and "Hank's Bat Wins Flag" (doc. 95) courtesy of Detroit Free Press.

"Always Something Exciting" (doc. 98) excerpted from a copy of Kenosha Comets 1946 Year Book held by the Joyce Sports Research Collection, Notre Dame.

"Players' Guild Formed Here to Bargain With Ball Clubs" by Hy Hurwitz, April 18, 1946 (doc. 100), reprinted courtesy of The Boston Globe.

"George Lynden Eighth Bus Crash Fatality" (doc. 101) courtesy of The Spokesman-Review.

"Baseball History in Gift to Library" and "Baseball down the Years" (doc. 102) copyright © 1946 by The New York Times Co. Reprinted by permission.

Index

DATE DUE